EQUALITY IN EARLY CHILDHOOD:
Linking Theory and Practice

EQUALITY IN EARLY CHILDHOOD
Linking Theory and Practice

Jennie Lindon

Hodder Arnold
A MEMBER OF THE HODDER HEADLINE GROUP

Dedication

In loving memory of my father, the Celtic part of my heritage

Orders: please contact Bookpoint Ltd, 130 Milton Park, Abingdon, Oxon OX14 4SB. Telephone: +44 (0)1235 827720. Fax: +44 (0)1235 400454. Lines are open 9.00–6.00, Monday to Saturday, with a 24-hour message answering service. You can also order through our website www.hoddereducation.co.uk.

If you have any comments to make about this, or any of our other titles, please send them to educationenquiries@hodder.co.uk

British Library Cataloguing in Publication Data
A catalogue record for this title is available from the British Library

ISBN-10: 0 340 913 479
ISBN-13: 978 0 340 913 475

This Edition Published 2006
Impression number 10 9 8 7 6 5 4 3 2 1
Year 2009 2008 2007 2006

Hodder Headline's policy is to use papers that are natural, renewable and recyclable products and made from wood grown in sustainable forests. The logging and manufacturing processes are expected to conform to the environmental regulations of the country of origin.

Cover photo from Lottie Davies/Digital Vision.
Typeset by Servis Filmsetting Ltd, Manchester
Printed in Great Britain for Hodder Arnold, an imprint of Hodder Education, a member of the Hodder Headline Group, 338 Euston Road, London NW1 3BH by Martins the Printer, Berwick upon Tweed

CONTENTS

FOREWORD

In any book about childhood some general decisions need to be made about words. I use the non-specific term *practitioner* to include the different kinds of professionals who take responsibility for children in early years provision, school and out-of-school facilities and the childminding service. It will be clear when I am talking about a particular type of provision. The word *parents* covers anyone who takes the main family responsibility for children. Please assume the word always includes 'and other family carers'.

I have benefited from conversations over the years with many fellow early years professionals, college tutors and advisers and with a wide range of practitioners working directly with children. I have drawn from conversations with children as well as adults, and from my own observations, to develop fictional people and places for the scenarios in this book. In my research for this completely revised edition, I appreciated guidance via telephone and email from advisers at many of the organisations I have referenced. Heartfelt thanks are also due to the invisible people who have created some really informative websites. Please note that all website addresses were correct at the time of writing (summer/autumn 2005).

Many thanks to the practitioners, children and parents of the settings where I took the photographs: Windham – a Partnership for Children (Richmond), the Randolph Beresford Early Years Centre (West London) and the Balham Family Centre.

We live in interesting times, and initiatives and legislation were in process when I completed the book. I have indicated where this situation applies. I take the usual responsibility for the content of my book, the ideas within it and any errors I have failed to recognise. Please let me know if you identify any mistakes or misunderstandings and I will correct them as soon as possible.

Part 1

Equality: principles and practice

Equality practice is built from many aspects. This part of the book addresses early childhood within the context of UK society. Everyone needs to be well-grounded in how young children learn attitudes and their images of themselves and others. Chapter 1 focuses on the need for practitioners to reflect on their own assumptions and current knowledge. What happens within early childhood, so in what ways should equality practice be focused over those years?

Chapter 2 covers the legal framework and guidance expectations for equality. Law matters but legal requirements are effective only through daily actions and experiences. Other parts of the book cover strands of practice that matter just as much as what is said in law. All the strands blend together for a fully rounded approach to equality that can make a difference.

Many early years practitioners in the UK have been inspired by the bicultural early years curriculum in New Zealand. This framework is known as *Te Whāriki*, a Māori term that describes a woven mat upon which all may stand. The concept is used to symbolise the inclusive nature of the curriculum, but also that many equally important strands are interwoven for good practice. The woven mat is an excellent concept, yet it arises from a culture on the other side of the world to the UK.

I propose to take the symbolism of Celtic knotwork: an art form indigenous to the UK and with a long history shared with other countries in western Europe. The continuous and interlocking shapes are created in different ways and one pattern is reproduced here. All parts of the pattern are equally important for the strength of the whole. It does not matter where you start, so long as your progress encompasses and respects all the strands.

1 Equality for early childhood practice

Equality is a crucial practice issue for early years, school and playwork professionals. There are legal obligations around equality, but the moral responsibility is just as important. Babies are not born prejudiced or bigoted, yet children are enthusiastic learners – they imitate the words and actions of familiar adults and of other children. Adult divisions can be reflected in children's choice of language, their expressed beliefs about groups in society, including their own sources of identity and their choice of play companions. Practitioners share with children's families the responsibility of raising the next generation.

> **The main sections of this chapter cover:**
> * **reflective practice**
> * **equality and childhood.**

REFLECTIVE PRACTICE

Young children are in the process of developing their attitudes, so early years, school and out-of-school practitioners are expected to be active in the following ways.

- Promoting equal opportunities to the best of their ability for all children and families who are in contact with the service.
- Working to equalise opportunities for those children and families whose situation or group identity may place them at a disadvantage.
- Fostering respect and mutual understanding between children and families who see themselves as different from each other. Such respect is always a two-way street. I do not accept, as good practice, assumptions that offensive attitudes emerge only from one direction.
- Extending their own knowledge and understanding of equality issues in practice around gender, ethnic group and cultural background, faith and disability.

Working as a reflective practitioner

Good practice for equality is partly a focus on the individual children and families who are currently attending your setting or service. So your work naturally reflects your immediate community and local environment. But good equality practice also covers the image of the world that you are giving children: the big picture that extends beyond their own back yard. You, as a practitioner, should not feel responsible for matters of inequality

3

or discrimination outside your control. However, you are definitely responsible for what children learn while they are within your care in early years centres of different types, school, after-school club or your home if you are a childminder.

Practitioners who work with children tend to be the kind of professionals who focus on practical details and action. In nursery, club or your own home, you will often have to deal with tricky situations by making swift personal decisions about what to say and do, or whether to ignore an event. Increasingly, training and continued professional development have fostered the approach of being a reflective practitioner: that is, one who is willing and able to think over options and discuss with team or network colleagues. Equality in practice is definitely an area that benefits from some reflection, as outlined below.

■ You need to be willing to acknowledge what you learned within your own childhood, as well as adulthood sources of your beliefs and assumptions.

■ Discussion with team or network colleagues is important for airing ideas, sharing knowledge and, with support, addressing areas of practice that are less comfortable to face.

■ Childminders, who usually work alone, need reflection, and a chance to discuss issues, in order to be consistent over time in their reactions with children. Childminders who work with an assistant, or couples registered together, need to discuss ways of handling sensitive situations.

■ Within group settings it is essential that the whole team reaches an informed commitment over policy and, just as important, a shared understanding about what policy means in daily practice.

■ There must be consistency between individual practitioners on key issues around how to handle types of situation that arise with children, in communication with parents or with fellow professionals.

Without a doubt, effective equality practice cannot stay with reflective discussion, however detailed, about getting the policy right or what might be done or said. Everyone needs to get to that point where something is actually said or done. For this reason, you will find sections in this book that offer direct suggestions. Of course, these examples are not ordering you to use those actual words and nothing else – my aim is to give you material with which to work.

You will never be able to anticipate all possibilities. So good professional practice has to be led by willingness to talk over situations that you have already handled. Sometimes you will need to inform a colleague about what you did or said. Sometimes you will welcome a chance to reflect on whether, with hindsight, you could have taken a different route. Be kind to yourself; it is hard to think quickly when faced with a difficult situation. You can learn from reflection and take a different option next time.

Approaches to equality

Many people now work within equality as trainers, writers and advisers. Over the past decades varied approaches have developed and sometimes dominated in different areas of equality. Professional practice evolves and a grasp of social history is useful, if only to challenge any assumption that the current face of equality practice is completely right and will not change. At several points in this book I will need to be clear about my value stance. Now is one of those times . . .

- Good practice over equality does not mean blaming people for the past. A positive approach looks to the future. You are not responsible for what happened before you were even born. However, you are responsible for your own attitudes now and your willingness, or resistance, to learn more and to reflect on your views.
- A culture of blame and attribution of guilt soured some approaches to anti-racist and anti-sexist initiatives over the 1980s. In some cases, blunt criticism of workshop delegates or accusatory behaviour set a negative, divisive model for how to address the issues, and led to defensive reactions.
- Since that time, there has been a constructive shift to methods more likely to bring about reflection and change in outlook and actions. Effective challenge, rather than attack, leaves fellow professionals able to save face, find common ground and opt to change rather than focus on self-defence.

Over the 1990s, policy statements on equality grew ever longer as more and more groups were added to the list of people who could be vulnerable to discrimination. Identifying every group that might need active support was well-intentioned, but the approach developed a less than useful victim ideology. Such an approach can swiftly become underpinned by pity, rather than the fellow-feeling of empathy. Additionally, it was soon time to ask who was not on the lists. The obvious group was 'white', middle-class, heterosexual males without any disability. Some materials for early years practitioners still pinpoint this group as unlikely to understand discrimination from a personal viewpoint. Since men are the most striking minority group in the early years workforce, this stance is wide open to challenge.

Action for equality should bring all groups on board in an even-handed way. Inclusive practice can never be about claiming that 'everyone is the same'; clearly they are not. Good practice rests upon ensuring that nobody is excluded, that children and families have equal chances to be acknowledged, respected and included in authentic ways. Existing social inequalities will mean that not all families have the same starting point. So broad intentions in equality practice need to be fine-tuned for the particular situation.

Equality practice for children needs to consider their current experiences. Children especially should not be expected to make up for past inequalities, nor those that still exist. They cannot be held responsible for the society into which they were born. But children can appreciate the impact now of their own words and actions, and learn a more open approach than seemed possible for previous generations. Equality means everyone. Here are some examples.

- Disabled children deserve to be treated as children first, and their child status brings responsibilities as well as rights. It is in nobody's interests if disabled children are excused fair boundaries for their behaviour.
- Girls need to show consideration to boys as well as vice versa, and a largely female workforce needs to take care in respecting boys' choices and preferences.
- Traveller or Gypsy children cannot be excused from offensive remarks to children from settled families because the latter do not belong to a defined minority ethnic group.
- Putting equality into practice is not a competitive exercise. Paying attention to one faith does not require pushing aside another. Celebrating Divali does not necessitate 'banning Christmas'.

Acknowledging differences does not have to entail judgement that one group or way of life is better than another. Within your practice all children, and their families, have the right to be treated with equal respect, attention and, when appropriate, concern for their wellbeing.

The impact of adult attitudes on behaviour

All adults have developed attitudes about other people and the groups to which they belong. Attitudes are partly made up of feelings about other people or whole groups. But there is also an intellectual part that is formed by beliefs, expectations and assumptions. These are supported by information and the conviction that particular facts are true: the sense of 'everyone knows that . . .'. You cannot see people's attitudes, but they emerge through behaviour: their actions and chosen words.

TAKE ANOTHER PERSPECTIVE

There is often no neat and easy logic about people's attitudes. Adults who are themselves on the receiving end of offensive behaviour may in their turn hold highly negative attitudes about people from other ethnic or social groups. Those adults may not feel that their outlook is in any way illogical. The confident rationale is probably that they are always the people in the right.

Everyone holds attitudes. Some are mainly positive, some may be mildly rejecting of others, but some may be intensely offensive towards particular individuals, defined by gender, social class, faith or ethnic group. Attitudes are learned throughout childhood and some adults resist later change as emotionally challenging. Change is that much harder if someone's sense of self-worth depends strongly upon feeling superior to specific other people, defined as the 'wrong' sex, skin colour, faith, social class or other group marker. However, adults continue to learn and are potentially capable of rethinking their views and assumptions about others.

Stereotyping

Firm attitudes about other groups are usually supported by stereotypes. This word describes simple, relatively fixed, beliefs about the characteristics shared by individuals of an identified group.

- Stereotypes are usually unfavourable. For instance, 'Women are always so emotional', 'Muslims are fanatical about their religion', 'He's so irresponsible – typical working class.'
- Apparently complimentary stereotypes can have a serious sting in the tail, when they restrict an individual's options to those that fit the stereotype. Examples would be, 'Disabled people are so brave' or 'Black boys are such natural athletes.'

Stereotypes are usually applied to groups to which the individuals speaking do not themselves belong. The development and maintenance of stereotypes depend on a belief that other groups have less variety than one's own.

- People are more ready to say of another social or ethnic group 'They're all . . .' or 'She's a typical . . .' . But they will say of their own group, 'It all depends' or 'People differ, you can't say that about everybody.' Listen to daily conversations and you will notice this pattern.
- Stereotypes are often built from a particular event or experience, which is then generalised well beyond the original context of place and time. Firmly-held stereotypes then shape the interpretation placed on experiences with individuals from the given group.

Adults create a warm emotional atmosphere

- People who appear to fit the stereotype are taken as further evidence of this person's beliefs. The experience of individuals who clearly do not fit is discounted as a reason to adjust beliefs because, 'You're my friend, I don't count you' or 'Well, most of them aren't like her.'
- People who object to having stereotypes imposed upon them are frequently further labelled as 'touchy' or 'having a chip on their shoulder'.

Stereotypes are partly learned during childhood because children hear familiar adults, in the family or outside, expressing simplistic, fixed views about other people. Children remember these beliefs along with other information that they have gained from key adults in their lives. They repeat the beliefs unless experience leads them to question these views.

WHAT DOES IT MEAN?

- **Stereotypes:** simplistic beliefs, that are resistant to change, about the characteristics allegedly shared by individuals of an identified group.
- **Stereotyping:** the process of using such beliefs to shape expectations of individuals, who belong, or are presumed to belong, to a given group, in order to predict or explain their actions.

LOOK, LISTEN, NOTE, LEARN

Look at the examples that follow.

- What kind of underlying beliefs are the speakers expressing? And what seems to be the source of their conviction that they are correct?

- What might be the consequences if the comments go unchallenged? Silence from other adults will most likely be taken as agreement.

1 'Don't ask May's grandma to help the children on the computer. Older people aren't computer-literate and she'll get all worried about it.'

2 'We let the boys run around and burn off their energy. There's no point in trying to make them sit and learn, they only fidget all the time.'

3 'Nur's parents shouldn't be trying to teach the child two languages at the same time. She should be learning English like everyone else. Nur can learn Turkish when she gets older and she's ready.'

4 'I don't care what you say. We'll never be able to work together with Prods. What on earth have we got in common with those Protestants?'

5 'Sunita looks a bit tired with the new baby, but she'll be fine. Asians always have extended families, don't they? There'll be loads of aunties helping out.'

6 'I'll wait until Liam's mother comes in tomorrow. His father has this dreadful stammer and any conversation takes forever. It's so embarrassing and I don't think he understands half of what I say.'

7 'I'm really not sure about asking Isaac's father about the Hanukkah celebrations. Jewish people are so touchy, aren't they? Don't you remember Rebecca's mother?'

8 'I give the children a proper balanced diet here, none of this vegetarian nonsense. They need to have a normal diet when they're little; they can choose for themselves when they get older.'

9 'We've got some city children visiting us next week. I bet none of them has seen a cow before, let alone walked up a hill. These families never take their children anywhere.'

Language reflects attitudes

Attitudes are represented through choice of words and phrases, even when adults are not conscious of the implications of what they say. Words matter because they are a reflection of deeply-entrenched attitudes in our society.

- Historically there have been more negative associations with 'black' than 'white'. Despite greater awareness, people still talk or write of 'blackening' someone's reputation, 'blackmail' and the weird phrase 'black comedy', which seems to apply to films or plays where the amusement depends on events that are miserable or semi-tragic for some characters.

- Something pure and clean has been and is still sometimes described as 'whiter than white'. The whole 'Black is beautiful' movement originating in the United States from the 1960s was a concerted attempt to reclaim the word and create positive associations.

- People who avoid racist remarks based directly on skin colour still sometimes use, perhaps without thinking, other offensive phrases like 'dirty little Arab' or 'acting Jewish' (an implication of meanness) or 'Welshing on a deal' (untrustworthiness).

- A range of insults are based on a negative view of being female: 'fussing like an old woman'; or upset boys are criticised for 'acting just like a girl'. Some spoken and written examples still use a generic 'he' to cover both sexes, or terms like 'mankind', when the discussion is about everyone.

- Words like 'cripple' or 'spastic' are less often used now as general insults. But you will notice comments like 'He's deaf as a post' or 'You blind or something?!' used to criticise someone for general inattention.

Changing the words people use does not magically change their attitudes. However, an awareness of your use of words is a valuable part of a more general willingness to consider your attitudes.

Unquestioned habits of language also extend to beliefs about those groups about which it is considered fine to make jokes. In mainland Britain there has been a tradition of 'Irish jokes', in which the punchline

LOOK, LISTEN, NOTE, LEARN

Be observant for examples of use of words that carry apparently positive or potentially negative meanings. In case any readers think this issue is all past history, I provide an example I read while writing this chapter.

Marcus Linklater wrote a feature in *The Times* (3 August 2005) in which he commented on racism and the murder of Anthony Walker under the heading 'A black day for Britain's self-image'. The choice of headline was bizarre and apparently not intended to convey some level of irony. (The writer may not have chosen the title; newspaper editors tend to determine headings.)

depends on a belief that Irish people are stupid. Similar patterns can be found in other countries, except that the ethnic or national group targeted varies. For example, in the United States this kind of barbed witticism has been known as the 'Polish joke' and in Scandinavia it is the 'Norwegian joke'. Traditionally, members of the given ethnic group can choose to tell such jokes. The longest run of 'Irish jokes' I have ever heard was during a convivial post-conference evening with the delegation from Belfast (and they did regard themselves as Irish; see page 77).

TAKE ANOTHER PERSPECTIVE

Previous generations in Britain expressed a casual anti-Semitism and disdain of 'foreigners', and the language became part of ordinary conversation. Try some Agatha Christie books written in the 1920s or 1930s. You'll soon notice that the heroes and heroines – not the villains – use what reads now as anti-Semitism and dismissive terms for anyone who is not British.

Attitudes about foreigners and 'black' ethnic groups also affected books written for children. The views were also very clear in children's comics well up to the 1960s and early 1970s. Comics may not be seen as real literature by adults, but children read them with great enthusiasm.

Words matter

Responsible practitioners are observant of reactions to their spoken language and adjust in the light of feedback, even if they had no intention of being impolite or operating to exclude. However, it is important to avoid getting stuck in endless debates over words as an alternative to useful action.

Offhand or offensive language needs to be challenged, but in ways that still leave anyone – children, young people or fellow adults – with the ability to save face and make a choice to change for the future (see page 142 or 209). Otherwise, it is not productive to behave as if there are 'right' and 'wrong' words in absolute terms. People sometimes boost their own sense of worthiness by getting on a verbal high horse about terms: accusing others of racism, sexism and various other -isms. But equality and good relations between different groups are not promoted when well-intentioned practitioners, or other people, are criticised solely for their choice of words.

Knowledge of social history over equality issues soon tells you that preferred words or phrases change. Some people are left with 'out-of-date' phrases that they continue to use with courteous, not offensive, intentions. Here are some examples.

- Some parts of the UK population hold to the word 'coloured' to refer to anyone not of 'white' appearance. The word is felt to be a polite term, although other phrases are usually preferred within the relevant ethnic groups. Interestingly, another version emerged as acceptable in the early twenty-first century in the United States: the phrase 'people of color'.

- In the UK the word 'handicapped' is experienced as offensive by many people involved with disability rights. The word has associations with begging for money or other help – the colloquial phrase 'going cap in hand'. However, these negative implications are not felt in all English-speaking countries. So you may find the term in recent books published outside the UK. Many adults in the general UK population use 'handicapped' in order to avoid terms they feel are impolite such as 'cripple' or 'retarded'.

Discussion with the group(s) in question is often the best way to make choices around words. Consultation often highlights that there is no single verbal route that will please everyone. However, within reason, people within any groups, however defined, usually care more about how they and their children are treated than the exact terminology and presence or absence of capital letters – sometimes also an issue.

The concept of political correctness

I doubt this phrase was ever useful, but it has now certainly passed its sell-by date. During the 1980s an initially sensible challenge to common words was made – for instance, over the language habit of assuming the entire population was male and to address negative associations with 'black'. Some of the wilder, newsworthy stories were myth; others were only slightly exaggerated, because some professionals became enmeshed in words alone. Responsible practitioners use words that are accurate, step aside from avoidable offence and use terms acceptable to most members of the relevant group.

The term 'politically correct' is now most linked to disagreement with initiatives responsive to the rights of a 'minority' or any group that has experienced some level of inequality. The phrase 'It's just political correctness' (or PC) is thrown at discussions around children's rights, as much as changes to improve access for disabled members of the population. The words have also become the lazy way to avoid any discussion: a playground way of implying 'You're stupid!' Some commentators to and for the media dismiss an event (often misreported anyway) as 'political correctness gone mad'. I have yet to hear a definition from such spokespeople of 'sane' political correctness.

Key words and phrases

Writers and advisers, with equivalent commitment and experience, do not all agree on the exact meaning for key terms within equality practice. There follows a list of the definitions I have used in this book.

General terms

- **Equality practice:** a move towards the common ground for different group identities of promoting equality in an active way and dealing with issues that undermine equality or operate in a discriminatory way.

- **Promoting equality/equal opportunities:** actions integral to regular practice in order to ensure that all children are enabled to have positive experiences supporting personal identity. Action is taken if children's opportunities are blocked in ways that practitioners can directly address.

- **Anti-discriminatory practice:** an active attempt to promote positive attitudes and behaviour, to challenge and change negative outlooks and actions, on the basis of any group identity. This approach stresses that practitioners should take the initiative and not wait for issues to arise.

- **Anti-bias practice or curriculum:** a framework of activities, play materials and experiences that avoid stereotypes and actively promote understanding and knowledge of all groups within society.

- **Inclusion:** this term, along with **an inclusive approach**, was initially developed with reference to disability. These terms, and also **social inclusion**, often now refer to general practice about equality. The terms mean an active effort to address ways in which children or adults may be excluded from services or experiences, whether this result was intentional or the result of unreflective practice. Inclusion is still used sometimes to refer specifically to equality issues over disability.

Race and racial equality

- **Race:** There is no scientific basis for the concept of race. Genetic research has consistently shown a high level of variation within any of the groupings that have been tried. The word is used within equality practice to cover a social, rather than genetic, concept of ethnic group.

- **Racial equality:** this phrase is used to describe promoting equal opportunities and challenging discrimination on the basis of racial/ethnic group as defined by legislation (see page 29).

- **Racism:** the set of attitudes, actions and practice that subordinates a group of people because of their skin colour, culture or ethnic group. Racist beliefs are used to justify **racial discrimination** – the denial or restriction of opportunities to individuals from the defined group.

- **'White' and 'black':** racial discrimination can still be a blunt instrument set against anyone who looks different by skin colour. I have chosen to use inverted commas, as a reminder that these are broad, often inaccurate, terms.

Ethnicity and ethnic group identity

- **Ethnic group:** a grouping of people who have a shared heritage of customs, language and possibly faith. People within a group have their national or cultural origins in common.

- **Minority ethnic group:** an ethnic group with a relatively small number of individuals, in comparison with the national population. The group might comprise the majority within a particular neighbourhood.

- **Black and Minority Ethnic (BME):** a term that has emerged since the first edition of this book. The phrase is used to cover people visibly identified by a 'black' skin colour whose ethnic group identity is Caribbean, African or Asian. Not everyone is at ease with the phrase and that includes me. The full phrase is often shortened to BME, which loses any personal sense and is uncomfortably close to BSE ('mad cow disease'). I choose to avoid the phrase, unless quoting from material that uses the term.

Culture and cultural identity

- **Culture:** describes the particular patterns of behaviour and associated beliefs that are shared by the individuals within a given group. Not all individuals will necessarily follow these patterns in exactly the same way. The term **cultural identity** is often used where, previously, people might have talked of a national identity.

- **Cultural diversity:** the sense that a society includes a myriad of cultural sources and people who locate their identity in different cultural backgrounds. There is usually a great deal of within-group variation as well as broad differences between groups and overlap.

■ **Multicultural:** a word to describe a society, like that of the UK, in which the population is drawn from many distinct cultural backgrounds. The word is often misapplied, rather like 'ethnic', to mean not 'white' European.

Faiths and religious belief

■ **Faith** or **religion:** a set of beliefs and practices built around one or more deities or individuals with paranormal powers.

■ **Sects:** the subdivisions that have formed within most world faiths after disagreements over detail of belief or religious practice.

■ **Religious intolerance:** hostility expressed by members of one faith towards a different faith, or between those who hold to a faith and people who do not follow any religious faith.

■ **Anti-Semitism:** religious intolerance and discrimination targeted at people of the Jewish faith and/or cultural background.

■ **Sectarianism:** intolerance expressed towards members of another denomination of the same religious faith. This form of discrimination can occur at an individual, group, cultural and institutional level.

■ **Anti-sectarianism:** the active attempt to challenge bigotry and inequalities that arise from a sectarian outlook and from religious intolerance of other types.

Sex and gender

■ **Sex and sex differences:** refer to the biological differences, created by the genes when babies are conceived, between boys and girls, men and women.

■ **Gender:** describes the psychological identity of being male or female, and the awareness of what sex differences mean within the social context.

■ **Gender equality:** aims and practice to promote equalising of opportunities on the basis of sex. Some writers prefer 'gender equity'.

■ **Gender stereotypes:** firm beliefs about the characteristics, behaviour, talents or weaknesses of individuals on the basis of their male or female identity.

■ **Sexism:** an outlook of prejudiced attitudes and discriminatory behaviour towards individuals on the basis of their sex.

■ **Sexual orientation:** the preference about sex of partner made by young people or adults.

Disability

- **Disabled children** or **children with disabilities:** children who live with any kind of continuing sensory impairment or chronic health condition that affects their development and/or daily life.

- **Children with special needs:** the same meaning as disabled children. The phrase can be unclear, since all children have individual wishes and specific needs. The phrase originally included gifted children, but in practice has been applied to disability and chronic ill health.

EQUALITY AND CHILDHOOD

An understanding of how children learn has to underpin effective good practice for equality. During early childhood, children learn an impressive range of skills and a large body of knowledge. By middle childhood, they still have a great deal to learn, but they already have a firm basis to their view of the world. They have developed, and will continue to develop, their social attitudes about other children and people in general. By four or five years of age, young children have developed opinions about and expectations of others, whom they judge to be like them or unfamiliar from what they already know. Children have also established views, which are still open to change, about their own place in their social world, their personal identity and sense of self-worth.

Awareness of differences

Children are visually curious; they look at and are interested in people and the events around them. As they learn to talk, children comment out loud on what has caught their interest. What young children say will depend on their experiences so far, based mainly on their own neighbourhood and family.

Four- and five-year-olds tend to remark on physical differences and contrasts with children or adults who do not fit their experience so far. They notice and often share their observations with familiar adults, with the assumption that you will be interested as well. Sometimes what children have seen or heard leads them to ask a question, but not always. Here are some examples.

- Children may point out an adult who is strikingly tall or heavy in comparison with the adults in their social network. They may comment, 'That lady looks awfully old' or 'Why is that man so little?' Part of adult responsibility is to explain courteously to a young child that their comments may be accurate but concern for other people's feelings means that observations should be made at less than top volume.

- Children are learning about boys and girls, and their observation of differences is often linked with trying to sort out what makes someone a girl or a boy. They may comment about another child, 'Is Nula really a girl? She's got very short hair.'

- As children encounter disabled peers or adults, they are likely to comment. A young child may say, 'Did you know that Andy in my playgroup has a thing to make his ears work?' or 'Marsha's daddy sits in a big buggy. Now why does he do that?'

- In a diverse neighbourhood, children may remark that some of their play companions are different in skin colour to themselves. Many parts of the UK have some level of ethnic group diversity but the variation is not reflected in skin colour. So young children may make an accurate observation that seeing a 'black' child is unusual or that an adult is dressed in an unfamiliar way.

Childhood is a time of busy learning

Change and stability

Adults who pay close attention to what children say and to their questions can learn a great deal about the development of children's thinking, as well as their current knowledge. The observations of parents and practitioners may be a source of endearing stories about children, but they are also a window onto children's emotional and intellectual world.

One area of children's learning focuses on what changes and what does not. Children observe that other people differ in many respects, but they are working out which physical characteristics will change as they grow older. Children are initially grounded in the present and what they personally know. So it can be a revelation to a boy that he will not always be a child; one day he will be a man, rather like his daddy, but he will not be able to become a mummy. In a similar way, children are often surprised to realise, perhaps by looking in the family photograph album, that grandma was once a young person, even a child.

When children realise that some features change, they begin to wonder whether everything can change. They have to learn about those characteristics that are stable throughout life. So it is not surprising if some children allow for the possibility that their sex or skin colour, or that of their friends, might change as they get older or because of circumstances. Children are learning about health, illness and disability and it is not obvious to them which are the conditions from which people can recover. So a child might reasonably ask, 'When will Andy's ears get better?' You may explain to a child that comments about people are usually best made in a quieter voice. It is a different situation from calling out, 'Hey, look at the big, yellow lorry!' because lorries do not have feelings.

From awareness to prejudice

Children who notice physical differences do not immediately assume that some characteristics are more valued. However, they are able to learn negative attitudes with the same ease that they are learning so many other ideas in their young life. Children will use the prejudiced words and actions of adults, or other children, to build negative images of people from a given faith or ethnic group, or people with visible disabilities. Attitudes of rejection can limit children's choice of friends and show in their words and behaviour towards children, or adults, from the defined group whom they have learned to dismiss.

Children who live in divided communities learn the religious or social distinctions that are important to local adults, even when outsiders would be hard-pressed to distinguish between the groups. Some writers are very aware of how anti-Muslim feeling has been absorbed by children over the early years of the twenty-first century. However, more than one generation of children has grown up with the conflict in Northern Ireland. Honest observation and research have documented the ease with which young children learn the bigotry that supports sectarianism. They become alert to symbols, such as flags or choice of sports, used to tell Catholic from Protestant. Sectarianism is also a serious issue in some parts of Scotland.

Children's personal identity

Young children steadily develop a sense of themselves as a unique person. Their personal identity builds from many aspects:

- their own name and an understanding of whether they are a girl or a boy
- their immediate family, and their place in relation to their parents, brothers and sisters and other close relatives
- how they look and how people react to their looks
- what they can do and what they cannot do, and whether this seems to matter to other people
- a growing sense of 'what we do in my family' – children's experience of cultural tradition and religious faith or other significant beliefs within their daily life.

Children's sense of identity and their sense of self-esteem will depend a great deal on their experience of other people – children and adults – and their own social world. Children may feel mainly positive about themselves, that they are worthwhile individuals and valued by others. Or they may doubt themselves and wonder if some of the sources of their personal identity, perhaps being a girl or having a visible disability, make them less valuable than other children. All children have the right to feel confident that their ethnic group and cultural background are valuable and of potential interest to their peers, as well as people who share the same or a very similar background.

Mixed heritage

Men and women have married, or formed long-standing partnerships, across every social, ethnic, faith and other group boundary. Personal

---

WHAT DOES IT MEAN?

There is not full agreement about a general term for children or adults whose family background brings together two or more ethnic group backgrounds. Phrases include 'mixed parentage', 'dual heritage' and 'multiple heritage'. If you need to know about individuals, invite them to self-describe.

The term 'mixed race' tends to be avoided by professionals working in equality, because of problems with the word 'race' – although, oddly, 'race equality' remains acceptable. The term 'half-caste' is definitely regarded as offensive. However, both phrases may be used by people outside equality professional boundaries, without obvious intention to offend.

commitments have been made in communities where such behaviour provokes disapproval, rejection and violence, even when the union has been illegal. Children's identity is then potentially a blend of their heritage from both parents. Adults aware of racist attitudes in society have sometimes taken the view that children with a 'white' and a 'black' parent must commit to one side or the other. Children from inter-faith relationships are sometimes given a similar stark choice. Increasingly it seems that children and young people are standing firm to determine their own identity, and that can include an insistence on valuing all sources of their family heritage.

In the UK, a considerable number of couples bridge various ethnic, social and faith-group boundaries. Some live with the full support of their extended family and community, but not all. External pressures can be very strong on families, and some fragment under the strain. Children of mixed ethnic group parentage are over-represented in the population of looked-after children (those who have become the responsibility of their local authority), as are children of inter-faith couples in Northern Ireland.

Positive pride rather than superiority

Children deserve a sense of pride in their own sources of personal identity, but it is unjust if they achieve their own confidence at the cost of other children's self-esteem. Some children learn to boost their sense of self-worth by being disdainful about a child of the opposite sex, rude about a disabled child or rejecting of a child from an ethnic group different from their own.

This pattern can be learned through childhood from the family. Adults who experience a socially deprived position in life can be especially vulnerable to building an identity mainly through disparaging other social or ethnic groups. This pattern is not exclusive to 'white' ethnic groups. Children may hear adults who are keen to blame another group for their misfortunes. In an economically hard-pressed neighbourhood, one group may be convinced that other people have gained unfair advantages. Offensive attitudes are not, of course, restricted to those families who have few sources of positive identity. People with no financial worries and a secure social position can be breathtakingly dismissive of others not in their social class or ethnic group.

Adult beliefs about children's attitudes

Some adults are still resistant to considering equality issues as they apply to childhood, especially early childhood. This resistance is reflected in the most ill-informed newspaper stories about equality practice. This section addresses some assumptions and mistaken beliefs about how young children learn. You may be thinking through some of these assumptions yourself or parents may ask you what your setting does about equality and why.

'Children do not notice'

Some adults claim that children are 'innocent' and do not notice social or ethnic group differences, so they cannot develop attitudes based on such visible differences. But how could children not notice and learn? Adults responsible for young children base much of their everyday contact on the belief that children are alert to their surroundings, that they learn from what they hear and see.

TAKE ANOTHER PERSPECTIVE

Some years ago a nursery teacher shared an observation with me of two boys, one 'white' European and one 'black' African in family origins. She had overheard the two boys laughing as they conspired together to swap their winter coats 'so that everybody will think you're me'. The teacher's interpretation of this anecdote was that young children literally did not notice differences in skin colour.

I disagreed with her viewpoint; it seemed more likely that the boys were alert to differences in colour and other descriptive features. Otherwise, how did they think everyone would be fooled by exchanging coats? It seemed more probable that these children had not yet realised the great significance placed on skin colour by many adults. They believed their trick could work, because a large winter coat would be much more noticeable than a small face.

What do you think?

'To notice is the same as being prejudiced'

Adults may prefer to believe children do not notice those aspects of the world that the adults themselves would rather remained outside children's experience. Adults are especially uneasy if they believe that noticing a difference is the same as saying the difference matters and makes some people better than others.

Many adults, and that still includes some practitioners, believe that if you say that children notice ethnic group differences, like skin colour, then you must also be saying that the children are prejudiced, but this is not the case. Adults can no longer easily distinguish awareness and prejudice; children are still learning. In a similar way, a child who notices another child's disability is not automatically being offensive about that individual, nor about disability in general. It depends so much on what is said and in what way.

Another source of adult unease arises from lack of confidence about how to react when children express curiosity, express potential prejudices about others or show distress at offence aimed at themselves. It feels easier to take the approach that alert and curious young children do not notice any of the visible differences of sex, ethnic group or disability.

'Children only learn what you deliberately teach them'

For a long time, many practitioners claimed that, since they never touched upon social or ethnic group differences, then they could not possibly exert any influence over children's developing attitudes. This approach was sometimes linked with the claim that talking about such topics destroys childhood 'innocence'.

Even limited observation of young children soon shows that they do not just learn what adults intend them to learn through deliberate telling or showing. Children are busy building their attitudes from what they see in their immediate play environment and, by implication, from what is absent. They learn from what adults say, but also from topics of conversation that adults avoid or with which they look uncomfortable.

'You should treat children all the same'

Some adults still claim that they do not notice any differences between the children for whom they are responsible, that 'I treat them all the same.' This belief muddles up fair treatment of young children with behaving as if they lack individuality. Children are not all the same and adults have a serious problem if they genuinely do not notice the ethnic group, sex or ability differences that make children into unique individuals. Reflective and good practice over equality is to work out in what ways it is appropriate to treat children as different, but with equal attention and respect offered to all children and their families.

'Children's attitudes are not our business'

Occasionally, a team or individuals argue that they should not get involved in children's attitudes over gender, ethnic group and culture because that would be interference, perhaps even 'brainwashing'. Yet the same practitioners are concerned to promote sharing or considerate behaviour at mealtimes – examples of attitudes linked with behaviour. Adult choices are shaped by what they believe to be important. Facing the responsibilities raised by equality certainly does not mean imposing values onto a setting that was previously a value-free zone.

TAKE ANOTHER PERSPECTIVE

Be honest with yourself and about your own staff team. Do you tend to make any of the comments highlighted in this section? If you are a student, have you heard similar comments expressed confidently to shut down a discussion about equality? Take one or two comments and ask yourself, or discuss with someone else, the following questions.

- What does this comment actually mean?
- Do we really put such sentiments into practice and what would happen if we did?
- In what ways are we possibly blocking children's experience or their developing self-esteem?

If you want to find out more:

✥ *Children's Play Information Service (CPIS).* Tel: 020 7843 6303; www.ncb.org.uk/library/cpis.

✥ *Early Childhood Unit*, 8 Wakley Street, London EC1V 7QE. Tel: 020 7843 6449. Download a range of topics on the website (www.earlychildhood.org.uk), as well as the series *Listening as a Way of Life*.

✥ *Early Years Equality* (*EYE*) PO Box 3428, Chester CH1 9BX. Tel: 01244 310569; www.earlyyearsequality.org. Focuses on race equality.

✥ *Learning and Teaching Scotland.* Tel: 01382 443600; www.ltscotland.org.uk. Valuable resource for anyone in the UK; online resources including *Early Years Matters*.

✥ *Sure Start*, www.surestart.gov.uk. The website has briefing papers to download; the 'Birth to three matters' section has three Resource Guides you can download, relating to children from minority ethnic groups, disabled children and working in partnership with families.

Individual practitioners and teams need to keep up-to-date with events affecting professional practice. But you also need accessible sources for ideas.

The following magazines and journals are useful in different ways for supporting good practice, including equality issues.

❖ *Children Now.* Tel: 020 8606 7500; www.childrennow.co.uk. Weekly magazine with news, updates and features; part of the National Children's Bureau subscription, otherwise pay by subscription.

❖ *Nursery World* and its regular supplements like *Out of School.* Tel: 01454 642480; www.nursery-world.com.

❖ *Practical Pre-School* and *Practical Professional Child Care* published by Step Forward Publishing. Tel: 01926420046; www.practicalpreschool.com.

❖ *Play Today* from the Children's Play Council. Tel: 020 7843 6016.

❖ *Race Equality Teaching* published by Trentham Books, www.trenthambooks.co.uk. The journal started life as *Multicultural Teaching* and was relaunched in 2002; you can buy back issues of the journal.

2 Equality law, guidance and policy

Professional practice requires a grasp of the main laws within the UK that relate to equality. This chapter describes, in brief, how legislation affects work with children and families. It is your professional responsibility, especially for team leaders or advisers, to know how to find out more. However, you need to seek proper legal advice if you face a challenge based on requirements by law.

> **The main sections of this chapter cover:**
>
> ✴ **a legal framework**
>
> ✴ **equality in law**
>
> ✴ **policy for equality.**

A LEGAL FRAMEWORK

Legislation does not automatically change behaviour or attitudes, but laws make a public statement about what is acceptable or unacceptable within a given society. Good practice for equality is considerably broader than the requirements of any of the laws described here. There are moral issues around what you judge to be the right way to deal with daily situations. All the fine details of legislation will not cover everything in your practice.

Where laws apply

Laws create a framework for all residents of the UK by defining some boundaries around what must or must not be done. The UK comprises four nations: England, Wales, Scotland and Northern Ireland. The central government determines some legislation that applies across the UK and passes through Parliament at Westminster, London. Historically Scotland has operated with a high level of self-determination and can set legislation through the Scottish Parliament in Edinburgh. Devolution of control towards the end of the twentieth century gave more power to Wales through the National Assembly at Cardiff. Wales does not have the power to make primary legislation, but can determine national applications. At the time of writing (autumn 2005) the Assembly in Northern Ireland remains suspended and any legislation in process has been frozen, when it is not the type of law that can pass through Westminster as an Order in Council.

You will first hear about possible laws when they are debated in Parliament or Assembly. Proposed primary legislation is usually known as a Bill. When it has passed to become law, the legislation tends to be known as an Act in England, Wales and Scotland, and an Order in Northern Ireland. You will often hear or read about Bills that are in process, so it is important to recall that proposed sections often get modified during the debate. Some proposed Bills are defeated and do not become law – at least not this time around.

Law, guidance and advice

The laws described in this section are primary legislation and the requirements built into the laws must be obeyed. However, legal language is not expressed in a way that allows straightforward application to daily life.

- In the years after any new law has been passed, there are often court cases that test sections that are open to more than one interpretation. Legal decisions following this challenge build a resource called case law. This information sets definite precedents for when a similar disagreement arises in the future. You may see case law quoted in newspapers or information leaflets in the format of 'Green versus Bloggs' or 'Bloggs versus the Crown'.

- Sometimes the relevant government department issues further information through books of guidance or codes of practice. These documents do not have the same force as primary legislation, but they are described as statutory. It is required that local authorities or

In what kind of society do you want her to grow up?

relevant organisations follow the details of statutory guidance or a code.

- Some good practice guidance is recommended, meaning that the associated government department strongly advises that the suggestions and examples are followed. An example is the difference between two Commission for Racial Equality (CRE) papers: *Race equality duty: code of practice*, which is statutory guidance, and *A guide for schools: the duty to promote race equality*, which is non-statutory advice (download from www.cre.gov.uk).

WHAT DOES IT MEAN?

Primary legislation: The term used for laws that have been passed for a given country. The detail of law defines what is legally required or has been made illegal. The name of a law is given, with the date that it was passed by Parliament or Assembly.

Statutory guidance: Issued by the relevant government department to explain some laws in less legal language. Such guidance describes what must be done or not done.

Good practice guidance: Often issued to support professionals and organisations to put law and statutory guidance into daily practice. These publications may be 'recommended' by the relevant government department or 'commended' in a foreword by a Minister.

Case law: Built through court cases when individuals or organisations challenge the interpretation of a law. The legal decision at the end of the case establishes a **precedent** that can be used in the future.

Key concepts within equality legislation

Legislation relevant to equality was initially most concerned with identifying discriminatory actions and making them unlawful. In recent years there has been a significant shift towards legislation that also establishes an active duty to promote equality and equal treatment. The laws described briefly in this chapter are not identical in their provisions, but there is now enough commonality that it is useful to explain those shared concepts that apply in much, but not all, legal provision that covers equality.

The following terms are used regularly within the legal framework for equality. Any legal challenge against behaviour would have to demonstrate that action, or inaction, was unlawful. Defence or justification would have to show that there were sound, non-discriminatory reasons for the behaviour.

- **Direct discrimination** – rejecting or favouring someone, for instance for a service or employment, on the basis of their group identity. The motive for such behaviour is irrelevant; what matters is the discriminatory result.

- **Indirect discrimination** – imposing conditions on everyone that effectively mean that individuals are favoured or put at a disadvantage because of their group identity. It is not regarded as an excuse that practices have a long history or were not intended as discriminatory. The legal requirement is increasingly that organisations must actively explore the impact of any policy or rules. Such behaviour can be unlawful, unless differential treatment can be shown to be a justifiable method to meet a legitimate aim.

- **Victimisation** – treating people, or those close to them (like children), in a negative way as a consequence of their challenge to discriminatory treatment.

- **Harassment** – behaving towards people in a consistently negative way in line with their group identity, such as to create an intimidating or hostile environment for them.

- **Segregation** – separating a person from others, or making distinctions in a service that effectively separate on the basis of group identity, and with no justifiable reason that would be beneficial to that person.

- **Promoting equality of opportunity** – this concept has been common within guidance. New equality legislation now frequently goes beyond a legal requirement to avoid discriminatory behaviour. There is increasingly a legal obligation actively to ensure equality of opportunity, in all relevant ways, with special attention to groups who could easily be disadvantaged.

Legislation applies to all residents of the country, including children, unless a specific exclusion has been made.

EQUALITY IN LAW

Gender equality

The Equal Pay Act 1970 and the Sex Discrimination Act 1975 were applied across the UK in response to widespread discrimination against women within society in terms of employment and pay, use of services or in reference to a woman's marital status. The Equal Opportunities Commission (EOC), with offices in England, Wales and Scotland, monitors the implementation of these Acts. In Northern Ireland the Equality Commission is responsible for the implications of legislation: Equal Pay Act (Northern Ireland) 1970, Sex Discrimination (Northern Ireland) Order 1976.

The laws make it illegal to discriminate against people on the grounds of their sex. Although the law was introduced in response to discrimination against women, protection in law applies equally to men. So early years settings cannot decide to turn away male applicants for posts, any more than a company can refuse to employ women, nor offer less favourable conditions for the same post depending on the sex of the applicant. Nor would it be lawful to have different job descriptions or roles exclusively on the grounds of sex.

Sometimes discriminatory behaviour is less obvious. Illegal indirect discrimination occurs when an employer applies a condition for a job or rules for promotion that mean one sex is less likely to be able to meet the condition. Exceptions can be made only if the sex of an employee can be justified as a genuine occupational qualification (GOQ). Special encouragement or training can be offered to people of a sex under-represented in an area of work, but employers cannot discriminate positively at the point of offering a job – for example, by having a quota.

The sex discrimination legislation was developed with adults in mind, especially in connection with employment. The law was not designed to relate to practice issues that arise directly with children. However, the EOC has been active in commissioning reviews and guidance of direct relevance to early years, school and out-of-school practitioners. EOC Scotland offers papers on its website about the position of fathers as well as mothers, the early years workforce and children's learning in the early years.

Further legal regulations have been issued in response to the European Employment Directive in 2000 from the European Union. The Employment Equality (Sexual Orientation) Regulations 2003 have made it illegal for employers across the UK to discriminate on the grounds of sexual orientation.

Race equality

The Race Relations Act 1976 was a response to substantial discrimination on racial grounds within society. The Act applies to England, Wales and Scotland with the aim of defining discrimination and making such behaviour illegal. The Commission for Racial Equality (CRE) was created as part of the 1976 Act. The Act made it unlawful to discriminate on racial grounds, which cover skin colour, race and nationality, including citizenship, ethnic or national origins. Case law has further established that some groups are, or are not, defined as a distinct racial group. For instance, Sikhs, Jews and Travellers, or Gypsies, have been defined legally as distinct ethnic groups and so are covered by the Act. Religious faith was not included in this legislation.

Discriminatory behaviour was defined in four broad ways and examples are given here that are relevant to services for children and families.

- Direct discrimination – refusing to admit a child to a nursery because he is Chinese or to employ a new member of staff because she is Egyptian. The Act applies to everyone, so an all-Asian staff group could not decide to avoid employing non-Asian colleagues.

- Indirect discrimination – applying any condition that in practice favours one group over another. Groups that judge they need a team member of a particular ethnic group have to justify the need on non-racial grounds – for instance, a bilingual practitioner to support bilingual children. The job specification has to establish a GOQ, in the same way as for gender.

- Segregation – for instance, a school that is organised so that children from Traveller or Gypsy families have to sit on a different table from other children, with no genuine care or educational reason for this pattern.

- Victimisation – if children are excluded from an after-school club, or treated badly by team members, as a consequence of complaints by their families about earlier discrimination.

Like other equality legislation, the Race Relations Act 1976 was not concerned with people's motives or intentions; the focus is entirely on what happens as a result of behaviour or organisational rules put into practice. Like any law, the Act does not enable anyone to insist that a person or group has acted illegally, in a racist manner, without offering objective proof. Any possible prosecutions only go forward after careful consideration of evidence.

The Race Relations (Amendment) Act 2000 extended the legal requirements of the 1976 act to require that all listed public authorities must work to:

- eliminate unlawful racial discrimination
- promote equality of opportunity
- promote good relations between people of different racial groups.

Effectively the Amendment has required a more proactive role for any public bodies, including care and education, to work towards racial equality. The legal duties apply to all early years, school and out-of-school care settings that are the responsibility of the local authority or who are in any way overseen by it. The Amendment requires settings to monitor how their services are used and experienced with regard to different ethnic groups. This requirement means that a school has to monitor the academic achievements of pupils and patterns of school exclusion rates. Information needs to show whether there are significant differences by ethnic group identity. The school would then have to explore the reasons for the differences, and take effective and appropriate action to resolve the anomaly.

Voluntary, independent and private services do not have the same additional legal duty. However, the same steps would be regarded as good practice and, of course, these settings and individual childminders are still subject to the existing anti-discrimination legislation.

The two Race Relations Acts just described do not apply in Northern Ireland. However, the Race Relations (NI) Order 1997 covers similar ground and is monitored by the Equality Commission for Northern Ireland. The Order specifically included the Irish Traveller community as a racial group.

Religion and equality

This race-equality legislation does not extend to religion. Jews and Sikhs are covered on the basis of shared racial identity, not through their faith. Muslims are not covered in the same way, because Islam is a faith followed by people from many different ethnic groups. The Equality Bill (see page 34) being debated in Westminster over 2005 has included group identity by religion.

In Northern Ireland, religious affiliation has divided Protestant and Catholic Christians. The Fair Employment and Treatment (Northern Ireland) Order 1998 requires organisations to avoid direct or indirect discrimination and victimisation on the basis of religious or political affiliation, or supposed affiliation. Legal requirements exist for monitoring job recruitment by religious (or community) affiliation and the possibility of affirmative action. The rest of the UK did not have similar law until the Employment Equality (Religion or Belief) Regulations 2003 (another result of the European Employment Directive 2000 from the European Union). It is now illegal for employers to discriminate on the grounds of a person's religion or belief in England, Scotland and Wales.

The Criminal Justice (Scotland) Act 2003 made specific provision for offences aggravated by religious hatred in that the offender showed malice on the basis of the victim's religious membership or presumed affiliation. This provision arose at least in part because some areas of Scotland experience Protestant–Catholic sectarianism. During 2005 there has been fierce debate over the proposed Racial and Religious Hatred Bill for England and Wales, which aims to extend existing laws against incitement to racial hatred to cover all religious faiths. This possible legislation was still being debated when this book went to press.

Disability and equality

The Disability Discrimination Act 1995 (DDA), applicable to England, Wales and Scotland, established the rights of disabled people, including children, to be able to access services. The DDA applied to childcare settings but educational establishments were exempt until the passing of the Special Educational Needs and Disability Act (SENDA) 2001. The Disability Discrimination Act 2005 removed some remaining exemptions and strengthened the legal obligation to promote equality for disabled people. Three key duties are directly relevant to services for children and families:

1   not to treat disabled children less favourably in any way than their peers
2   to make reasonable adjustments to enable the inclusion and full involvement of disabled children
3   to make reasonable adjustment to enable access by disabled adults – parents or professionals.

These duties create the legal situation that it is unlawful to discriminate against disabled children in such a way that they cannot access care and educational services. Disability is defined as having an impairment that has a substantial and long-term adverse effect on children's ability to perform daily tasks. The impairment could be a disabling condition like cerebral palsy or a chronic health condition like epilepsy. The legislation also covers conditions that affect mental health.

SENDA also required that all early years settings have a written SEN policy, a designated member of staff with responsibility for SEN (the SENCO) and arrangements for continued professional development using training made available by the LEA or Partnership. These requirements built upon a series of Education Acts applicable to England, Wales and Scotland that shaped provision for disabled children and their families. The Children Acts and Order (see page 33) are also relevant to disabled children.

An SEN Code of Practice applies to England and Wales. In Scotland the Education (Additional Support for Learning) (Scotland) Act 2004 has now created the broader concept of 'additional support needs'. Practice covers help for any children, including those with disabilities, that is necessary if they are to be able to make the most of their educational experience.

The situation in Northern Ireland has differed from the rest of the UK. The Equality (Disability etc.) (Northern Ireland) Order 2000 expanded the duties and powers of the Equality Commission to be much more active in promoting equalisation of opportunities for disabled people in Northern Ireland. The Special Educational Needs and Disability Order 2005

(SENDO) aims to establish for disabled children the same rights to mainstream education as is required in the rest of the UK. The legal details are very similar to those of SENDA, but also include enforceable disability discrimination legislation applicable to schools and higher education.

Legislation affecting the welfare of children

Several key pieces of UK legislation affect children's overall welfare and have implications for equality in practice. These are:

- the Children Act 1989 for England and Wales
- the Children (Scotland) Act 1995
- the Children (Northern Ireland) Order 1995
- the UN Convention on the Rights of the Child 1989.

The first three pieces of primary legislation have similarities but are not identical and of course operate within the social welfare and early years services of the four nations of the UK.

None of the Children Acts or Order is legislation specifically about equality. However, they all introduced the requirement to respond to the religious persuasion, racial origin, and cultural and linguistic background of individual children. This requirement is applied in the process of making decisions about children when responsibility has shifted to include non-family members, provision of services for children in need, and the registration and inspection of early years services. The Scottish legislation extended the approach of the Children Act 1989 and integrated the concept of children's rights.

The UN Convention on the Rights of the Child 1989 was the first international agreement in which the rights of children worldwide were detailed in one document. The UK signed the Convention in 1991. Consequently, central government has to ensure that the laws and practice regarding children meet the standards established in the Convention. The UN Convention is organised by a series of articles, describing the rights of children and young people up to the age of 18 years. Some relevant statements include the following.

- **Article 2:** the right of non-discrimination and that all the rights within the Convention apply to all children equally, whatever their race, sex, religion, language, disability, opinion or family background.
- **Article 14:** parents have a duty to provide children with guidance. However, children have the right to choose their own religion and to express their own views as soon as they are able to decide for themselves.

33

- **Article 20:** when children cannot be cared for within their own family, the children's race, religion, culture and language must all be taken into consideration in decisions about an alternative home.
- **Article 30:** Children of minority communities and indigenous populations have the right to enjoy their own culture and to practise their own religion and language.

Single equality bills

A Single Equality Bill was developed in Northern Ireland, but progress stalled with the suspension of the Assembly. The aim of the Bill was to take account of developments in the rest of the UK, European Union directives and to address civil rights and religious liberties for Northern Ireland.

At the time of writing (autumn 2005) an Equality Bill is being debated in Parliament at Westminster. This Bill aims to provide the framework for a broad-based 'culture of respect'. The proposed new legislation will, if passed, make the following main changes for England, Wales and Scotland.

- Create a Commission for Equality and Human Rights (CEHR) that would become the regulatory body to ensure equality, human rights and anti-discrimination.
- Over a specified time span, the CEHR would take responsibility for race, gender and disability equality covered by existing legislation. But the Bill also brings in equality and anti-discrimination over sexual orientation, religion or belief and age.
- The details of the Bill are not explicitly about children and young people. There is scope for the CEHR to promote good relations between communities and to ensure that every individual has an equal opportunity to participate in society.
- Human rights are key to the operation of a new Commission, but it is too early to tell how provisions would actually work. Children's Commissioners for each part of the UK will remain separate from the CEHR.

If you want to find out more:

You will often find useful links through a good search engine like Google. I have found the following organisations and website links especially helpful.

- ❖ *Children's Legal Centre,* University of Essex, Wivenhoe Park, Colchester, Essex. Tel: 01206 873820; www.childrenslegalcentre.com.

✤ *Commission for Racial Equality (CRE)*; www.cre.gov.uk. A website with many links, including to CRE Scotland and CRE Wales; provides useful briefing papers about laws and relevant legislation in process.

✤ *Department of Trade and Industry*; www.dti.gov.uk/er/equality. Information about employment regulations in England, Wales and Scotland.

✤ *Equal Opportunities Commission (EOC)*; www.eoc.org.uk. Links including to EOC Wales and EOC Scotland.

✤ *Equality Commission for Northern Ireland*, Equality House, 7–9 Shaftesbury Square, Belfast BT2 7DP. Tel: 028 90 500600; www.equalityni.org.

✤ *4 Nations Child Policy Network*; www.childpolicy.org.uk. Covers the whole of the UK and includes legislation in process.

✤ *UNICEF*; www.unicef.org/crc/crc.htm. Has a section for the UN Convention on the Rights of the Child.

Much has changed since the mid-twentieth century

POLICY FOR EQUALITY

The early years of the twenty-first century have seen a significant shift towards equality as an active approach and integral to all aspects of practice.

Equality regarding any group identity cannot be treated as an afterthought or optional add-on activity. Effective equality practice does not stop with addressing negative views or removing inappropriate resources. Professional practice has to be that you actively promote a positive outlook and are ready to deal with possible blocks to inclusion before a situation becomes significant.

Guidance on learning

Every setting needs a clear policy on equality issues as they affect everyday practice. In some cases such a policy is a legal requirement, otherwise a clear policy is an integral part of good and effective equality practice. Each nation in the UK has an early years curriculum. Equality issues are raised in each guidance document about supporting the learning of young children:

- the **Foundation Stage** in England for children from three years of age to the end of reception class when children are just five or nearly six years of age (www.qca.org.uk)
- the **Foundation Phase** in Wales, for children from three to seven years of age (www.learning.wales.gov.uk or www.accac.org.uk)
- the **Curriculum Framework for Children 3–5** in Scotland (www.ltscotland.org.uk/earlyyears/framechildren3to5.asp)
- the **Curricular Guidance for Pre-School Education** for three- and four-year-olds in Northern Ireland (www.deni.gov.uk/preschool/preschool_curricular.pdf); this guidance will be revised if the proposed Foundation Stage for children from three to six years of age is implemented (under discussion in 2005).

The exact wording differs, but each guidance document commits to ensuring equality of opportunity on the basis of gender, disability, ethnic group and cultural background. Descriptive examples of experiences and resources promote the twin aims of enabling young children to feel positive about their own sources of identity and steadily to extend their understanding of family backgrounds and perspectives that are less familiar. More specific examples tend to be within the area of learning related to emotional and social development, but also for 'Knowledge and understanding of world' in the English Foundation Stage and 'Bilingualism and multi-cultural understanding' in the Welsh Foundation Phase.

Two nations have additionally developed guidance for practitioners working with under-threes: *Birth to three matters* in England and *Birth to Three: supporting our youngest children* in Scotland. In ways appropriate for this youngest group, both sets of guidance promote an active approach to equality and emphasise the necessity of close partnership with families.

- Learning and Teaching Scotland, *Birth to Three: supporting our youngest children* 2005; www.ltscotland.org.uk/earlyyears/birthtothree
- Sure Start/DfES, *Birth to three matters: a framework to support children in their earliest years* 2002; www.surestart.gov.uk/resources/ childcareworkers/birthtothreematters.

A birth to five framework, the Early Years Foundation Stage, is in the process of development for England.

Written policy

You need to check for any local requirements, but it probably works best now to develop a general policy that clearly applies to all equality applications. There could be a great deal of repetition if you try to draft separate policies for ethnic group and culture, faith, language, gender and disability.

Neither group teams nor childminders should have to draft policies starting from a blank sheet of paper. You will find some general points in this section but you are strongly advised to use available resources from:

- advisers in your local area appropriate to your part of the early years, school and out-of-school services
- supportive materials from your local authority or partnership
- your coordinator for the local childminding network
- national professional organisations relevant to your part of services for children and families (see below).

If you want to find out more:

The following professional organisations offer information or publications to support your development of appropriate policies:

- ✤ National Childminding Association, Royal Court, 81 Tweedy Road, Bromley, Kent BR1 1TG. Tel: 0845 880 0044; www.ncma.org.uk.

- ✤ National Day Nurseries Association, Oak House, Woodvale Road, Brighouse, West Yorkshire HD6 4AB. Tel: 0870 774 4244; www.ndna.org.uk. NDNA publications are distributed by Featherstone Education: www.featherstone.uk.com.

- ✤ Playgroup Network, 391 West Road, Newcastle-upon-Tyne NE15 7PY. Tel: 0191 275 3837; www.playgroup-network.org.uk.

- ✤ Pre-school Learning Alliance, 69 Kings Cross Road, London WC1X 9LL. Tel: 020 7833 0991; www.pre-school.org.uk.

✢ 4Children, City Reach, 5 Greenwich View Place, London E14 9NN. Tel: 020 7512 2100; www.4Children.org.uk. Covers out-of-school care settings.

Policy and practice

Many settings are now required to have a SENCO and in some situations this role is merged to become a more general Equality Coordinator. The person who takes this kind of special responsibility offers a lead and should be ready to promote discussion. This practitioner does not take all responsibility for equality practice in a setting – any more than child protection is handed over totally to the named team specialist.

Any policy needs to be open to discussion and review, and an exchange of opinions within a team can raise important practical issues, as well as air misunderstandings or disagreements (see the examples in Chapter 9). Any policy can have real meaning only when it is put into practice day by day and an equality perspective affects all your work. If you are a practitioner in the childminding service you need to have equivalent policies that are a public statement about your service.

A written policy works as a clear statement of the commitment of the setting, or your personal commitment, to equality and, in brief, how such a commitment affects all aspects of your practice. You need to use words that communicate 'active recognition of . . .' different identities, rather than a phrase like 'regardless of . . .'. The second phrase can, unfortunately, suggest that you kindly overlook family or other identity. You might consider a key opening paragraph that focuses on children, perhaps to highlight that you aim to create a harmonious atmosphere in which individual differences are seen as assets and that you want all the children to feel proud of what contributes to their personal identity.

Different elements make up the whole framework for an early years, school or out-of-school service and would include that you strive to do the following.

- Organise every aspect of the service with careful attention to equality. A clear focus on equality includes where and how you promote the service. In group settings, equality affects your admissions system, staff recruitment, selection and training within a team.
- Ensure that all children are welcome and fully included in the regular routines and experiences of your service. Part of this commitment has to be about resolving any issues that prevent children being included.
- Offer personal care that meets the individual needs of children, always with emotional warmth, and that is attentive to their dignity and responsive to family preferences.

- Ensure that any individual care or learning needs will be met in ways that enable children to feel full members of your setting or service.

- Meet children's spiritual needs in ways that are respectful to everyone. Meeting those needs will not entail separate experiences unless this option is appropriate (for instance, a private room for prayer).

- Respect different ways of learning and ensure that individual children can access the resources and experiences on offer.

- Promote respect and courtesy between children through a positive approach to behaviour, including dealing with unacceptable words, actions or attempted ill-treatment.

- Create an accessible and balanced learning environment, with experiences and resources that actively show respect for all children and support an extension of their understanding beyond what is currently familiar.

- Work in an open and courteous partnership with each parent or family carer, being willing to describe what you do and why, dealing respectfully with any differences of opinion or belief and explaining if it is not possible to meet a family's preference.

Policy and strategy

Any policy has to work alongside reflective and good practice. No written policy will do the work alone; it has to be put into practice through the words and actions of practitioners. A policy is a statement of intentions for your practice or service. So policies lay out key principles and values that inform and guide your work. A strategy explains how good intentions will be put into practice, the details of procedures or the choices to be made under given circumstances. The strategy might also be called an implementation programme.

A broad strategy could be about exact steps to be followed, for instance if a team member persisted in biased communication practice that resulted in some families receiving considerably more attention than others. However, strategy that is understood and discussed could be more about the balance of what is done. An example would be that children who use offensive language are told firmly that the words are unacceptable and why, but that practitioners are still responsive in helping with any conflict that provoked the words.

WHAT DOES IT MEAN?

Policy: Key intentions, values or principles that guide a given area of practice.

Strategy: Procedures, steps or preferred approaches for dealing with situations arising that are relevant to this policy.

A realistic view of policy that brings in strategy is not restricted to equality. For instance, your policy about health and safety will not itself keep children or adults safe – no matter how beautifully drafted or laminated. An acceptable level of health and safety is delivered by people who follow what has been agreed and are ready to ask questions for any situation that is unclear. Policy on equality and any related areas of practice has to come alive day by day and through professional practitioners reporting any dilemmas if the policy in practice appears to go counter to the requirements of another policy.

No policy will cover every conceivable situation in detail and it would be unwise to try.

- Focus on the positives in the wording of any policy – what do you strive to offer and to promote? Much like an effective policy on behaviour, you do not want an equality policy that is imbalanced towards listing all the situations you will not tolerate in the name of good practice.

- Your policy needs to state your commitment to clear communication with parents and other family carers, your willingness to listen and seek to understand what matters to each and every family. But avoid any wording that suggests partnership will always mean following parents' requests. Agreement will not always be possible and practitioners need to feel able to give themselves time to think, or consult in a team situation.

- Equality policy, linked with behaviour, may say that offensive badges, T-shirts or written material are not welcome within a school or after-school club. However, local conditions will determine the detail of decisions that need to be discussed.

- An inclusive approach to the physical care needs of children can raise issues around existing policies – for example, over medication or whether children are expected to be toilet-trained. You need a general statement of commitment and should be swift to review policy assumptions that unreasonably exclude a child.

Reflection and review

Part of policy and strategy has to be a shared understanding of how you recognise successful outcomes from the policy. Of course, success is not a one-off, or final 'We've done it!' Nor will it be effective practice for children if their important adults are weighed down by obligation to track and prove particular outcomes. However, all individuals or teams, allegedly committed to equality practice, need to explore what you will be pleased to see and hear in your time with children and families. You might consider the following questions.

▨ What current examples of practice, involving actual children and families, are able to show that your policy is working in an active way?

▨ Are the details of the policy clear to you and to everyone in the team? In what ways have questions or comments highlighted different interpretations of policy in daily practice?

▨ Are the details of the policy clear to the families who use your service? If conversation within partnership raises issues, is there good reason to revisit the policy?

▨ Are your policy and practice over equality clear to other local professionals with whom you work?

▨ In what ways do you use the opportunities of continued professional development, part of which can be from training?

▨ What are your information systems for ensuring that you are up-to-date with any changes in local or national guidance or how the law could affect you? You cannot assume that someone else will always tell you face to face.

LOOK, LISTEN, NOTE, LEARN

The written material of any setting has to be reasonably concise. It is expensive in time and money to produce many long documents, and few parents will get round to reading pages and pages of details. So it is almost inevitable that you will have brief phrases that sum up your approach. You need to be able to explain – to people who are not fellow professionals in your field – what the words mean in practice day by day in the setting.

Look at the following examples. What else would you need to say, perhaps to a parent, to bring these phrases alive? Ideally think of a good example within your own practice of 'What I do'. If these are phrases in a written policy, are there better ways to express that aim?

■ 'We celebrate diversity in the nursery.'

■ 'Here we work to empower disabled children.'

■ 'I show respect for every child's home language.'

■ 'We take a multicultural approach to caring.'

■ 'All nurseries in our company are committed to gender equality.'

■ 'We treat children differently in order to treat them equally.'

■ 'My aim is to treat all children with equal concern.'

■ 'We offer an anti-bias early years curriculum.'

■ 'I encourage all the children to respect faiths other than their own.'

■ 'We want to ensure that all children feel included.'

One way of evaluating equality practice can be to monitor and collect numerical data. Local or national legal obligations will sometimes raise the need to collect information about the group background of children, families or fellow professionals who attend training days. The central government for the UK is asking schools initially (but it seems likely to extend to any relevant service) to collect and record data about pupils' ethnicity, first language, faith or other personal belief, Traveller status and disability during 2006 in order to inform the Schools Census of 2007. The aim of collecting such statistics is to establish a reliable baseline from which to launch improvements and changes to services where any groups appear to be excluded. Parents will have access to the data of their own children and will provide the group identity choices for children of primary school age.

Part 2

Key areas for equality

When I wrote *Equal Opportunities in Practice* in 1997 I felt strongly that practitioners needed to explore the connections between equality issues on gender, disability, faith, and ethnic and cultural diversity. *Equality in Early Childhood* has taken that earlier edition as the core material for updating and revision. Now, in 2005, general discussion and practice around equality makes those links more explicitly. The issues are far from identical, but we need to see the common ground, as well as the divergence. In terms of the Celtic knotwork image, some strands flow in different directions, as well as touching at some points.

In this part of the book, three chapters take a specific and separate focus on the issues central to equality (and inequality) over gender, for ethnic group, cultural traditions and faith, and then on how equality arises for disability. Each of these broad areas has some shared values and concerns. However, there is a different backdrop created by the social history of each equality area. It is important for practitioners to tune in to something of the past, otherwise the concerns of the present will not make full sense.

In each, very broad, area of practice, there is also divergence, even intense disagreement, about priorities and what defines good and effective equality practice. Where appropriate, my aim has been to be clear about my values and any choices I have made, although I know everyone will not necessarily agree. Equality practice is about moral principles and decisions. People are different in many ways – the fact of diversity is not in question – the crucial issues arise from the meaning taken from differences.

Good and effective practice to promote equality, and address inequality, does not pretend differences do not exist. Choice over actions in practice is a moral statement that some interpretations about differences, and the personal and social consequences for children or adults, are unacceptable.

3 Active support for both sexes

All societies take a stance on how to raise girls and boys and how to ensure that they grow into the women and men wanted by this social or cultural group. UK society is no exception to this general rule and, until recent decades, the pattern was clearly one in which men and boys were more highly valued than women and girls. As with other equality areas, the key issues around gender do not make much sense without some social history.

> **The main sections of this chapter cover:**
>
> ✶ **the roots of inequality**
>
> ✶ **focus on childhood**
>
> ✶ **reflection on gender equality.**

THE ROOTS OF INEQUALITY

During the first half of the twentieth century, laws and entrenched social attitudes in the UK encouraged a view that women were less able, less responsible and less important in society than men. The decades from the end of the nineteenth century and into the first part of the twentieth saw some improvement from a situation in which women had scarcely higher legal status than children. Some basic rights, including being able to vote, were finally granted to half the adult population. However, many legal and social inequalities continued into the second half of the century – well into the memories of a proportion of early years practitioners and specialists.

The female role

Women were expected to care for their families and raise children. This role was allegedly respected, but most messages to women and girls told them loudly that the male role was much more valuable. Women taking family responsibility were routinely dismissed as 'just housewives'. The assumption was that women were characteristically less intelligent than men. Some official paperwork was still being sent in the 1970s with the instruction, 'If you are a married woman, your husband should complete this form as if it were addressed to him.'

It is unremarkable now to see and hear female newsreaders, yet I recall firm statements during the 1960s that such a situation was impossible 'because nobody would ever take the news seriously if read by a woman'. It was common to hear that women should not be in positions of responsibility because they were too emotional – meant as a criticism. Yet aggressive behaviour in boys or men was not treated as a dubious emotional reaction. The behaviour was more likely to be interpreted as 'decisive', evidence of the ability to manage others. Female leaders, on the other hand, risked being labelled as 'bossy' or 'shrill'. That risk still exists in the early twenty-first century.

Girls were expected to do less well in their education and many people argued against further education for girls on the grounds that 'They'll only get married, so what's the point?' Into the 1960s, it was still accepted that women had to resign from some professional jobs when they got married. The view that married women should not work conveniently overlooked the long tradition of working women in many factories and mills. It was considered reasonable that females should be paid less than males, even when they were employed in an identical job. The assumption was that men had, or would soon have, a family to support and that women just worked for extras. The legal situation was changed by legislation over equal pay and sexual discrimination (see page 28).

Some of the social attitudes still persist, although not always in the same format. In the twenty-first century, women who choose to put their energies into raising their own children are still vulnerable to criticism, sometimes made by fellow females. There are now many more fathers who are the main carer at home, at least for a while. They too experience, although in a different way, the social value that work really has to be paid in order to deserve respect. We still have some distance to go before the vital role of caring for children is genuinely valued for either sex in our society.

Social research and theory

During the twentieth century, broad social attitudes about men and women were reflected in the social sciences, despite their claim to be objective. Many prominent names from early psychology and sociology were men. Theories about personality development, moral reasoning and behaviour patterns such as aggression frequently took observations of men or boys as the norm. When a theory did not easily apply to female development or behaviour, then the reaction was rarely to change the theory. The explanation was far more often that the female pattern was a deviation from 'normal' development or a sign of problems.

During the 1970s there was a strong reaction against this bias within the social sciences. Many female psychologists and sociologists worked to value the different female patterns and to build theory and research that were a genuine reflection of both sexes. Feminist approaches are now well-established and in some ways have evened up the discussion. However, feminism subdivided into many strands and, frankly, some females readily show bias of their own. It is appropriate to challenge women who resist considering negative experiences for boys, or male practitioners in a largely female profession, or who assume that a masculine approach is inevitably violent. Sweeping assumptions and bigotry are unwelcome, whatever their source.

Different or better?

In a fair society it should be possible to ask why does it matter if females and males are different – surely any society benefits from diversity? However, it is still difficult to discuss female–male differences in a calm way. Part of the problem is historical. For many years, any apparent differences between females and males were interpreted as evidence of female inferiority. For decades, girls' achievements in the early years of school were dismissed through the view that boys were later developers. There are even indications that, when all children sat the 11+ examination, the pass level was made tougher for girls in some authorities, otherwise there would have been significantly more girls in the local grammar schools than boys.

Most children are keen to have adventures

Young boys may well be less advanced on average than some of their female peers on some aspects of development, but the point of this late development argument was that boys were just taking a while to show the natural male superiority. On the other hand, girls' under-achievements in maths or science at the secondary level were taken as proof that females were naturally deficient at subjects requiring objectivity or logic.

There are some signs that attitudes are changing towards a recognition that all parts of society, not least children, need a blend of perspectives and abilities, some of which may be more on the masculine side and some on the feminine. Different should not necessarily mean better or worse, superior or inferior. However, the sense of win/lose competitiveness still undermines a balanced discussion in this area.

TAKE ANOTHER PERSPECTIVE

Simon Baron-Cohen describes his extreme wariness about going into print with his research about male and female brain functioning. He presents findings that the male and female brains, on average, seem to work differently. Intriguingly, Baron-Cohen's starting point was that the male brain seems to be more prone to patterns that can create extremes: the type of obsessiveness that may be labelled as genius or within the autistic spectrum, depending on the focus of concentrated activity. Despite his careful explanation, Baron-Cohen's work has sometimes been misinterpreted: that the stronger male tendency to systemise and analyse must mean that men have a higher IQ. The stronger female tendency to empathise is an average difference, not a statement about overall intelligence in either direction.

Baron-Cohen, Simon (2003) *The Essential Difference: Men, Women and the Extreme Male Brain*. London: Allen Lane

FOCUS ON CHILDHOOD

There are several related questions about the development of the two sexes, and these issues are often muddled in conversation or argument. The first two questions are about research evidence.

1   Are boys and girls consistently different from each other? If so, then in what way(s) and how significant are any differences?
2   If there are predictable sex differences, then is this situation explained by biology and the genetic pattern (nature)? Or from experiences starting in very early childhood (nurture)? Or some combination of the two possibilities?

The second set of questions homes in on the social relevance of any differences. Regardless of the details of any reliable data:

1   In what ways does it matter if there are observable sex differences in behaviour, skills, brain functioning and other aspects?

2   Is there a problem about difference and why? Or could average differences have positive implications for appropriately different ways of how adults support children?

3   Should girls and boys be different from each other in behaviour, outlook or aspirations? Is it the responsibility of adults to nurture those differences, because males and females should not be similar?

This second set of questions relates to values, because the issues are to do with possible interpretation and social obligations. Some social, cultural or

LOOK, LISTEN, NOTE, LEARN

The first question asked by many adults when faced with a young baby is to enquire as to its sex. Even babies' behaviour is often interpreted in line with whether they are a boy or girl. Anecdotal evidence suggests that crying girl babies tend to be seen as needing comfort and cuddling, whereas crying boy babies need some physical action and distraction. This pattern of adult behaviour depends on what they are told is the sex of the child, which is not necessarily the truth.

Informal observation will show you that children's inclinations are often shaped by adult reactions, including those of their parents. When our son, Drew, was a few months old we visited friends who had a daughter of six years of age and a slightly older son. The young girl moved immediately towards Drew and asked to hold him. Her brother looked very interested, but from a slight distance. His father said confidently that girls were naturally more interested in babies. His wife asked her son if he wanted to hold the baby. He nodded firmly and showed just as much care as his sister as he cuddled and talked with our very young baby. It was hard not to conclude that this young boy had held back because of his father's confident views. Without his mother's intervention, this boy's reticence would have 'proved' his father's claim.

Comments

■   This example is from the early 1980s, but I have observed similar patterns being repeated with the current generation of young boys and girls.

■   Watch out for your own examples of how adult beliefs and expectations work to encourage, or discourage, children in similar ways to that described in this anecdote.

faith traditions promote a very clear division between male and female roles in life. Parents and other adults within those groups will actively encourage differentiation between boys and girls, perhaps from early childhood, but definitely from puberty: the bridge into adulthood. In other social and cultural groups, there can be much more overlap between expectations for girls and boys, but there may still be subtle differences in how the sexes are treated and assumptions about appropriate behaviour in adult life.

In a nutshell, there do seem to be some differences between the sexes that start very early on in childhood, with babies. Males and females as a group seem to be intrinsically inclined to behave in broadly different ways. However, each individual girl or boy, man or woman, does not inevitably behave in the same way, nor have the same pattern of abilities. Some of these differences start so young that a biological explanation seems most likely. Yet there is also strong evidence that adult behaviour towards young girls and boys exaggerates the existing differences to fit socially-preferred patterns.

Are boys and girls different from each other?

In one important way girls and boys are very different from each other. The significant pattern of changes brought about by puberty means that girls grow up into young women and boys grow into young men. A very small minority of children are born with indeterminate sex. Some other children and young people come to question their sexual identity and may seek to change. But most children will start and remain one sex, and they all need a positive outlook on the adults they will eventually become.

Careful research into children's development and behaviour has established no absolute differences between boys and girls in their development or behaviour. There is no basis for saying that 'all boys' are better at these particular skills or that 'all girls' behave in this particular way. When a difference is found by studying groups, the sex difference is usually small, and is not always found consistently.

Research into aggressive patterns of behaviour suggests the interplay between nature and nurture. Many studies have shown a pattern which reveals that, from a young age, boys tend to hit and insult each other more than girls. Boys also tend to react more swiftly and strongly if they are hit or insulted. Boys are more likely than girls to engage in general rough and tumble and play fighting. The observation that the physically more lively pattern emerges so young in boys raises the possibility of some biological basis to their behaviour. However, observation of adults has shown how they frequently behave differently towards very young children, depending on the child's sex. Boys are more likely to be encouraged towards more active physical behaviour, which is not necessarily aggressive. Adults also seem to tolerate more dominant or aggressive behaviour in boys before it is regarded as a problem.

TAKE ANOTHER PERSPECTIVE

Children will not be supported in developing a strong sense of personal identity if practitioners believe equality practice means overlooking differences. Good practice over ethnic group or cultural identity has challenged the cliché of 'I treat them all the same.' There has been a delay in challenging that kind of unreflective thinking as applied to gender equality.

Early years practitioners have been directed by some childcare courses and textbooks to ignore the differences between boys and girls and focus on the similarities. But this recommendation makes no more sense in behaviour towards girls and boys than it ever did for an approach to children over ethnic group flagged up by skin colour. The end result of that kind of 'treating them all the same' was that, for too long, 'white' practitioners treated 'black' children as if they were 'white', or interpreted children's needs as special needs: a variation from the 'white' norm.

Is there not a real risk in terms of gender that female practitioners will treat boys as children who do not fit the 'girl' pattern? Boys deserve to be treated as young males, respected for any differences and not repackaged as noisy little girls who stand up to pee! Reflective practitioners and teams are ready to think about assumptions and actions.

Observations and assessment of children have shown a great deal of variety within the sexes and, in many ways, girls and boys are more similar than unalike. On most aspects of development and behaviour both sexes are represented across the full range of abilities and difficulties. However, boys tend to cluster more at the extremes. There are, for example, three to four times as many boys coping with dyslexia as there are girls. So if you are working in the early years of school, you could expect to encounter more boys with this learning disability than girls. But it would be poor practice to overlook this possibility for girls, because some will need useful strategies to cope with dyslexia.

Study of language development has suggested that, on average, girls tend to talk more and in slightly longer sentences than boys in early childhood.

This average difference lasts into middle childhood when girls as a group do slightly better than boys on verbal reasoning and brain teasers based on words. Girls often seem to be more able to put feelings into words and to talk about emotions. However, observation of parents and practitioners often shows that adults are more inclined to talk about feelings with girls and to offer explanations that focus on feelings. So if there is an underlying sex difference, it is being strengthened by adult behaviour.

Observed differences in behaviour seem to be related to some average differences between how male and female brains develop. Computer imaging techniques have opened up possibilities of studying brain function and there do seem to be some broad sex differences. A further reason for open-mindedness about basic biology is that several decades of dedicated attempts to smooth out boy/girl differences in early years provision have made limited noticeable difference to their dominant play choices.

The human brain has two halves – the left and right hemispheres – that become effectively joined within early childhood by a bundle of nerve fibres called the corpus callosum. Boys (but also some girls) have greater activity in the right hemisphere, which is more dedicated to large physical movements and handling visual and spatial information. The consequence of this

LOOK, LISTEN, NOTE, LEARN

Whatever research suggests, there is no doubt that many people believe that girls and boys are reliably different. Over a period of two to three weeks, listen in to conversations in your working and personal life and gather examples of firm views on such differences. It might be the confident statement that 'Of course, girl babies are so much easier' or 'He's into everything – a real boy.'

Look over the examples you have gathered and, if possible, compare with colleagues or fellow students who have completed the same activity.

- What images are emerging of girls and boys?

- How did any of the speakers deal with disagreement? For instance, somebody saying, 'Well, I had a much harder time when my daughter was a baby. My son was the easy one.'

- In what ways do you think any of the speakers' actions might work to support and prove their beliefs? Perhaps their non-verbal behaviour that accompanies requests for children to help?

- Do some adults use different words to apply to girls and boys: who is (or is not) brave, chatty, tough, thoughtful, pretty, strong or kind?

average difference seems to be that boys can be more adept with constructional materials and large body movements in some physical games. The link between the two hemispheres seems often to be stronger in girls and women. The result seems to be that males may focus more strongly on the task at hand. But what is won in single-mindedness can bring less ability to undertake tasks that overlap or to blend rational thoughts and feelings.

REFLECTION ON GENDER EQUALITY

Given the historical background, it is not surprising that the foremost concerns of the feminist movement in the 1960s and 1970s were to gain equality for women. Similarly, the first focus in applying ideas to childhood was to address how girls were given messages that would restrict their options and development. Any movement that is concerned with good practice must be ready to reflect, and that is what has happened in some quarters over gender equality. There has been an increasing awareness of the messages being given to boys and the possible negative effects on their development.

It does not really matter what the sources are of generally observed differences between boys and girls. A fair and even-handed approach is to show equal levels of care, respect and concern for all children. Girls and boys deserve active support, so they can feel positive about their personal identity by gender. Neither sex should be weighed in the balance and found wanting because their interests or behaviour do not fit an adult-imposed pattern.

A female early years world?

The early years professional world, and many primary schools, are overwhelmingly female. This sex imbalance is not the result of some plot by women, so recognition of this fact implies no criticism whatsoever. The main reasons for such a female profession include social views that still judge working with young children as more 'women's work'. Contact with younger children is often seen as less valuable than teaching late primary or secondary pupils, with the consequent lower status, pay and conditions of many of the jobs. However, the end result is that it is easy for unreflective female teams to slip into judging boys against their own childhood memories and current professional concerns.

TAKE ANOTHER PERSPECTIVE

Of course, female childhoods vary. Some, like my own, were dominated by digging holes, climbing trees, building dens and go-karts, as well as taking immense pleasure in dolls, books, cooking and dressing-up.

In recent decades, more active and outdoor pursuits have been forced to stage a comeback against pressures to get many young children to sit quietly, 'do their learning' indoors and tolerate a great deal of adult direction of their play. In the name of early education, there has been a great deal of talk within early years (much less in the playwork professional area) of 'play with a purpose', 'well-structured play' and a lot about 'learning outcomes' and 'intentions'. The purposes, structure and intentions have, in too many instances, been those of adults, not envisaged and chosen by children themselves.

The end result of over-direction by adults has been negative for many children. But it has probably had the greatest adverse impact on the more lively, physically enthusiastic, outdoor-loving children, and many of these have been boys.

Awareness of your own behaviour

You and your colleagues, as well as the parents with whom you have contact, have all been influenced during childhood. There is no need to feel personally at fault about assumptions and expectations learned in your childhood. On the other hand, you are responsible now for

Boys and girls sometimes choose to play together

LOOK, LISTEN, NOTE, LEARN

Children learn from what they experience directly, so they do not necessarily learn gender stereotypes if they observe a different pattern.

In a family I knew, the mother worked as an electrical engineer and the father in personnel management. The children were used to their mother tackling anything electrical in the house and this was normal life as far as they were concerned. On one occasion their father was in charge for the day and a kitchen appliance needed a new plug. As soon as the children saw their father with a screwdriver, they became concerned. Did daddy know what he was doing? Mummy did plugs and things like that – shouldn't he wait until she got home? Their father persevered and changed the plug, watched by two anxious children who could not wait to tell their mother and be reassured that everything was all right.

Comments

- Until they have a broader experience, children tend to assume that everyone's family life runs in a similar way to their own. Do you have examples where children's conversation shows how they generalise from their own life?

- Young children build gender stereotypes from many sources, not only their own family life. Perhaps their mother works as a doctor, but the children still say 'Men are doctors and women are nurses.' How do you think this happens?

thinking about your views, being willing to question some of them and to adjust how you behave as a grown-up towards this generation of young children.

Children look towards adults for guidance on what is a normal or generally acceptable way to behave. Girls and boys need positive input from adults of both sexes and they look towards the adults of their own sex for an idea of what it is to be a grown-up. What you say matters, but your actions speak as loudly as your words. Fine sentiments about 'Girls can do anything that boys can' will be undermined if you (as a female) act as if you are hopeless and cannot learn when faced with a traditionally male task. It is of limited use to say, 'Men can be just as caring as women', if misplaced anxiety about child protection leads a nursery or school to place suspicious limits on the role of male practitioners (see also page 224).

Gender equality in practice

Your aim is that both sexes feel positive about their own identity. Girls' view of their skills needs to be far removed from any sense of 'just a girl'. All girls will have some pattern of confident talents, mixed with some doubts. Adult support is important to check any beliefs about not being good at something 'because I'm a girl', or that there is no point in trying 'because only boys are good at that'. But it is equally important for boys' sense of self-worth that they experience adults who show genuine interest in what enthuses the children. Boys' sense of identity is undermined if early years practitioners show that they believe the boys' games are noisy and disruptive, or their interests are empty of adult-valued learning.

- How are boys and girls treated during their experiences in nursery, after-school club or your home if you are a childminder? Are there patterns (intended or not) that are different, depending on whether a child is a girl or a boy?
- How do practitioners behave, what do they say about children or about their own, adult abilities? What role model do the children see from the adults?
- What activities are available and how are children encouraged to use, or discouraged from using potential experiences?
- What resources are available for children, and what kind of social world and adult opportunities do they show?

TAKE ANOTHER PERSPECTIVE

Imagine you are listening in to adult conversation in an early years setting. What would you guess is the sex of the children mentioned in these comments?

- 'A is so sensitive. What can we do about it? Mum's worried too.'
- 'B is always so helpful and so ready to be caring with the little ones.'
- 'Have you noticed how C has hardly any pretend play? It's never the home corner, just cars all the time.'

You might say there is no way of knowing: the children could be boys or girls. Of course, there is no certainty from the quoted adult words, but given the underlying assumptions still held by many adults, including practitioners:

- Child A is more likely to be a boy; in many social and cultural groups in the UK boys are expected to be 'tougher', so a young boy who shows his 'softer' emotions may be seen as out of the ordinary and some adults genuinely worry that he will have problems.

- It will often be assumed that child B is a girl, because little girls are allegedly so ready to help; but, as many practitioners know well, in an encouraging setting or family home, individual boys can be considerate and competent helpers.
- Child C is probably a boy and the adult words are most likely spoken by an unreflective female practitioner; there is no basis for counting absorption in the home corner as a more valuable type of pretend play than choosing to concentrate on cars or other kinds of vehicle.

Questions

1. Use the examples to reflect on your own practice and, if you work with colleagues, in your team.
2. If you are honest, might you be tempted to see the behaviour of children A and C as a bit of a problem?

Gender equality and other values

The concerns that underlie gender equality share some important common ground with other areas for equality covered in this part of the book. However, what has developed as good practice in gender equality within early years, out-of-school and school services is a direct challenge to some cultural traditions, including some 'white' UK social groups. It may be impossible to develop what you regard as equal treatment of girls and boys and still follow every parent's preferences. Some cultures, and social groups within a culture, express deeply-held beliefs that boys and girls should be treated differently.

Girls need confidence and self-esteem, but boys too need a positive sense of themselves and their interests that does not depend on undermining girls or women. Parts of UK society still value males over females, and such beliefs are justified through social habit, interpretation of research and, in some cases, through particular interpretations of world faiths, including sects within Islam, Judaism and Christianity. Putting gender equality into practice can present practitioners with dilemmas that have to be resolved (see, for example, page 252). The stance in this book is that it is possible, and definitely preferable, that boys develop a sense of self-worth that is personal, not one dependent on the belief that 'I'm better simply because I was born a boy.'

Teams and home-based childminders can address this potential conflict between practice for equality and partnership with parents in several ways, as outlined below.

■ Be clear and honest in your policy statements about how you aim to treat boys and girls, and the ways in which equal opportunities on gender are approached positively in your setting or family home.

■ Be ready to talk with parents about what you do and why, and also what you do not do. For instance, you are not saying that girls and boys are all the same – if you are implying there is no difference, please rethink. Nor are you 'banning' resources or activities that have traditionally been associated more with one sex than the other.

■ Some parents will agree with your approach or see the value when you explain. Others, from a variety of cultural backgrounds, may continue to disagree. You will show respect for parents' views by listening and demonstrating that you wish to understand their point of view.

■ However, some parents' preferences may be against your policy and values: that their son has no involvement in cooking or that their daughter is firmly dissuaded from getting 'dirty' in the garden. Professionalism is met when you are honest about 'what happens here'. It will be a family choice whether the child continues to attend your setting or home as childminder.

It can be useful to recall that parents will not agree with all your values or approaches, not just on gender equality. Sometimes you will hear about the disagreement; sometimes you will never realise, because parents decide they are mainly satisfied with what you offer and are willing to compromise on this issue.

Be alert to assumptions and language

You should be wary of describing the same, or very similar, behaviour in different ways just because the child is a girl or a boy. A child who is a confident organiser and leader in a group is not 'bossy' just because she is female. A child who is sensitive to events and easily moved to tears is not 'immature' because he is a boy. If in doubt, think about whether you would use this description about a child of the opposite sex and same age. If not, do you have any sound reason for your comment about this child? Your words reflect your attitudes about gender and how it is appropriate to react to boys and girls. Within any team it is worth listening out for what you all say and finding friendly ways to alert colleagues to assumptions, and to listen to comments about your own reactions.

SCENARIO

Maria attends a regular discussion group of the local childminding network. The group has managed to move on from any feeling of 'You mustn't say that!' to exploring alternative ways to handle situations that could impose gender stereotypes on young children. Here are some recent examples.

- Instead of asking, 'I need a strong boy to shift this box', it is just as easy to say, 'This box is heavy, I need some strong hands to help me.'

- Some childminders in the group became aware that they tended to compliment girls more on their hair or clothes (appearance) and boys more about their skills (what they could do). They realised that boys also liked to hear, 'That's a fine hat!' and girls soon appreciated, 'You have done a grand job with that digging.'

- The group also began to recognise that they were more inclined to tell girls to watch out on the climbing frame or even to suggest, 'That's too high' at an earlier stage than they did for boys. On the other hand, the boys were more likely to be watched and told, 'Now be very careful' if they are doing something domestic or handling a breakable item.

In this discussion group, it was important that none of the childminders felt criticised and judged. The atmosphere was friendly and discussion highlighted how many assumptions had been laid down in adults' own childhood.

Questions

Consider in your own practice whether some unconsidered remarks just pop out without thought. How might you reflect on your own practice?

1. Do you catch yourself expressing surprise when a girl has built something mechanical or when a boy has shown intense interest in baby animals?

2. Do you express surprise that a boy is not keen to get his hands dirty, when a girl's reluctance might be seen as more likely?

3. Are you more likely to ask a girl to be a buddy to a disabled peer? If you ask one of the boys, do you hear yourself explaining with more care than you might for a girl?

LOOK, LISTEN, NOTE, LEARN

A couple of decades ago, toy stores were firmly divided into different sections for 'girls' toys' and 'boys' toys'. Manufacturers and retailers are no longer so blunt, but a significant amount of gender stereotyping remains.

On your own, or with a colleague, visit a large toy store or warehouse and make observations. Explore the messages that could be given to children and their parents about the appropriateness of different play materials for the two sexes. Some suggestions for your observations follow.

- Look at how the toys are organised into different sections. What is the basis for this organisation?

- Look at the packaging of toys and play materials. If children are shown on the boxes, are they boys, girls or both? What are they doing?

- If you were a child, might you conclude that some toys and kinds of equipment were more for the opposite sex?

- Are there different versions of the same item of play equipment? For instance, are bikes or scooters offered in different colours or styles, apparently to appeal to one sex or the other?

- Are there some sections that seem genuinely for both sexes? What are they?

- If possible, take a child who is five years or older with you on this trip (your own child or a niece or nephew, perhaps). Ask the child for his or her opinion, including which toys are supposed to be for boys or girls.

If you want to find out more:

❖ Featherstone, Sally and Bayley, Ros (2005) *Boys and Girls Come out to Play: Not Better or Worse, Just Different*. Husbands Bosworth: Featherstone Education.

❖ Healy, Jane (2004) *Your Child's Growing Mind: Brain Development and Learning from Birth to Adolescence*. New York: Broadway.

❖ Holland, Penny (2003) *We Don't Play With Guns Here: War, Weapon and Superhero Play in the Early Years*. Maidenhead: Open University Press.

❖ Lindon, Jennie (2001) *Understanding Children's Play*. Cheltenham: Nelson Thornes.

❖ Skelton, Christine and Hall, Elaine (2001) *The Development of Gender Roles in Young Children*: *A Review of Policy and the Literature*. Equal Opportunities Commission, www.eoc.org.uk.

4 Ethnic group, culture and faith

Everyone has a sense of personal and family identity arising from their own ethnic group, which may be viewed more as a cultural or national background. From your childhood you will also have developed an affinity with one or more family languages and may have committed to a particular world faith. All these sources of identity meet along blurry boundaries.

> **The main sections of this chapter cover:**
> * a history of ethnic group diversity
> * learning from childhood
> * religious faith and personal beliefs.

A HISTORY OF ETHNIC GROUP DIVERSITY

Current ethnic group diversity in the UK did not arise solely as the result of population movements in the second half of the twentieth century. The origins of many 'white' families are far from 100 per cent English. Many families have at least mixed European and Celtic or Gaelic origins. The UK also had many thriving ports, at which sailors and overseas visitors landed and often stayed. Most of these arrivals were men; they married local women and over the generations their ethnic origins became less and less obvious in their descendants.

From the sixteenth century, written accounts and paintings document that many Africans lived in London and other cities. Some of these residents were servants, or slaves over the period when Britain was active in the slave trade. After emancipation, ordinary people whose origins were African were part of the UK in different jobs or as students. Traces of an earlier 'black' population are sometimes left – for instance, in the West Country surname of Blackmore, which is allegedly a reference to North African 'moors' and 'blackamoors'. There are also Chinese communities with a long history in several cities of the UK.

After the Second World War increasing numbers of people chose to leave their country of origin and migrate to the UK for work and/or study. Some economic migrants always planned to return to their country of birth and succeeded in doing so. Some waited to establish themselves in the UK and then were joined by their families, or met partners who were already resident here. Many of the migrants were from areas like the Caribbean or India, which had been influenced by the

British presence through the years of imperialism. Arrivals in the 1950s and 1960s from the Caribbean islands and mainland often felt a strong affinity with Britain, using phrases like 'the mother country' or 'a home from home'. This emotional connection made it even more shocking for them to face racial prejudice as blatant as notices in boarding houses saying, 'No coloureds'. Additionally some men and women had been invited to come to Britain, recruited specifically for jobs in sectors such as transport.

People continued to come to the UK, temporarily or on a more permanent basis, in the hopes of a more secure life. Increasingly some more recent arrivals have fled disruption or war in their countries of origin.

The past in the present

The present for any society is shaped in many ways by what has happened in the past. In previous centuries Britain was a dominant force in the world, in competition with other European nations. (I have used the word Britain, rather than the UK, because Ireland was seen as separate.) Britain was actively involved in the slave trade when huge numbers of people from Africa were forcibly taken across the Atlantic to the Caribbean and what later became the United States. The wish to secure trade and further desire for expansion led to the colonisation of large and small countries around the world to form what became known as the British Empire.

At the time of these events, and for many years afterwards, the prevailing view was that British activities were justified for economic reasons and that the colonised peoples benefited from a civilising influence. The dominant attitude was that British culture, religious beliefs, education and social systems were superior and that indigenous peoples were definitely inferior, the only question being just how 'primitive' or 'uncivilised'. Such views became an integral part of British culture and were reflected in material for children, for instance within school textbooks.

Books published within the first decades of the twentieth century present the glory of the British Empire, with no doubts whatsoever. During the 1960s and 1970s the emphasis was still on the allegedly civilising effect of the British presence, with very limited respect for pre-existing traditions, or even a recognition that colonised countries had a real culture. The slave trade, although not justified completely, was often presented as an unfortunate economic necessity.

So generations of children grew up with a conviction that the 'white' British way of life was not only the best, but had brought light into the darkness (a very common image) of 'primitive' countries. A liberal outlook was that people from the African or Indian continent and the Caribbean could be educated and therefore 'more like us'. An overtly racist outlook was that 'non-white' peoples were inherently inferior, always would be and were not welcome as residents in the UK. The legacy of history has been that 'black' residents of the UK have frequently met prejudiced attitudes and active discrimination. By the 1970s and onwards, enough people ('white' as well as 'black') felt strongly that the situation was completely unacceptable and that positive action had to be taken, through legislation and direct challenge to people's attitudes in action.

Racist attitudes entered the way that organisations and administration worked on a daily basis. Systems and procedures have to be developed originally by individuals. Those people may have been explicitly racist, but were just as likely to have made decisions on the basis of assumptions that they simply never questioned. Once discriminatory systems are in place, they give support to individuals who are openly racist. The sense of 'but this is how we do it' encourages a sense of inertia for those who are much less racist in outlook or intention. It is hard work to challenge a set of procedures that carries the weight of tradition and is presented as normal. There are strong parallels with how assumptions about gender and disability can become deeply rooted in administrative or employment practices, creating institutional blocks to equality.

For understandable historical reasons, a considerable amount of emphasis in racial equality has been on racist attitudes held by 'white' people about 'black' ethnic groups. Some sources of racial bigotry continue in that blunt vein. However, equality practice within a highly diverse society, as is now the case with the UK, has to be even-handed and recognise that members of ethnic groups, who experience discrimination, can themselves be bigoted and rejecting about other groups. Such an outlook sits uncomfortably with a simplistic equality perspective. But a more honest approach about human behaviour is necessary, especially when the aim is to promote positive attitudes and behaviour from early childhood.

Furthermore, racial bigotry has not been restricted to differences based on skin colour. Anti-Semitism has a long and shameful history in the UK, as well as in other European countries. Non-English ethnic groups in Britain, such as the Welsh or Scots, can also look back on a history of oppression of their culture and language. It is very usual now, for instance, to hear a wide range of accents on the television or radio. But generations of people unlearned their Irish, Cornish or other so-called 'regional' accents to increase acceptance and avoid offensive remarks presented as jokes.

Language and culture

Cultural traditions are passed on within families and communities partly through a shared language. Linguistic tradition is therefore part of cultural and ethnic group identity. So respect for family language(s) and accent has to be an integral part of any approach to equality.

Around the world bilingualism is common and many children grow up learning two or more languages. In countries on mainland Europe, confident use of two languages is normal for many people. However, it is often overlooked that there is a long history in the UK of bilingualism for speakers who have combined knowledge of English with fluency in Welsh, Scottish Gaelic (pronounced 'gallic') and Irish Gaelic. Cornish and Manx (on the Isle of Man) went into decline as daily spoken languages, although both have an active heritage movement.

Yet, until recent decades, the common view in England was that the only 'normal' language development was for children to learn English and then to study one or more 'foreign' languages at secondary school. The language movements in Wales and Scotland struggled against active attempts to suppress daily use of languages other than English. For instance, within the first half of the twentieth century some school teams in Wales felt justified in a policy of caning children for speaking Welsh in ordinary conversation.

It was therefore not surprising that many professionals took a negative approach to families from minority ethnic groups who became resident through immigration from the 1960s and whose first language was not English. Bilingualism was treated as a problem by service providers who were blinkered by their own monolingual situation. Parents were told that they must speak only English to their children, otherwise the children's language development would be disrupted. A fluent home language was often ignored and children's emerging English was treated as their only language, leading to assessment of speaking children as having 'poor' or 'no' language. School pupils could end up in remedial classes for no reason other than lack of fluent English.

Over the second half of the twentieth century, there was a slow but significant change in official treatment of languages other than English. Active bilingual movements took root in Wales, Scotland and Ireland. Welsh, in particular, is the success story of Europe's regional languages. From a precarious existence in mid-Wales, the language is now prominent in the early years and school curriculum, and established in all aspects of public life.

A revision of views of good practice, combined with research about bilingual children, has led to a more accurate, and respectful, approach to all families with more than one fluent language. However, reflective practitioners need to remain alert about assumptions. I still hear children sometimes described as 'not talking much', when the problem is more accurately that the practitioner cannot understand what children are saying in their home language.

Families with a travelling lifestyle

The history of travelling families within Europe goes back many centuries, and the travelling lifestyle has more than one origin. Over the 1990s in equality practice, 'traveller' was considered the most courteous term to describe anyone who chose the nomadic form of life. The word 'gypsy' was avoided, because historically it had been used as a term of abuse by some members of the settled population. (The latter word appears to have derived from 'Egyptian' at a time when the settled population believed that to be the country of origin of the Roma peoples.)

However, the travelling community is a diverse set of groups, some of whom absolutely wanted to be called gypsies. The intention was sometimes to distinguish their Romany origins from the Irish travelling community or from newer arrivals such as new age travellers. Some of this latter group took to the road over the 1960s–70s, but some Londoners who fled the bombing during the Second World War had already become permanent travellers. Currently, the terms Traveller, Irish Traveller or Gypsy tend to be given initial capital letters in order to indicate that the terms cover a distinct ethnic group identity. The word Roma is sometimes added to Traveller.

Gypsies and Irish Travellers have been fully recognised as ethnic groups, because they have a shared culture, language and beliefs. They are therefore covered legally against discrimination. The cultural code of many Romany communities is guided by *romaniya* (Gypsy laws) customs and rules that distinguish behaviour that is *vujo* (pure) and that which is *marime* (polluted). Romany/Roma Gypsies and Irish Travellers each have distinct and different languages.

Travellers from any of the nomadic groups frequently experience hostility from the settled population. Poor relations are often provoked by lack of proper sites on which travelling families can stop. The situation was aggravated by the removal in 1994 of a legal duty on local authorities to provide sites. Some long-standing travelling groups themselves harbour deep suspicions about the settled population, whom they call 'gaujos' or 'gorgios'. This wariness is sometimes fuelled by specific ill-treatment of their children in schools or general fears about the dangers to the children outside the immediate protection of their family.

Early years or school staff have sometimes been less than enthusiastic about children from travelling families because of the conviction that the families will soon move on: 'So what's the point?' This outlook is unacceptable practice. Families sometimes stay in one location for some or most of a calendar year. Some family movements follow a planned circuit involved in running a travelling circus or fairground, taking seasonal work on a circuit of farms or moving by canal barge. You would not avoid making an effort for a child whose parents' professional commitments might move them on in the near future, so there is no justification for being less than fully attentive to Gypsy and Traveller children.

Even if families do move on, a positive experience for child and parent in your setting will support the whole family when they make a relationship with the next early years centre or school. Many local authorities now have support services for Gypsy and Traveller families, either as a dedicated team or as part of services for families from a range of minority ethnic groups.

If you want to find out more:

- ✛ The Travellers' School Charity: www.travellerschool.plus.com.

- ✛ Traveller Law Research Unit: www.law.cf.ac.uk/tlru.

- ✛ Using a search engine like Google, type in 'Traveller Education Service' and you will bring up many local services around the UK; some have developed books, photo resources and posters that they are happy to share or sell.

- ✛ Trentham Books offers several titles; check its website to see which may be most relevant to your work: www.trentham-books.co.uk.

Refugee families and asylum seekers

The word 'refugee' has a specific legal meaning under the 1951 UN Convention Relating to the Status of Refugees. Refugees are people who have left their own country and are unable to return 'owing to a well-founded fear of being persecuted for reasons of race, religion, nationality, membership of a particular social group or political opinion'. In order to stay in the UK, individuals or families who arrive as asylum seekers have to apply for official refugee status. Children and young people under the age of 18 years, who arrive unaccompanied by a parent or other adult carer, automatically become the responsibility of the local authority. From the 1990s asylum seekers increasingly came to the UK from such different countries as the former Yugoslavia, Sri Lanka, Turkey (Turkish Kurds), Somalia, Nigeria and Iraq.

WHAT DOES IT MEAN?

Refugees: People who have left their own country out of fear of persecution and who seek safety in another country.

Asylum seekers: People who have left their country of origin and crossed international borders in search of safety and refugee status in another country.

In addition to becoming accustomed to a new country, some families have left their homes under distressing circumstances and perhaps with very little chance to prepare their children. Adults and children may have traumatic memories of the disruptions that turned them into refugees. Even very young children may have seen terrible sights and know that members of their family, immediate or more extended, are still living or fighting in dangerous areas. The refugee families may be living in temporary accommodation with uncertainty about where they will live in the near future and whether the family will be allowed to stay in the UK.

The Immigration and Asylum Act 1999 led to increased dispersal of refugee and asylum seeker families away from London and the south-east of England where many had settled after arrival. The aim was to relieve the pressure on a few local authorities who were heavily responsible for the families and saying ever more loudly that the duty of care was a national issue. Whatever the intentions, the resulting relocation was often far from smooth.

Support and understanding will be essential to help both the children and their parents. It is also possible that tensions may develop in the local neighbourhood, from resistance to the families' arrival and possibly fuelled by beliefs that refugee families are getting material advantages not available to existing residents. Sudden relocation of families around the UK has not helped local services to ease their entry. However, some areas, like Glasgow (one of the three UK cities other than London with more than 2000 school pupils from refugee and asylum seeker families), have worked hard to support early years and school services. The city has also created facilities, like play areas, that clearly support the whole local community and offer a chance for adults to come together over the common ground of having children.

If you want to find out more

❖ Refugee Council; Tel: 020 7820 3000 www.refugeecouncil.org.uk.

❖ Rutter, Jill (2003) *Supporting Refugee Children in 21st Century Britain*. Stoke-on-Trent: Trentham Books; www.trentham-books.co.uk.

❖ The Children's Legal Centre Home Page for Refugee and Asylum Seeking Children's Project: www.childrenslegalcentre.com.

❖ Hyder, Tina (2004) *War, Conflict and Play: Working with Refugee Children in the Early Years*. Buckingham: Open University Press.

LEARNING FROM CHILDHOOD

Children tend to assume that the family life of other people is much the same as their own, until experience shows them the level of diversity. For anyone, what they know best can seem to be the natural or obvious way of organising a life or raising children. If adults remain with relatively narrow horizons, then different ways may be judged as odd, exotic or suspect. Early years professionals have a responsibility to address narrow views or rejection of less familiar ways.

Children are interested in physical differences

Cultural traditions affect everyone

Unreflective adults may take the stance that they talk 'normally'; it is other people who have a 'strong accent'. Or people say in a puzzled way, 'I bring up my children the way I was raised; I don't have a cultural tradition.' But experience of culture is not something that just happens to other people; everyone has a cultural background, just as everyone has an ethnic group to which they belong.

TAKE ANOTHER PERSPECTIVE

Please consider your own ethnic group identity and sense of cultural heritage.

- How would you describe yourself in words? What are your family origins in terms of ethnic group and/or nationality?
- Within your daily life, in what ways do your habits and choices reflect your own cultural background?
- If you find it hard to get started, you might think about food and drink, how you dress, what you do in your leisure time or the family celebrations in which you are involved.
- Reflect on your childhood, whether it was within your birth family or an alternative form of upbringing. In what ways did you build an understanding of your identity and family allegiances. What made 'you'?
- If possible, share some of these ideas and memories with colleagues or fellow students. Take care to show active respect for the reflections and reminiscences of everyone.

Everyone has their own source of ethnicity; all people have their own ethnic origins. So individuals of Celtic origin, Gaelic or Scandinavian are an ethnic group just as much as people of Thai, Moroccan or Bangladeshi origin. Cultural traditions can affect everyday behaviour as well as influence the details of special occasions or festivals. Diet and style of eating, personal hygiene and habits, forms of spoken and non-verbal communication can all be shaped by cultural traditions. Some aspects of culture are rooted in the religious beliefs that have shaped the traditions of a given society or social group. Some patterns of behaviour can therefore persist, even when individuals are not active followers of a particular religious faith. However, 'Muslim' is not a description of ethnic group identity, any more than 'Christian'. People who share a faith that has spread over much of the world will differ in ethnic group, language and cultural tradition.

TAKE ANOTHER PERSPECTIVE

Misuse of the word 'ethnic' can highlight narrow or dismissive views of cultures other than that of the person speaking. In some instances the term is used effectively to mean 'exotic' or non-European. If tandoori chicken is an example of 'ethnic food', then so is steak and kidney pie. English country dancing is an example of cultural tradition just as much as Greek dances. My most ridiculous example so far was a household catalogue that featured 'ethnic tables' – apparently the words indicated that the style was Indian.

Unfortunate choice of language in some catalogues for play resources perpetuates the idea that there is 'our culture' and there are 'other cultures'. Even companies that offer good-quality resources sometimes have an odd way with words. The words 'multicultural' or 'ethnic' are often used to mean any non-European or 'non-white' source.

- 'Multicultural hats' – what does such a phrase mean exactly? What is the message when the display of hats I saw for sale were all from non-European traditions? They did not include, for instance, flat caps or silky headscarves, as worn by many English women, including the Queen of England.

- Some companies specify an outfit for a Nigerian child but many propose the cover-all of 'African child'. This huge continent is made up of many countries, cultures, languages, faiths and ways of dressing. General terms like 'Oriental' or 'Asian' are no more accurate. What assumptions are revealed by this choice of words?

- Whatever your own cultural background, try collecting a set of clothes to meet the aim of dressing up as a 'European' child or adult. Is it possible? Does it make any sense at all?

Find some examples of your own and discuss them with colleagues or fellow students.

A meeting of traditions can lead to surprise or interest. The feelings may be more of uneasiness and uncertainty, followed by adjustment. Alternatively, the difference in culture may be taken as a reason to reject the other group and take up an ethnocentric outlook. Individuals who persist in this kind of selective perception are currently unable, or unwilling, to acknowledge that other traditions, practices and values could be worthy of respect. Those with an ethnocentric outlook insist on taking their own traditions as the measure of what is 'normal' and probably superior. An ethnocentric approach can be part of a restricted view, when practitioners from a range of ethnic groups would object to being described as racist.

WHAT DOES IT MEAN?

Ethnocentric: An outlook based very firmly in individuals' own perspective, with the strong belief that their own group and traditions are superior to those of others. This outlook has also been called cultural racism and can arise within any group towards any group.

Adult responsibilities

Young children do not automatically assume that skin colour or other visible group differences mean that people are more or less worthy. However, children who are exposed to bigoted attitudes and actions soon use what they have heard, or the behaviour they have watched. Young children can build a negative image associated with a darker skin colour, or other indicators of ethnic origin, cultural difference or faith.

Prejudice has an impact on how children feel about themselves, as well as their attitude towards others. Those children who are part of the dominant ethnic or cultural group may boost their sense of self-worth by disparaging others. Their pride in their own group, and in themselves as a member of that group, is supported largely by feelings of superiority or by ridiculing others. Negative views learned by some children will gain a stronger hold, like any kind of rejection of other people, if responsible adults do not counteract the dismissive sense of arrogance.

The children who are part of the group to which the prejudice is directed are soon fully aware of this rejection. They are at risk of low self-esteem and doubts about their own self-worth. Young children who are emotionally abused can develop a very fragile sense of self-worth. The additional risk from an attack based on group identity is that children may cope by rejecting a part of their identity.

Research in the United States and the UK up to the 1970s established that some 'black' children, as young as four and five years old, had already encountered sufficiently racist beliefs that they expressed the preference to be 'white'. Children's views were usually invited through their reactions to dolls or pictures. Similar research has not continued and both societies have changed, not least with very active movements to support a positive identity for 'black' children from a diversity of ethnic group backgrounds. There is every reason to suppose that young children still pick up on the attitudes around them and that 'black' children are still vulnerable, because of crass prejudice linked with skin colour. However, possible reactions could well include the choice to attack verbally in return, rather than assume that bigots are correct.

Practitioners in mainly 'white' areas

Some areas of the UK show very little evidence of ethnic diversity, especially if the focus is on skin colour. The national, cultural and religious origins of local families may have many sources of diversity. However, this fact is not immediately obvious because the majority of the population is 'white'. Some practitioners share the views of other local residents that equality issues around race and cultural tradition are relevant only for urban areas with their 'inner-city race problems'. This mistaken outlook about cities can be as misguided as the naïve views held by some urban dwellers about country life. Communities with ethnic group diversity are not all disrupted on a regular basis, although it makes striking newspaper headlines.

In mainly 'white' areas, even the more thoughtful practitioners can feel that ethnic group and cultural equality issues are more theoretical than real. The advantages of a mixed local area are undoubtedly that there are real children and families who experience differences in dress, beliefs, diet and language. The challenge in a non-diverse area is to present materials to extend children's horizons, while showing that daily life is different not so very far away, perhaps no more than an hour or so by car or train. You have a responsibility to show children something of the world beyond their own back door. You also have a responsibility for the future; many children will travel and leave their current local community. The details of equality over ethnic group and cultural tradition should be adjusted to reflect local reality, but any team or advisory service needs to distinguish between what is appropriate adjustment and what is sneaky avoidance of the issues.

There can be genuine practical problems of finding resources in an area with limited ethnic diversity. Local book shops or toy suppliers may offer a range that assumes everyone is 'white' or otherwise exotic, temporary visitors. You may need to obtain materials through the many mail-order book or play resources suppliers (see page 200). Many settings in diverse areas face the same situation, however – high-street stores do not necessarily reflect the full variety of families living locally.

SCENARIO

The Whittons Nursery is located in a neighbourhood where there is limited obvious ethnic group diversity; most of the local faces are 'white'. Clare, the manager, wants to use partnership with all parents. She is aware that the previous manager was well-intentioned, but made the few parents from non-European backgrounds feel like walking visual aids for some nursery topics.

Li-Fong's family are very busy running their restaurant, but had felt under great pressure to be active in the nursery's celebration of Chinese New Year. They are relieved that Clare would like to repeat the experience but is not giving the message that it is for Li-Fong rather than all her peers. Clare is also working hard to challenge the belief that has built up in the Whittons team that contact with one family from a particular ethnic group or faith is sufficient to inform everyone about that background or set of beliefs.

With support, the team are now developing a more inclusive outlook on this aspect to their equality practice. For instance, the dolls with African features are an integral part of pretend play resources. They are not on display because Rafat has now joined the group. Once Rafat's family had come to know the team, Clare felt ready to invite suggestions from his mother for stories or music that could complement the nursery's existing resources. Friendly conversation over the weeks is helping Clare to know more about the family. There is no expectation that Rafat's parents will be a source of information about the whole of Africa, when their country of origin is Uganda and the family relocated to England when Rafat's parents were children.

Questions

1. **Do you work in a neighbourhood with limited obvious ethnic group diversity? In what ways do you address the kind of issues faced by the Whittons team?**

2. **Are there views in your team that need to be challenged in a firm but professional way? Perhaps that families are asked if they really want 'special' dolls or books for their children? Families who are very much in the minority locally would have to feel really self-assured to say 'Yes', especially since the message could be that limited financial resources are being stretched just for them.**

TAKE ANOTHER PERSPECTIVE

Sometimes a team in a mainly 'white' area will say that equality over ethnic group and culture is 'nothing to do with us'. Since the children do not apparently experience cultural variation, practitioners claim it should not enter the early years curriculum. If such feelings are strong in some of your team or childminding network, try the following exercise.

Find a map and draw a circle 20 miles in all directions around your setting or family home. Now, imagine that you have to remove anything from your centre or home that children could neither see nor hear within that circle.

- Are you within 20 miles of the sea? If not, then out go any books, jigsaws or pictures about the seaside, sea fishing or seagoing boats. And perhaps the sand tray should be removed as well!

- Take away any books and pictures showing animals or birds, unless children can see the real thing locally. The same goes for flowers, trees and shrubs.

- Remove anything that relates to castles, forts or palaces, unless you have a real one nearby.

- Remove any books, pictures, construction materials, play people or dressing-up clothes that reflect anything that children could not directly observe within the 20-mile boundary.

- And what if the children are not allowed to draw anything they could not observe in their own everyday lives?

You will probably not get far into the activity (making a list or an actual pile of resources) before people say that it is ridiculous to remove all these learning resources from children. Of course, it would be very foolish to organise a group setting, nursery or childminder's home in this way. Children's learning is seriously restricted if the only permitted sources of play and ideas are those that can be personally experienced locally. All children need resources and experiences that extend their understanding beyond their immediate daily life in ways that make sense to them.

Respect for cultural identity

Play and learning resources matter in every early years, school or out-of-school service. Your aim is to reflect the cultural traditions of children who currently attend your provision. Children, and their families, need to see themselves represented throughout resources and events. Children need to feel that they belong as individuals through those experiences that create their ethnic group and cultural identity. An equally important aim is to extend the horizons of all the children. So you will need to make some choices, but will not be restricted to cultural traditions represented locally.

All traditions should be approached with respect and you should avoid any implication that the main traditions within the current group are more 'normal' than the other 'exotic' or 'odd' traditions that you explore briefly. This approach is sometimes called a 'tourist curriculum', because the impression given is that the activities are not related to real life. Whatever the background of individuals in your provision, practitioners are responsible for encouraging attitudes of respect as well as interest. It would be no more acceptable for a mainly African-Caribbean group of children to ridicule Japanese clothes or food than it would be to allow such behaviour from a mainly 'white' European group of children.

Positive identity for all children

Early years professionals are responsible for supporting a positive identity by cultural group for all the children. Written material about equality through resources often focuses most on supporting the personal identity of children from minority ethnic groups. This focus is understandable, given a past history of inadequacy of resources to reflect non-European traditions. However, the current generation of young children all need to develop a positive sense of history and culture for the group(s) to which they and their families belong.

An enthusiastic use of 'special' resources from non-European cultural traditions can leave 'white' children feeling that all the interesting material comes from cultures other than their own. I have known some 'white' children who have expressed the wish to be 'Indian' because, 'they have really interesting dances and painting and things'. Such a feeling is not as emotionally destructive as a 'black' child who wishes to be 'white', but I think it is still a matter of regret and deserves attention.

Children learn from 'me and my friends'

Studies of 'white' UK children in socially deprived areas have highlighted that they may have no obvious sources of positive identity unless they are disdainful and rejecting of 'black' groups. An approach that stresses 'other cultures' increases feelings of 'them and us' and gives the underlying message that the 'other' contrasts with some kind of 'normal'. Any equality approach has to be fully inclusive, and that means helping potentially disaffected 'white' children. Some boys and girls really need to explore their own sources of personal, family and cultural identity in ways that boost their self-esteem, without bigoted feelings of superiority that desperately boil down to, 'At least I'm not a . . .'.

TAKE ANOTHER PERSPECTIVE

Experiences and resources matter to help children of any minority ethnic group establish a sense of positive identity and explore a shared history. Equality is not a competitive exercise and any concerns can be grounded in an overview of how all children are likely to gain a sense of pride in their origins.

- One of the problems has been that a generation of professionals (including me!) first approached equality from the 1960s–70s through sharp awareness of the racial and cultural bias in so many textbooks, stories and play resources. Those problems are not fully resolved, but there has been considerable improvement.

- We need now to be truly inclusive in equality practice and that means weaving in an active appreciation of cultural, historical, linguistic and other sources of a personal identity rooted in the UK.

- Children have a right to develop a pride in being English, Welsh, Scottish or Irish. Even those divisions for identity have further meaning. As readers from Northern Ireland will know very well, a serious division between communities in that part of the UK falls between a wish to be seen as British or Irish.

If you want to find out more:

⁜ Commission for Racial Equality: www.cre.gov.uk.

⁜ Connolly, Paul and Troyna, Barry (eds.) (1998) *Researching Racism in Education: Policies, Theory and Practice*. Buckingham: Open University Press (for readers who wish to explore the complexities of research in this area).

✢ Gaine, Chris (2005) *We're all White, Thanks: The Persisting Myth about White Schools*. Stoke-on-Trent: Trentham Books.

✢ Gaine, Chris and Lamley, Kirstin (2003) *Racism and the Dorset Idyll: A Report of the Experiences of Black and Minority Ethnic People in Bournemouth, Dorset and Poole*. Dorset Race Equality Council.

✢ Milner, David (1983) *Children and Race: Ten Years On*. London: Ward Lock Educational (useful summary of research up to the 1980s that provides an insight into social history for readers whose adulthood started more recently).

RELIGIOUS FAITH AND PERSONAL BELIEFS

Family life and the raising of children can be influenced by parents' religious faith and by personal belief systems that matter a great deal but are not religious in origin. Identity by faith is often intermingled with ethnic group and cultural traditions. Some adults, and by association their children, prefer to identify themselves by faith than by ethnic group or nationality.

Attempts to gather statistics by ethnicity or other groupings face difficulties because people have clear preferences about how they wish to self-describe. Some UK residents are content to identify themselves as 'British Asian'. However, Asia is a large continent comprising different countries, languages, faiths and cultural traditions. Some people definitely wish to choose 'British Muslim' or 'British Hindu'. Distinctions and the sources of family ways can be less than obvious to people who are unfamiliar with the group. Ignorance, misunderstanding and stereotyping can also undermine or derail harmonious relationships across these group boundaries.

Negative blurring of boundaries worsens in times of social stress and fear, such as the London bombings of July 2005. Media reporting, let alone ordinary conversation, frequently muddles broad ethnicity, as in 'Asian', with faith, as in 'Muslim' – not to mention the untrue implication that all, or most, followers of Islam are 'extremist' or 'fundamentalist'. Aggressive reactions to events show evidence of this ignorance, stereotyping and failure to see diversity in a group to which writers or speakers do not themselves belong.

Faith and culture

Religious beliefs and practices have shaped societies around the world. When there has been a long history of a particular faith associated with a country, then religious practices become merged with the culture and can affect virtually every aspect of a society: social, moral and political. What was originally rooted in religious faith becomes seen as 'normal' life. Habits are absorbed into everyday language, expected ways of behaving and celebrations by people who are no longer active members of the particular religious faith.

Additionally, faiths like Christianity, Buddhism or Islam have spread far beyond their historical roots. Versions of the main faith have developed varied cultural traditions in the details of religious observance or applications to daily life. For example, modest dress is a requirement within Islam, but many different styles of modest dress for women have evolved within different Muslim communities across the world.

The UK as an example

The four nations of the UK have a long history of being shaped by Christianity. The faith arrived in the fifth century, most likely brought by St Patrick to Ireland, and steadily gained followers, absorbing some of the pre-existing Celtic beliefs. A major schism was provoked by Henry VIII in the sixteenth century, when he broke from the religious leadership of the Pope in Rome. An alternative denomination of Christianity developed in England, known as Protestant to be distinguished from Catholic. The Church of England became the established church and the monarch retains the title Defender of the Faith.

Throughout the twentieth century, being 'C of E' was regarded by many people as much the same as being 'English'. There are different denominations within Christianity and England is not the only country in the UK. I recall as a child visiting the Welsh half of my family and being kindly corrected by my grandmother, who explained that in the valleys people did not go to church, they went to chapel. The Church of England was the English faith and the local community was Welsh Methodist by tradition. The Scottish Presbyterian Church also has distinct practices.

Even if you work in a diverse neighbourhood, you may find an unquestioned assumption within a team that families are nominally Christian unless they definitely say otherwise. I am not the only parent to have left a deliberate blank in the space asking for family religion in their child's school information sheet, only to find later that someone in the school office had filled in 'Christian' without further consultation.

SCENARIOS

The merging of religious and cultural tradition is relevant for practitioners. Even adults who no longer practise the faith in which they were raised often prefer to follow patterns established in their own childhood.

1
At Crest Road Early Years Centre, Chloe and her mother are keen to show staff some photos of the new baby's christening. This conversation is the first time either parent has mentioned the Christian faith. They are not regular church-goers but feel more comfortable having baby Jessica christened.

2
When Aaron and his parents first visited the Whittons Nursery, they explained that Aaron was not to be given any pork or shellfish. Clare, the manager, commented that there was no synagogue in the town and it became clear that Aaron's family was not active in the Jewish faith. His parents simply preferred to follow the diet in which they had been raised.

Questions

1. In each setting the comments and requests from parents were taken seriously. In Chloe's case an important family event was shared and in Aaron's case the request about diet was respected.

2. Have similar situations arisen within your own setting or service as a childminder?

TAKE ANOTHER PERSPECTIVE

If your childhood was spent in the UK, or another culture strongly influenced by Christianity, you may never have questioned a feeling that it is normal to believe in one god (monotheism) and that religions that have more than one deity are therefore strange. You may make other, similar assumptions.

I recall working with an early years team that was very diverse by ethnic group, but most of the team had a Christian background, even if they were no longer active. Conversation turned to Hinduism during one session and several people turned to their only Indian colleague to say with great surprise, 'But you don't believe in reincarnation, do you?' She replied, 'Of course I do.' The group clearly had to adjust to the experience that a fellow practitioner, who was very much 'one of us', believed in an idea that most of the team had learned was out of the ordinary.

Diversity within faiths

Six main world faiths are often featured most prominently within supporting materials for early years, school and playwork professionals.

1. **Hinduism** is the oldest major world faith, established about 5000 years ago in India. The specific name dates from about 800 years ago, when followers were identified as Hindu, the Persian word for Indian.

2. **Judaism** has existed for about 3500 years and developed in the area known from a European perspective as the Middle East. It is the first faith known to be monotheistic (belief in a single deity).

3. **Buddhism** stretches back some 2500 years to its origins in India, where it was founded by Gautama, who became the Buddha, meaning 'The Enlightened One'.

4. **Christianity** evolved about 2000 years ago in part of the Middle East then known as Palestine. Believers worship one god whom they believe created the world and took human form as Jesus Christ (the Messiah).

5. **Islam** emerged as a world faith, in what is now Saudi Arabia, about 1400 years ago, led by the Prophet Muhammad (always said with the Arabic phrase meaning 'peace and blessings of Allah upon him').

6. **Sikhism** developed over 500 years ago within the Punjab (an area stretching from what became Pakistan into north-west India). The movement was started by Guru Nanak.

All the faiths spread beyond their point of origin, sometimes because of population movements. However, some followers deliberately travelled to other countries in order to convert members of that population. World faiths have developed variations in different locations. Sometimes followers have absorbed the practices of pre-existing religions in the culture. Buddhism in India differs from the faith in Japan, because the latter developed in co-existence with Shintoism, an ancient religion based in animist beliefs of a supernatural force within all natural objects. Differences also arise because of unresolved divisions within the faith. The Orthodox Church in eastern Europe split over questions of belief long before the schism that divided Protestant from Catholic Christianity in western Europe.

You will be aware of sects within the world faith most familiar to you. However, diversity is a feature of every major world faith. There is disagreement, sometimes significant, over core beliefs, interpretations of the main holy book(s), the details of daily practice like diet or dress, aspects of worship and related cultural tradition. For no faith can you confidently say 'Everyone believes that . . .' or 'Everyone behaves in this way'. It is also unjust to generalise from the behaviour of the more uncompromising groups in any faith to claim that intolerance is part of that religion.

Disagreements can turn vicious between followers of different faiths – for example, the continuing violence between some Hindus and some Muslims in India. Some of the massacres that occurred through the early 1990s in the former Yugoslavia were determined along Christian–Muslim divisions, sometimes between people who had co-existed as neighbours for decades. However, the sectarian divisions between the Protestant and Catholic denominations of Christianity in Northern Ireland are thoroughly entangled with historical, political and social factors. The resulting ill feeling, violence and social disruption are yet to be resolved.

Uncompromising versions of a faith are sometimes called fundamentalist. The term seemed first to arise from Christian sects that took the Bible as literal truth. In contrast, other Christians regard the Old and New Testaments as more symbolic and open to different interpretations. The term fundamentalist has increasingly been used to mean a follower of any faith whose allegiance involves rejection of everyone who does not agree with their faith or with this specific version. The word is sometimes applied indiscriminately to followers of Islam. Muslims are not all fundamentalists in this sense, any more than the allegation can legitimately be made of all Christians.

Diversity of faith in the UK

For many centuries the different denominations of Christianity were by far the most prominent faith in the UK. However, Judaism has been present for many centuries because there were Jewish communities in many cities. These settlements experienced periodic violence and persecution as a direct result of their faith. Other sources of religious diversity mainly developed with the population movements of the twentieth century.

Many migrants from the Caribbean and the African continent were active Christians or, like other residents of the UK, shared that faith as a cultural backdrop to daily life. Migrants from some countries in Africa, Asia and Malaysia followed Islam. Some migrants, and refugees, from parts of Europe, are also Muslim. Migrants from the Punjab are frequently Sikh by faith. Buddhism is a widely-dispersed faith and followers may originate from many parts of the world, not only India or China. Through the 1960s and 1970s some UK residents became intrigued by eastern mysticism and became committed to the faith.

Faith and professional practice

Knowledge and understanding

You are not expected to be an expert about religions. Your responsibility in good practice is to be aware of the gaps in what you know and ready to learn more. You should also be willing to check your understanding, even when colleagues share the same assumptions. You may all have misunderstood the real significance of a religious festival or the reason for particular practices. There is no shame in admitting to confusion or having misunderstood. It is, however, unprofessional if practitioners shut their mind to that possibility.

If you keep an open mind, you will extend your learning about faiths that are unfamiliar to you, but you are also likely to learn more about the religious faith that is most familiar, perhaps a faith in which you were raised or which you still practise. It can be hard to stand back from beliefs that seem part of everyday life, and it can be valuable to grasp finally, 'Oh, that's why we do that!' This opportunity to continue to learn applies whatever the faith that is most familiar to you.

Respect and belief

You will not be in tune with everyone over religious faith or personal belief systems. You are not expected to agree, or pretend to agree, with every colleague or parent who expresses their personal beliefs. Good practice includes the following.

- Having a clear policy that includes matters of faith within how you address equality in your daily practice.
- Creating opportunities to discuss within a team any confusion or disagreement that arises through conversations with parents, or indeed from diversity of belief within the team. Childminders benefit from being part of a local network and having easy contact with local support advisers.
- Acknowledging differences and showing respect for beliefs and practices that you may not share. Respect applies regardless of whether you currently have contact with a family that follows the faith in question.
- Showing respect through an active attempt to understand any requests that parents make based on religious or other personal beliefs. If the setting genuinely cannot meet parents' requests, then you should be honest and seek a compromise, if possible.

Mutual respect

The way in which you approach experiences within your practice should demonstrate that you value faiths equally. Nobody should behave in their professional life as if one religion is more important or true than any other.

Practitioners and policy makers are sometimes concerned that offence will be given to followers of one faith by the sheer presence of celebrations or symbols linked with another faith. It is important to be aware of the significance of events or symbols, and to ensure that the resources and experiences you offer children are balanced. Such sensitivity is a significant part of equality practice in Northern Ireland, which addresses sectarianism. Young children in that part of the UK become aware of how flags, sporting allegiance and events like marches carry symbolic meaning for Catholic and Protestant sects.

Part of religious faith for some followers is that they are definitely right and anyone who does not share their beliefs, or this version of the faith, is definitely wrong. This evaluative judgement is not necessarily hostile to non-believers. Indeed the conviction leads some faith members towards active attempts to convert other people: an evangelical stance. However, some sects within different world faiths are more dogmatic than others and some are utterly rejecting of outsiders, as well as any divergence of opinion within the same faith. This situation can shock people unfamiliar with the group beliefs and complicates good practice on equality. Respect for anyone's beliefs has to be balanced with an awareness that nobody is to impose their beliefs on colleagues, parents or children in the service or setting.

Personal beliefs and spirituality

Policy and practice on equality over faith must also recognise that parents who do not actively follow a particular faith can still have strong beliefs about how to behave and raise their children. It is disrespectful to assume that families with no specific religious beliefs lack moral values to guide their decisions.

If people have religious beliefs, then their sense of spirituality is very likely to be interwoven with their faith. However, 'religious' is not inevitably the same as 'spiritual'. It is possible and appropriate to address the spiritual aspect of children's development through awareness of human experience that does not have to answer to rational analysis. Whatever the family faith or belief system, children can be encouraged in a sense of wonder, often through enchantment about the natural world, and peaceful contemplation.

Religious affiliation

If a group setting has no definite religious affiliation, then any parent, practitioner or volunteer needs to understand policy and practice on equality. Adults have the right to their own beliefs, and team members will show respect, including flexibility in connection with requests arising from religious practice. However, rights are accompanied by the responsibility to show respect in their turn and no practitioner should tell children that only this single faith or sect is true. The early years curriculum frameworks around the UK are consistent in promoting mutual respect and avoiding any specific religious allegiance. Childminders who have committed to a particular religion may have symbols of their faith within the home. It would be expected that, whatever the faith, practitioners would not push forward their own beliefs. In your own home, as in any group setting, it is appropriate to answer any questions or comments put by children themselves.

Some early years settings are linked with a specific place of worship and therefore religious faith or denomination. The situation must be made clear in the brochure or other form of written material about the setting. Registered early years settings and providers are still obliged to show respect for religions other than the faith followed by staff.

Religious education is a feature of the school curriculum throughout the UK. Use of the term 'education' rather than 'religious instruction' reflects the focus that it is a teacher's role to educate children about faith in general and not to instruct them in specific religious beliefs or practices. Schools are expected to organise a regular experience of collective worship of a broadly Christian nature unless the school has been given permission to vary this format (usually because a significant proportion of pupils follow another world faith).

The general approach is that children will experience this part of the curriculum together and not subdivided by belief. Parents have the right to withdraw their children from RE or the collective worship. Faith schools may offer, separately, to organise specific religious instruction in preparation for events such as confirmation, a ceremony of personal dedication to faith for some Christian denominations.

In England, Wales and Scotland the majority of state schools do not have a specific religious affiliation. Most faith schools have allegiance to Protestant (Church of England) or Catholic denominations of Christianity. There are a small number of Jewish schools and a very few Muslim and Sikh schools. The situation is reversed in Northern Ireland, where most schools are affiliated along Christian denominational lines: Protestant or Catholic.

Since 1981 the Integrated Education Movement has steadily set up nurseries, playgroups and schools integrated by denomination. Demand for places still exceeds supply.

If you want to find out more:

❖ Community Relations Council (Northern Ireland): www.community-relations.org.uk. Material explaining an anti-sectarian approach.

❖ Connolly, Paul, Smith, Alan and Kelly, Berni (2002) *Too Young to Notice: The Cultural and Political Awareness of 3–6-Year-Olds in Northern Ireland*. Belfast: Community Relations Council.

❖ Learning and Teaching Scotland: www.ltscotland.org.uk/antisectarian.

❖ Lindon, Jennie (1999) *Understanding World Religions in Early Years Practice*. London: Hodder & Stoughton.

❖ Qualifications and Curriculum Authority (QCA): *Religious Education: Glossary of Terms*; www.qca.org.uk/downloads/6148_re_glossary.pdf.

5 Disability and health

Some children cope with the difference made to daily life by learning, physical or emotional disabilities, or a continuing health condition that leaves them feeling ill on a regular or permanent basis. Equality practice over disability has much in common with other aspects of inclusion. However, like gender, ethnic group and faith, there are some issues that benefit from a separate discussion. Disabled children should be seen and recognised as children, not seen only through their disability or health condition, and practitioners need to explore how to manage that aim.

> **The main areas covered by this chapter are:**
>
> ✳ **disabled children in society**
>
> ✳ **the range of disability and chronic ill health**
>
> ✳ **special support for disabled children.**

DISABLED CHILDREN IN SOCIETY

Into the 1980s, the dominant approach in the UK to disabled children and their families was to focus on disability mainly in medical terms: diagnosis, treatment and management of the condition when, as often, no cure was possible. A re-evaluation of this approach was provoked by disabled adults sharing their memories and views of how they had been treated as children. Parents of disabled children were also critical of services that treated their son or daughter as a medical case, rather than an individual child. Some of the objections about lack of information, disrespect (to parents and children) and conflicting advice from different medical professionals are shared by families who do not have a disabled child. The 'patients rather than people' model can still undermine good health-care practice.

Challenges to a medical model

An alternative social model of disability has been promoted that focuses on the child as an individual. This model also highlights social conditions, outside the child's specific disability, that cause the child to be further disabled unnecessarily. The approach through a social model does not deny the value of appropriate treatments or medication, but stresses that children's lives should not be driven by the disability label they are given, nor by a regime of treatment. Disabled children have individual needs, wants, interests and views about what happens to them, just like any other children.

TAKE ANOTHER PERSPECTIVE

A shift from a predominantly medical to a social model makes a significant difference from the point of view of a child or young person. Practitioners working implicitly with a medical model would say (or think), 'Andy can't join in because he's deaf and won't understand.' The shift to a social model recognises how adult attitudes are disabling Andy. Practitioners need to move the point of responsibility to Andy's legitimate perspective of, 'I could join in, if people here were able to sign with me.'

A challenge to the medical model also brought in the need for coherence for parents of children with complex health needs. Families were too often left trying to balance the different, sometimes conflicting, advice from several professionals or agencies. Now, at least in theory, families are supported towards a more holistic view of care and family life, which can also involve striving to find time for the siblings of a disabled or very sick child.

WHAT DOES IT MEAN?

Medical model of disability: An approach to disabled children that focuses exclusively on diagnosis and medical management of the condition.

Social model of disability: An approach that focuses on disabled children as individuals, and on ways in which they can be disabled by social circumstances and attitudes.

Inclusive approach or inclusion: A commitment to enable disabled children to join mainstream settings and play facilities, with suitable adjustment or support as necessary.

Responsibility for active inclusion

A couple of generations ago, disabled children were largely segregated from their peers, often in residential accommodation. Carers and decision-makers often had low expectations for what children could manage and little respect for what they might want. The situation has changed in that parents across the UK now have the legal right to seek mainstream provision, including schooling, for their disabled child, supported by additional services appropriate to the child.

Children with special learning, educational or health needs have been affected by a wide range of laws. Disability discrimination legislation across England, Wales and Scotland has made educational and other services responsible for enabling inclusion and accessibility in all its forms. Northern Ireland was the last nation of the UK to pass this type of legislation (2005) and changes are now likely in accepted practice to meet special educational needs.

- The law does not require settings to run up huge bills for structural alterations to buildings, but a nursery or school is required to look ahead – for instance, in anticipating the needs of wheelchair users. It is not an acceptable excuse to say that no child or parent currently involved with the provision has serious mobility problems.

- It is good practice for settings or childminders to consider how they would adjust to the needs of a child with profound hearing loss or whose behaviour fell within the autistic spectrum.

- It is unacceptable for any practitioner or team simply to refuse children in the belief that their health or learning needs will be 'too difficult' or that other children or their parents allegedly 'wouldn't like it'.

- If you genuinely doubt your ability to provide for a child, then you must be able to give sound reasons, explained in terms of the child's needs, the premises or practical details of the service the family seeks.

The requirements arising from laws against disability discrimination have meant that some teams have had to revisit assumed ground rules such as 'We don't give medication here' or 'All children must be toilet-trained'. For some children daily medication is part of normal life, not temporary illness for which 'they should be at home'. Some children with disabilities will take longer to attain self-care skills; some may always need considerable help. (There is more on this in Chapter 6.)

Disabled children have the right to enjoy all the events and resources within early years, school or out-of-school provision. It is unacceptable for practitioners simply to decide to exclude a child from an activity or an outing. Such actions are discriminatory and therefore illegal. The main aim of the laws and related guidance documents is to encourage a 'can-do' outlook. Practitioners need to be ready and able to access advice in order to ensure that they are confident in dealing with a child's daily health issues. Teams may need support to find ways to include children fully in activities that look problematic at the outset or provoke adult anxiety about children's safety.

Inclusion is a continuing process that depends on alert adult observation and listening to the views of the children themselves. They are the best judges of whether they feel welcome and an easy partner in experiences. Disabled children need to feel able to make genuine choices within their play and, of course, that will sometimes mean declining an invitation to join an activity. Practitioners need to get to know any disabled children as individuals and build partnership with their families. Of course, disabled children still all have their own temperaments and it is important to avoid stereotypes.

SCENARIOS

1

Crest Road Early Years Centre learned a great deal when Freddy, who has Down's syndrome, first joined the setting. Two team members expressed surprise that Freddy became easily upset. Liz, the manager, carefully explored these practitioners' stereotyped belief that all children with Down's syndrome had a sunny disposition. Freddy was happy with much of what he saw at Crest Road, but was quick to express his displeasure at routines he found unfamiliar.

It also became clear in the early weeks that Alicia, Freddy's mother, had given an over-optimistic description of what her son could manage. Nell, Freddy's key person, started again with Alicia. She had been worried Freddy would not get a place if she was honest about the significant delay in her son's development. The experience made the Crest Road team think even more carefully about first meetings with families.

2

There were serious concerns in the Whittons team when Max's family first approached the nursery. Some practitioners recalled a very unhappy experience with Deanna, who was also diagnosed within autistic spectrum disorder. There was pressure on Clare, who had arrived as manager since that time, to refuse a place to Max. Staff recalled how Deanna 'was impossible – wrecked the place – she needed one-to-one all the time' and 'Her mother was worse – kept banging on about disability rights.' Clare took a firm stand that it was not appropriate to generalise from Deanna to Max. Nor was it all right to make sweeping assumptions about parents of disabled children. Clare reassured the team there would be a thorough discussion with Max's father and that she would get advice from the local SEN advisory team.

Comments

- Not all disabled children need one-to-one support but some children will only be able to benefit from group provision with a personal support worker.
- Be ready to ask for practical advice and support from your local special needs adviser or team. Early years and school professionals need to extend their knowledge, but you are not expected to know everything.
- It is important that all practitioners get beyond the label with disabled children and connect with them, and their families, as individuals.

Is inclusion always the best way?

The inclusive perspective on the care and education of disabled children stresses the value of enabling children to remain within mainstream provision. There has been serious concern about the impact of dividing disabled children from their peers. But there are also misgivings about uncompromising policy, or financial decisions, which result in the closure of special units or schools. You will find disagreement, as well as harmony, among professionals and parents who are active on behalf of their disabled children.

There are certainly legitimate concerns about whether mainstream schools will have the facilities and give appropriate personal attention to some children with specific or profound disabilities. For instance, some parents of deaf children have been keen not to lose the advantages of special units. Parents have been very concerned about proper support for children with autistic spectrum disorder. Without appropriate care and understanding, children can be confused and frightened by the usual bustle of a nursery or primary group. On the hand, a child's experience can be transformed with the continued support of an adult, like a Specialist Teaching Assistant. Early years and school practitioners in their turn are very aware of the impact on a group of children of a child with severe emotional and behavioural difficulties. There are no easy answers.

Yet mixing together has definite advantages for all children. Young children can be very straightforward about other children who are disabled. They want to know what is happening and to hear simple answers to reasonable questions. Their experience of disabled friends can help to shift images in society in which disabled or very sick children may effectively be invisible. In the past, children with physical disabilities got bored and frustrated when placed in an all-purpose 'special unit' alongside children with severe learning disabilities. The physically disabled children often lacked conversation, challenge and play with their intellectual equals.

An inclusive approach is not some magical option and children will not be helped if the positive opportunities are stressed with limited attention paid to practicalities.

- There needs to be a proper assessment of the needs of an individual child. What does the child need, who will deliver it and to what extent can her or his needs be met within your setting or family home?
- Specific needs, arising through a disability or health condition, should be assessed carefully and met as far as possible through enabling disabled children to play and learn with other children.

■ Neither the physical environment of the setting, nor the behaviour of practitioners or other adults, should lead children to be further disabled by what is offered or not offered to meet their needs.

Child-friendly health care

Hospital stays

Some disabled children will spend a lot of time in hospital – either in many short bursts or for longer periods of time. Over the last decades of the twentieth century there was a substantial change in attitudes and practice towards children in hospital. The organisation that became Action for Sick Children has been very influential in making health practice more responsive to the needs of children, including easy continued contact with their families. The development of a profession of hospital play therapists has been supportive for all children who are separated from family life, for one or more hospital stays.

Dealing with chronic pain

Some children who live with chronic pain are unable to express what they feel in words. They also may have no idea that this 'normal' condition for them could be alleviated. Unfortunately, children and their parents have not always been taken seriously by health professionals when asked to prescribe medication for pain control.

LOOK, LISTEN, NOTE, LEARN

Some practitioners have diverse career routes before reaching work in early years, school and out-of-school service. But few readers are likely to be health care specialists. The issue of chronic pain and pain control for children is a good example of an area that you might need to research, so that you can more effectively support children and families.

Gather some practical information that could support your practice. Here are some starting points:

■ Action Research (www.actionresearch.org.uk) and the Royal College of Nursing (www.rcn.org.uk) have developed guidelines to help parents and professionals notice and assess children's pain.

■ You will also find useful information on www.painrelieffoundation. org.uk.

If you want to find out more:

- ❖ *ACT*, Orchard House, Orchard Lane, Bristol BS1 5DT. Tel: 0117 922 1556; www.act.org.uk. Promotes palliative care for children, and offers support and resources for children with life-threatening or terminal conditions, and their families.

- ❖ *Action for Sick Children*, 8 Wakley Street, London EC1V 7QE. Tel: 020 7843 6444; www.actionforsickchildren.org. Supports good care for children in hospital, and their families.

THE RANGE OF DISABILITY AND CHRONIC ILL HEALTH

It would be unrealistic for you to aim to know about every possible health condition or disability that you might encounter within your entire career. Furthermore, new research and reviews of practice often mean that the information and advice of ten, or even five, years ago is overtaken. A realistic approach and good practice is to be:

- ▪ willing to find out, to listen and to learn – from parents, the children themselves, other professionals and the many organisations that are keen to inform and advise

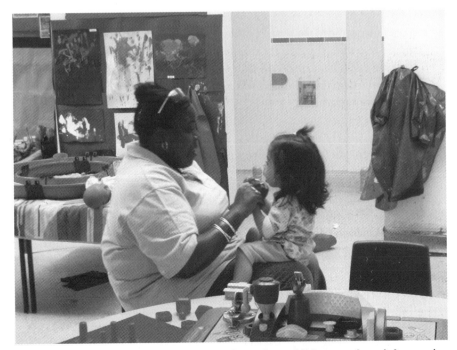

Sometimes children need special attention

- ready to consider your expectations for disabled children and to assess your assumptions, some of which may be neither accurate nor helpful.

There are many different kinds of disability and the aim of this section is to give you a sense of the range. A website reference is given the first time each condition is mentioned in this chapter. Details of further resources can be found on page 104.

Some children are mainly or wholly physically disabled and the effect may be anything from mild to very severe. Here are some examples.

- **Muscular dystrophy** is a progressive disease in which children's muscles waste away. There are variations of the condition, but Duchenne is the form more commonly identified within early childhood and directly affects only boys (www.muscular-dystrophy. org.uk).

- Children who are **blind** or **deaf** live with a disability of the senses that affects the way in which they learn in other areas of development. Children learn to cope, with appropriate support, in a society that usually assumes people can see and hear (www.rnib.org.uk and www.ndcs.org.uk).

Some physical disabilities have associated learning difficulties.

- Children with **cerebral palsy** share a condition in which their brain is failing to send the appropriate signals to their limbs. Some children experience no more than mild difficulties in hand control, others struggle to stand or move their limbs in a planned, deliberate way. There may also be damage to other parts of the brain such that some children are deaf, blind or live with severe learning disabilities (www.scope.org.uk).

Children may largely experience learning disabilities and again the severity of the condition can vary for individuals.

- Children with **Down's syndrome** (also referred to as Down syndrome) can have mild through to severe learning disabilities. The condition sometimes brings associated physical disabilities: heart problems, which may require surgery, or difficulties with hearing and vision (www.downs-syndrome.org.uk).

TAKE ANOTHER PERSPECTIVE

The experience of children with Down's syndrome and that of their families are a good example of significant social changes. Even in the

1960s, it would have been regarded as wildly optimistic to propose that children with Down's syndrome could attend mainstream primary and secondary school, learn to read and in some cases emerge with qualifications. Many children and young people with Down's have now shown what is possible with appropriate support. Had they been born into earlier generations, they would have been placed in residential schools, with minimal expectations for their progress or an independent adult life.

Some children with Down's and other kinds of disability were hidden by their families through a sense of shame. Parents sometimes felt they were personally responsible for having produced a child who was not 'normal'. I spoke with social workers as late as the 1970s who were still very occasionally finding older children or teenagers with Down's syndrome who had never been permitted to leave the family home.

Some social and cultural groups still have negative views about disability that locate the cause with personal failings, perhaps of the mother, or a more general cosmic backlash upon the family for wrongdoing. Supportive professionals need to grasp the sources of such feelings, without of course assuming that every member of this ethnic group or faith will share the wish to reject.

Children can have learning disabilities for a wide range of reasons, and there may not be a definite explanation and diagnosis for some families. Children who show difficulties in their learning may have experienced brain damage during a protracted and difficult birth, as a result of accidental damage to the head in childhood or as a consequence of serious illnesses such as meningitis or whooping cough.

Some disabilities affect social and emotional development as well as other aspects. Children with severe learning disabilities will struggle to make sense of social situations and adult expectations that are obvious to their age peers. Some conditions directly affect social understanding and behaviour.

- Some children cope within **autism spectrum disorder**. This condition is broadly a developmental disability that affects how a child's brain functions. Such children usually have difficulty with social and communication skills; some never learn spoken language (www.nas.org.uk).

You may care for children whose fragile health is a direct result of their disability. Some children will have a continuing health condition that affects their choices and how they run their lives.

- **Cystic fibrosis** is a life-threatening condition affecting children's respiratory and digestive systems. Thick mucus in children's lungs blocks the bronchial tubes and they are vulnerable to chest infections. Special needs in care, such as physiotherapy, arise from the condition, but cystic fibrosis does not affect learning abilities (www.cftrust.org.uk).

- **Asthma** is the most common chronic medical disorder in childhood. Some children experience mild attacks of breathlessness, but others have serious attacks in which they struggle desperately to take breath. A severe asthmatic attack can be fatal (www.asthma.org.uk).

- **Sickle cell disease** is a blood disorder, the most common and severe form being sickle cell anaemia. Children and adults experience bouts of illness, called crises, in which severe anaemia and pain require urgent hospital treatment (www.sicklecellsociety.org).

- **Epilepsy** is a condition in which electrical signals from one group of nerve cells overwhelm nearby parts of the brain. This sudden, excessive electrical discharge brings on an epileptic seizure. Some seizures cause obvious loss of consciousness but milder incidents can be misinterpreted as daydreaming. Epilepsy is a potentially life-threatening condition and severe seizures can cause brain damage (www.epilepsy.org.uk).

Experiencing disability

There is also great variation within any given diagnosed condition, so nobody is justified in comments like, 'All children with cerebral palsy will . . .' or 'Children with Down's syndrome will never . . .'. Your task as a supportive practitioner will always be to get to know the individual child and their family.

A whole family – parents and siblings – lives with disability or chronic ill health and not just the child directly affected. Some families have more than one child coping with a disability or, in some cases, an inherited condition. Some parents are themselves disabled: from a condition experienced from childhood, a progressive disease that started in adulthood or serious accidental injury. Across the UK, the Children Acts and Order define any disabled child as a child 'in need'. The Children Act (Scotland) 1995 extended this definition to children in a family where anyone is disabled.

Disabled children, young people and adults still experience thoughtless people, who assume any visible physical disability means this individual can neither communicate for themselves, nor understand what others say. Good practice is to ensure full and courteous communication with disabled children, or with disabled parents or colleagues. You may need to guide volunteers in your setting or parent helpers towards good practice. You can also show the peers of a disabled child, through your actions or explanations, ways to open up communication.

LOOK, LISTEN, NOTE, LEARN

I have known several college tutors who have sent out small groups of students into the local high street, with one individual in a wheelchair. The aim of this activity is to provoke a direct experience of the way that disabled people are sometimes treated in our society, as well as the difficulties that still exist in moving around shops and other public buildings. The usual result is that at least one group returns highly irritated at how their colleague has been treated, just because he or she is sitting in a wheelchair.

Some readers will not be surprised by the results of this experience – those of you who use wheelchairs or have family members who are independently mobile with this kind of support.

Possible causes of disability

There is no single cause for the different kinds of disability or chronic ill health. Practitioners need to be aware that families have very different experiences around the identification of disability or chronic ill health. Sometimes a diagnostic explanation is clear from very early in childhood. However, there can be a delay before the effects of a disability show themselves or are fully recognised. Some families never have a definite explanation of the cause of a child's severe language delay or a more general developmental disorder. Then, families need to get on with what supports their child and leave aside the nagging question of why this has happened.

Genetic causes

Sometimes either the sperm or the egg that combine in fertilisation contains genetic material that carries the information leading to a disability. The condition is then said to be genetic, or inherited through the genes. Some inherited conditions include Down's syndrome, cystic fibrosis and muscular dystrophy.

Some conditions are statistically more frequent within the gene pool of particular ethnic groups. Sickle cell disease is inherited and most common in families who originated from Africa or the Caribbean. But the condition also occurs in families from the eastern Mediterranean, the Middle East, India and Pakistan. Thalassaemia is a condition leading to an excess of iron in the body, and is more common in families of Mediterranean, African, Eastern, Far Eastern and Indian origin (see www.ukts.org). Both of these health conditions may have arisen because they give some protection against malaria. There was a survival value to having the condition for groups who lived in areas where malaria was endemic and life-threatening.

Congenital conditions

The word congenital means that a baby is born with a disability or health condition. Inherited conditions are therefore all congenital, but not all congenital conditions are inherited.

The human foetus is mostly well-protected in the womb, but some events can cause lasting damage. If women are infected with rubella (German measles) during the first three months of pregnancy, then there is permanent damage to the organs developing at that time, with resulting blindness, deafness or cerebral palsy (see www.sense.org.uk). Excessive use of alcohol crosses the placenta throughout pregnancy and causes the damage of foetal alcohol syndrome, which can include learning disabilities. Use of addictive drugs like heroin also affects the foetus and babies can be born drug-dependent (see www.fasaware.co.uk).

Traumatic or very premature birth

Lack of oxygen at birth can arise from a number of different reasons and cause brain damage in babies. The exact consequences will depend on the severity of the brain damage and what parts of the brain are affected. Oxygen deprivation can be dangerous for children at any age, or for adults, and may lead to brain damage and consequent disability.

WHAT DOES IT MEAN?

Genetic causes of disability: When a child inherits a condition from the genes of their parent(s).

Congenital causes of disability: When pre-birth conditions lead to a disability or health condition, so that the baby is born with this condition.

Birth trauma: Unexpected events during childbirth, such as being deprived of oxygen, that create high risk to the future wellbeing of the unborn baby.

Premature babies: Any infant born before a pregnancy has lasted 37 weeks. (Full-term is around 40 weeks.) Some babies of 22–23 weeks' gestation have survived. Once a pregnancy passes 26 weeks, the prospects for a newborn improve steadily.

The difficulty for very premature babies is that vital organs and their brain have to continue to develop outside the ideal environment of their mother's womb. Advances in intensive care have improved the prospects of tiny babies, who are not ready for an independent existence. Nevertheless, newspaper stories of 'miracle babies' rarely follow them into childhood. Mild to severe physical and/or learning disabilities often become clear as a baby or child struggles with the skills of development in early childhood.

Illness and accidents after birth

Very serious illnesses within childhood can have permanent consequences even when children survive the illness itself. Meningitis can leave children with hearing difficulties (the most common possible after-effect), brain injury or epilepsy (see www.meningitis-trust.org.uk).

Some children's physical or learning disabilities result from injuries, especially damage to the head and therefore to the brain. Children may be involved in traffic accidents, or may have serious falls at home or at play. Serious head injuries can lead to the development of cerebral palsy. Much damage is accidental, but some children are maltreated by parents or other carers.

Multiple possible causes or unknown

There is sometimes no clear pattern of cause and effect. For example, epilepsy can result from brain injury at birth or from a serious accident. Some seizures may be caused by a faulty gene and so the condition is inherited for this child. However, for many people who have epilepsy there is no obvious cause.

There are few definite answers about how negative aspects of our environment may contribute to disability and health conditions. Certainly, the claim that poor air quality is the main explanation for rising levels of

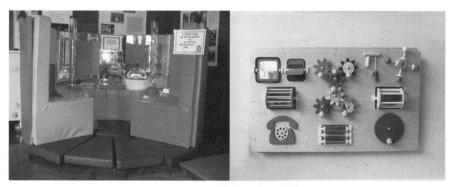

Many 'special' resources are truly inclusive

asthma is not supported by studies in different countries. However, there are many other good reasons for tackling pollution. Lead poisoning can have an impact on learning disabilities – whether accidental by children sucking on a lead-coated object or from living in a neighbourhood with high lead levels in the air.

LOOK, LISTEN, NOTE, LEARN

Consider one of the conditions mentioned so far and imagine that a child with this disability or health condition is soon to join your setting. Gather some general information about the condition. A good first step would be to contact the relevant specialist organisation, through websites and other details given in this chapter.

Think over, and ideally discuss with colleagues or in your student group, the following questions.

- What do you need to know and understand in order to work well with this child? What can you do (not just a negative list of what you 'can't do' or 'problems')?

- What questions should you be ready to ask the parent(s) and how can you put your queries in a positive way?

- Do you need to prepare the existing group for the child's arrival? What sort of questions might the children ask? Consider the actual words you could use to reply with honesty and respect.

- Imagine this child as a part of your group. Are there gaps in the equipment or play materials? Does this child's arrival make you think about the range of activities, how the setting is organised or the kinds of books you have? You will find more ideas in Part 3.

SPECIAL SUPPORT FOR DISABLED CHILDREN

There is common ground across the UK in the law and practical ways to support disabled children and their families. Approaches are similar in England, Wales and Scotland, although not identical in the details. Equality practice for disability in Northern Ireland is at an earlier stage than in the rest of the UK.

Main strands of support

Each nation has a code of practice relating to provision for children with special educational needs. An SEN Code of Practice applies for England and Wales. The Supporting Children's Learning: Code of Practice applies in Scotland, where special educational needs are now addressed within the broader context of additional support needs.

Support for children with any type of special needs is seen as a process, in which there are steps along the way. In England and Wales a two-stage process starts with additional support within provision: Early Years Action and School Action. The next stage of Early Years Action Plus or School Action Plus is started if, despite your extra help, the child is still struggling in any identified area for behaviour or learning. In consultation with parents, and children themselves, you should then consider the possible involvement of specialist agencies outside the early years setting or school.

There is a common theme that children and family needs should be identified and assessed on an individual basis.

- Any kind of education plan is specific to this child; there is no sense of a one-size-fits-all in response to special needs.
- Any targets are discussed with parents, and the children themselves as soon as they are able to participate.
- Suitable additional help for children will often arise within the existing provision, and codes of good practice reflect the variety in suitable responses.
- Some special needs will be met through suitable adjustments to children's personal care and routines.
- Some, though not all, children will need special resources or equipment and practitioners may need additional training to support individual children.
- Special needs that show through children's behaviour may require careful adjustment of adult expectations. Children may need a steady approach to enable them to cope with daily life in nursery or school.

Of course, professionals working in any part of the UK may find that the best service for this child is in short supply, or even does not exist locally.

Each code of practice emphasises that families and professionals work together at every stage of support: identification, assessment, weighing up possibilities and any plan of action for the child. Parents should not be put in the position of having to juggle meetings, advice and requirements from a long list of interested parties. Good practice in England and Wales includes direct efforts to reduce the number of professionals and services with whom a family has to communicate about their child. In Scotland, the Educational Plans are supplemented with a Coordinated Support Plan, with a strong emphasis on bringing professionals and services into effective partnership for children and families. Arrangements have also to be in place to resolve disagreement or outright dispute between a family and the nursery, school or other services.

Inclusion is definitely viewed as education within mainstream provision whenever possible. This model of response is likely to require changes through the Northern Ireland Education and Library Boards. Research commissioned in 1998 by the Department of Education documented an inconsistent approach across schools to implementing the Code of Practice on the Identification and Assessment of Special Educational Needs. It appeared that the integrated schools in Northern Ireland were more likely to have inclusion of disabled children in the way that it is meant in England, Wales and Scotland. The majority of denominational schools (Protestant and Catholic) used an inclusion model that depended on provision for children outside mainstream classrooms. You can access the report, Research Brief 1998 (rb1998), at www.deni.gov.uk/facts_figures.

Building a relationship with disabled children

Too many people, when they look at a disabled child, see the condition rather than the child. Good practice in early years, in schools and out-of-school settings is to develop a personal relationship with a disabled child as you should with any children who are your responsibility. Of course, you and your colleagues need to understand the steps of special support as they apply to your part of the UK. But any guidance needs to be implemented in a personal way.

You will always need to learn what the disability or health condition means for this child, but you should put this knowledge into practice within the context of working with individual children and their families.

- You can have empathy and appreciation of children's frustrations, but avoid pity, either through sad looks or comments such as 'Poor little Louisa – if only she could talk properly.'
- As a childminder, you set the tone for your home in terms of language. In a group setting, team leaders need to ensure that all staff, including any volunteers or parent helpers, relate to children as individuals.
- It is positive to explain that 'Joshua has cerebral palsy', rather than use phrases like 'He suffers from cerebral palsy.' You are not pretending that cerebral palsy is a condition that anyone would

SCENARIO

Social relationships can take more careful building with children with autistic spectrum disorders. The world is a different place to four-year-old Max who has attended the Whittons Nursery over the last year.

Max's level of understanding is very literal. He is puzzled by the subtleties communicated by exactly how something is said or the social conventions of play that his peers have now learned. Max has needed a lot of personal support from Janice, his key person, in order to feel at ease with the nursery routine. He needs prior warning of any changes, because he experiences even minor disruptions as scary.

It has been important that Janice and her colleagues understand that children like Max can develop very rigid personal routines and play preferences in order to cope with anxiety and unpredictability. Janice, in close partnership with Max's father, has helped the young boy to begin to understand some of the non-verbal clues in play and to manage basic social skills. Max is still often perplexed by what is a joke and what is serious, as well as many aspects of pretend play.

Comments

- Children can be very straightforward about disabled peers, but they still want an atmosphere of fairness. Three- and four-year-olds get very annoyed if 'being special' means a child is allowed to break important rules.
- It is easy to take for granted the subtle social skills gained by most four-year-olds until you tune in to the struggles of children with autistic spectrum disorder. When you observe how a child unwittingly breaks the social rules of play, you realise how shared social assumptions underpin rich play between young children.
- Find out more from the National Autistic Society (www.nas.org.uk), which has direct information and suggestions for books and stories.

choose to have, but the way you talk about Joshua should leave nobody surprised that he has an absorbing interest in dinosaurs and a wicked sense of humour.

- Children should never be described just by their disability or health condition. This approach is disrespectful and chips away at children's individuality. It is discourteous to say of children, 'Megan is our little Down's' or 'You know Alric – the epileptic.'

If you want to find out more:

❖ *Advisory Centre for Education*, 1c Aberdeen Studios, 22 Highbury Grove, London N5 2DQ. Tel: 0808 800 5793; www.ace-ed.org.uk. Information about state-funded education for England and Wales.

❖ *Council for Disabled Children*, 8 Wakley Street, London EC1V 9QE. Tel: 020 7843 1900; www.ncb.org.uk/cdc. Information relevant to disabled children and their families.

❖ *David Fulton*: Tel: 020 7405 5606; www.fultonpublishers.com; and *Jessica Kingsley*: Tel: 020 7833 2307; www.jkp.com. Two publishing houses, each of which has a long list of books covering specific disabilities.

❖ *Department of Education* in Northern Ireland, Rathgael House, 43 Balloo Road, Bangor, Co Down BT19 7PR. Tel: 028 9127 9279; www.deni.gov.uk.

❖ *4 Nations Child Policy Network*: www.childpolicy.org.uk.

❖ *Hemihelp*: Tel: 0845 120 3713; www.hemihelp.org.uk. Offers advice and support to families whose children have hemiplegia (similar to cerebral palsy, but affecting one side of the body), as well as useful general fact-sheets.

❖ *Learning and Teaching Scotland*: Tel: 08700 100 297; www.ltscotland. org.uk/inclusiveeducation. Online information about practice in Scotland.

❖ *Scope*, PO Box 833, Milton Keynes MK12 5NY. Tel: 0808 800 3333; www.scope.org.uk/earlyyears/prof/resources. Information about living with cerebral palsy, but also offers general fact-sheets about disability.

❖ *Sure Start*: www.surestart.gov.uk. The website has sections on inclusion, SEN and disability.

❖ *Teacher Net*: www.teachernet.gov.uk. The website has a 'Special Needs' section.

Working well with children

Part 3 of the book focuses on equality issues as they directly affect children through the actions of their important adults, in this case practitioners. Policy can create a foundation for an effective approach on equality. However, policy comes alive only by what happens for and with children and their families, day by day and week by week: all the separate yet interweaving strands in the image of Celtic knotwork.

Good personal care for children is part of promoting equality through recognising individual needs and family preferences. Chapter 6 explores how practice as a whole with children and their families has to blend time and respectful attention to personal care with effective support for their learning. Equality issues can be approached effectively through communication, conversation and a positive approach to children's behaviour. Chapter 7 shows how equality is not a separate issue, nor should it be the last priority, tacked on after everything else. Effective and sensible practice for early childhood must also be well-grounded in knowledge of child development. What are children at different ages likely to understand and how will they make sense of fair approaches to how everyone behaves towards each other?

Childhood lasts for years and practitioners within the early years services need to see themselves as part of a learning process that moves onwards, in a smooth way, to be continued by professional colleagues in schools and out-of-school care. Chapter 8 explores how you offer good-quality resources that properly reflect diversity and the range of opportunities available. How can you extend appropriately from children's current grasp of how their world works? In what ways will resources and experiences support a positive sense of personal identity for all children?

6 Taking good care of children

Services in the UK for children developed historically with a division between what was called 'care' and the approach of 'education'. Childminders are able to offer a holistic service based upon a family home. Many group settings and teams have worked hard to avoid the anomalies that arise from the bizarre view that it is possible to have genuine care without education or vice versa. Equality practice will be undermined if attitudes persist that adult responsibilities labelled as 'care' are of less value and status than those categorised as 'education'.

> **The main sections of this chapter cover:**
>
> ✳ **respect for personal care**
>
> ✳ **organising care routines**
>
> ✳ **food and mealtimes**
>
> ✳ **disability and ill health.**

RESPECT FOR PERSONAL CARE

Children share many care needs in common, but there is also variation across the diversity of ethnic and cultural groups, and the requirements arising from some world faiths.

▓ All practitioners, even those who work in a very diverse neighbourhood, need to extend their existing experience when children come from social or cultural groups that are unfamiliar. There are many different ways of raising healthy, secure children.

▓ No practitioners, whatever their personal background, are justified in taking their own family approach as the only template for best care practice in their professional life.

▓ Practitioners who have so far lived in mainly 'white' areas may move to a different part of the country. Additionally, practitioners' assumptions have been challenged in some areas by the relocation of families who are refugees or asylum seekers.

▓ It would be offensive, not to mention poor practice, if any practitioners insisted on continuing to take 'white' European children as the benchmark for 'normal' personal care. Such a stance is also untenable given the diversity within such a broad ethnic grouping.

Some issues about personal care arise because of religious reasons, some of which have become intertwined with cultural tradition. Along with other information invited from parents, you need to know in what ways a family's religious faith or personal belief system affects the care of their child. Your way of asking parents communicates respect in wanting to understand what is important, in order for you to share the care of their child(ren).

- If you are unclear what parents want, then ask for further explanation or an example of what matters in personal care or food.
- Once you fully understand a parent's request, then you can make an honest commitment to follow what they want.
- Alternatively, you have the information to explain in what way their request is less than straightforward for you, or that you cannot commit to this aspect of care (see, for example, page 119).

Some issues around individual personal care arise because of a child's disability or continuing health condition. Equality legislation regarding disability requires that early years, schools and out-of-school settings make reasonable adjustments to ensure inclusion. One consequence is that teams and their leaders have to revisit any policies and daily assumptions that could work to exclude disabled children or children with chronic ill health. Settings and services will be open to challenge if staff refuse to make a reasonable adjustment for children's needs. Many personal care routines and some basic medical needs fall into this category.

Care of hair

Children, whose 'black' family origins are African or Caribbean, have hair that is of a different texture to most 'white' European hair. Children's, and adults', hair needs to be carefully combed to avoid damage to the strands. Hair styles may include plaiting or intricate braiding. Apart from being attractive, such styles have a practical value of avoiding tangles and so reduce damage to hair. Braided styles take a long time, sometimes hours, to complete. However, the style can then remain in place for weeks, even months, and children's hair can be washed with their normal toiletry products. Many families of different ethnic group background use conditioner on their own and their children's hair, but families of African, Caribbean and Asian origin may also use appropriate hair oil to protect and condition.

Complex braided hairstyles are a specialist skill, but practitioners can learn simple methods of plaiting and braiding. If nobody in a team or local group is able to share their skills, then organise for someone to visit and teach you the techniques. Depending on the ethnic group diversity of your neighbourhood, you could have easy opportunities to request help from parents or other family members. The skills could be useful in braiding dolls' hair, even if you will not care for the hair of individual children.

You can show equal respect and admiration for different styles, textures and colour of hair.

- Use the natural opportunities of doll play, looking at pictures as well as giving complimentary comments to actual children.
- Find discreet ways to support any children who have developed negative views that straight or fair hair is somehow better.
- Young children often like to touch adults' hair, not only when the texture is less familiar to them. You can gently stop a hefty tug from a child, but otherwise let them stroke your hair and you can answer any questions children want to ask you.

When children have braided hair, it is a daunting task to remove sand or other gritty substances without unravelling the entire style. You need to face this situation as a problem to be resolved. It is unfair to children if you restrict their access to enjoyable resources like an outdoor sand area. Talk with parents: some will be more relaxed about the potential problem than others. An option is to encourage children to wear a scarf or hat of their choice at the sand tray or when they enjoy other fine-grained materials.

Skin care and hygiene

A proportion of children have sensitive skin, but children whose skin is darker in tone often need to have cream applied, otherwise parts of the body become uncomfortably dry or cracked. Families use a range of over-the-counter creams and lotions, like coconut oil-based preparations. These are ordinary toiletries – not medication for eczema. Ask parents what they use and you will probably find it is a good hand and body lotion for everyone. You may not need to apply cream to some children unless you include swimming as one of your activities. In that case any 'white' child with sensitive skin will also appreciate lotion to counteract the dry itchy feeling provoked by chlorinated water. Children may also need to apply cream to their hands and lower arms if they have a long session at the water tray. Children with darker skin tones may feel irritation from perfumed soaps, and so will any children with sensitive skin. Unperfumed or basic baby soaps will be best for everyone.

Your approach should also encourage children to learn good hygiene habits. Some religious beliefs include a particular approach that should be respected. Muslim children, and some Sikhs and Hindus, are taught to use the right hand for eating and keep the left for dealing with personal hygiene. They are also shown important habits of hand washing before prayer.

Personal care extends to sun protection. Inexperienced 'white' practitioners sometimes assume that children with darker skin are fully protected against the risks of sunburn. Children with lighter skin tones will be the first to burn, if adults do not take proper care, but a darker skin tone gives only some additional protection. 'Black' children will get sunburned and suffer from heat stroke, unless practitioners take equivalent care with hats, sun protection cream and drinking water for everyone.

Differences in colouration

Some children, from a range of ethnic groups, have areas that are without melanin and so have no pigmentation. This condition is called vitiligo and may not be noticed in lighter-skinned children until they are out in the sun. The permanently pale areas of skin are more noticeable when children otherwise have a dark skin colour. Vitiligo is not in itself a problem for health, except that children need to be protected by sun block. These areas of skin do not tan at all and sunburn swiftly results. Children may, however, feel very self-conscious, when the different skin tones are obvious (see www.vitiligosociety.org.uk).

Children of African-Caribbean, Asian and Mediterranean origin sometimes have patches of darker skin that occur naturally. Historically, this condition has been called 'Mongolian blue spots'. Families and health workers fairly object to this phrase, because it arises from classifying children and families as being of the ' Mongoloid race'. The medical term is congenital dermal melanocytosis.

The darker areas are benign skin markings, but unfortunately can look, to the inexperienced eye, like bruising. These areas are a consistent slate blue in colour, unlike genuine bruising that varies in shade and changes over a period of days. However, the similarity has sometimes raised concerns of non-accidental injury. Good practice in child protection would always include a careful conversation with children and their parents. An open-ended approach will give children, and their parents, the opportunity to tell you that these differences in skin colouration are permanent.

TAKE ANOTHER PERSPECTIVE

None of the personal care routines discussed so far is 'special needs'; they are all ordinary, daily needs for many children. The attention only seems 'special' if practitioners lack previous experience. Individuals or teams may need to address unquestioned assumptions that have worked up until now.

Children enjoy helping you

Modest clothing and hair coverings

Some faiths have requirements about clothing that arise from considerations of modesty and religious and/or cultural tradition. As in any faith, some families will be stricter about their children's dress code than others. Problems arise if practitioners are insensitive to arrangements over changing for physical activities or what is worn.

You should be ready to consider children's dignity and desire for privacy, regardless of whether specific religious views have been expressed. Adults can be generally insensitive about young children's feelings, thinking that children will not mind communal changing rooms, or even changing in the primary school corridor.

- Some children seriously dislike the lack of privacy and object to being expected to do games or dance in their underwear, as still happens in some primary schools. After all, adults make a big fuss at other times about keeping clothes on properly and not flashing one's knickers!
- Children who live with skin conditions such as eczema or vitiligo can feel very self-conscious about undressing to reveal limbs. Those emotions are heightened if other children have made offhand or rude remarks.

111

- Respectful and good practice is to ensure that all children have options and nobody is made to feel 'silly' or that they are 'making a fuss about nothing'.

Several faiths have traditions that affect clothing and covering the hair. Muslim families, for instance, are likely to be concerned that girls in particular keep to modest styles of dress. However, families that follow Islam, like any other world faith, vary in how strictly they wish to follow codes of daily practice. The basic requirement from the Qur'an is for modest dress for both sexes. Different cultural traditions of clothing have arisen in Muslim communities from different parts of the world, so the aim of modesty is achieved by different kinds of head covering and overall clothing. Some groups are considerably more concerned about female than male forms of dress and the issues usually become more acute for older girls and teenagers.

However, Islam is not the only faith in which beliefs affect styles of dress.

- Some Jewish and Christian groups require women and girls to keep their head covered by a scarf, although all the hair may not have to be enclosed. Families are often concerned about appropriate dress for boys, although people outside the group may be more alert to requirements for girls.
- Jewish boys may wear a kippah, the small cap-type hat that covers the top of their head. Males wear a kippah during prayers, but some groups like the boys to wear it all the time.
- Rastafarian parents may ask that their daughters keep their hair neatly covered by a scarf and the sons with a hat in rasta colours (called a tam), which contains their dreadlocks. Strict Rastafarians neither cut nor comb their hair, which then twists naturally to form the dreadlocks.
- Sikhs do not cut their hair – neither females nor males. Girls and women will have different ways of styling their own long hair. Young boys have the hair plaited neatly around their head. When they are older, boys' hair is wound into a close circular style on top of the head (*jura*) contained by a small cloth covering (*patka*). Male teenagers will eventually have a turban.

Religious symbols

Children may sometimes wear items that have religious significance. Good practice is to ask parents and certainly not to insist on removal of an item just because it looks unimportant to you. Respect may also be undermined if your setting has an uncompromising 'no jewellery rule'. For example:

- some children of Christian families may wear a small crucifix on a chain around the neck
- Chinese children may wear charms that are associated with good fortune
- Hindu boys may wear a plaited red and gold bracelet (*Rakhi*) at the festival of Raksha Bandhan as a pledge to protect their sister or a close friend to whom they will act as a brother
- Sikh children may wear a steel band (*Kara*) on the right wrist, which is of great importance as one of the 'five Ks', symbols of the faith worn by Sikhs.

Practitioners may be anxious that an item could genuinely lead to safety problems, perhaps scratching another child during lively physical games. In that case, good practice is to resolve the problem through discussion with parents and the children themselves. You need to find a way to make an item safe or keep it safe, if there are agreed times when a child temporarily removes the item.

ORGANISING CARE ROUTINES

Some issues may arise around how you organise personal care routines, and assumptions about the regular routines of a day or session in a group setting or the home of a childminder.

Personal care and disability

Physical care is a vital means of communication with babies and young children. The same respectful approach is needed for children who continue to need help, because of physical or learning disabilities, beyond the age when their peers can manage independently.

- Children should be enabled to communicate their preferences over their personal care and adults should pay attention to whatever way these wishes are expressed.
- Children who need your help in the toilet, but also at the meal table, should be given time to adjust to the care routine. It is rude and disrespectful to handle children as if they have no feelings or personality.
- It takes only additional moments to smile or say what you are about to do for and with children. Good practice is always to talk directly with the child and never over their head to colleagues, as if adult conversation is more interesting and important.
- Children should be enabled to partake in their own care as much as possible. Good practice requires sufficient adult time and attention

113

and support for children as they learn. Some children will need self-care skills broken down into very fine steps.

- Be encouraging and positive about what children can manage, and acknowledge their frustrations with what they cannot do or cannot yet manage.
- Ask children (by words, signing, use of visuals) if they want some assistance, rather than assuming you know what will be most helpful. Avoid swooping in without words to wipe a nose or a bottom, or to push a child's arms into her coat when she is almost there through her own ability.

Disabled children should have a key person who attends to their intimate care needs. In some settings this carer may be their regular, daily support person. Children should be confident that only one, or at most two, people will help them in this way, so that care is offered within an affectionate and respectful relationship. A system in which any practitioner may deal with a child can lead to an expectation by disabled children that virtual strangers can touch them, and this increases their vulnerability to possible abuse.

You need to be aware of your own physical wellbeing, in particular to take care to protect your back when you lift or help a child to move who cannot help you much in supporting the weight. Practitioners who care for older, and therefore heavier, disabled children must have access to appropriate lifting equipment.

Support for self-reliance

It is important to encourage children to take care of their personal equipment: mobility aids, glasses, hearing aids and so on. You are helping them to learn skills of self-reliance and responsibility that are appropriate for all children. Disabled children who regularly manage to lose or break their equipment are not necessarily careless. Sometimes they are communicating their frustration or distress about their condition. You need to talk with and listen to the child, to understand why they are 'care-less' – try to avoid a focus only on the expense of replacements.

Depending on the child's disability, helpful adults will adjust how they support children in learning about self-care. Charlotte, who is blind, will appreciate a verbal description of what you are doing in dressing or helping her to eat a meal. She cannot see what you are doing, you need to tell her and guide her hands to be able to use touch. Peter's learning disabilities mean that he needs an activity like drinking or eating broken down into many fine steps of learning. He can then feel proud as he manages each fine skill.

Continence

Many three-year-olds can be reliably toilet-trained for daytime, so long as there are no physical or learning disabilities that slow the process. Getting dry for night-time soon follows with some children, but others can take many months, even years. Daytime toileting accidents still occur, even with children in the primary school years. When the process is likely to be extended, then professionals talk about achieving continence or issues around incontinence, the permanent or temporary inability to control bodily functions.

Legislation to remove discrimination on the basis of disability requires services to consider, and if necessary change, policies that could act to exclude disabled children. It is legitimate to challenge the admission requirement of many settings with minimum age limits of two to three years that children must be toilet-trained. Some settings have already rethought their stance, because of a pressing need to keep up numbers by welcoming the younger two-year-olds.

The Department of Health 2000 guidance on *Good Practice in Continence Services* makes it very clear (see Section 6 on www.doh.gov.uk) that local authorities must ensure children are not excluded from ordinary early years and school facilities solely because they are incontinent. The key point is that incontinence is regarded as a manageable condition, whether it arises from physical or learning disabilities or is related to a child's behavioural reaction to emotional difficulties. The guidance also stresses that care systems should preserve the dignity and independence of children and avoid any risks of ridicule or bullying.

Toilet facilities will have to be accessible for wheelchairs or other mobility aids. If children need direct adult help, there will have to be a pleasant space for changing that offers privacy and does not look like a baby-changing area. You will also need storage space for pads (older children will be insulted if you call them 'nappies') and changes of clothing.

If you want to find out more:

❖ *ERIC* (*Education and Resources for Improving Childhood Continence*), 34 Old School House, Britannia Road, Kingswood, Bristol BS15 8DB. Tel: 0117 960 3060; www.eric.org.uk. A good source of information and advice about all issues around toilet training and problems in achieving continence. The website has materials for children and young people as well as parents.

The DoH guidance on continence does not acknowledge the high level of anxiety in some teams over physical contact. Many schools and some early years settings have established guidelines that limit touching children, arising from fear of allegations of sexual abuse. Some anxious practitioners in sessional early years services now refuse to wipe the bottoms of young children or may telephone a parent whose child needs changing. Such limitations to care are not usually contemplated in full day settings; they would be so obviously neglectful.

Concerns about allegations arising from misunderstood physical contact all link with sexual abuse. Practitioners need to recall that child protection is not exclusively about this kind of abuse. Each Children Act or Order in the UK specifies the different types of risk to children from which the law must protect them. These are physical abuse, neglect, emotional abuse and sexual abuse. In Scotland, non-organic failure to thrive is distinguished from neglect, making for a fifth category of abuse. Good-quality care as a whole requires physical contact through respectful touch. Limitations on contact could well be seen as potential neglect but also a risk to children's emotional well-being.

If you want to find out more:

❖ Lindon, Jennie (2003) *Child Protection*. London: Hodder & Stoughton.

Unfamiliar routines

Part of good practice with all children is to give time and attention to helping them feel part of regular daily routines, such as what we do at tidying-up time or what it is like for special key person time in this nursery. Children are reassured when they experience predictability and become familiar with the daily rhythms of their time with you. Practitioners should never assume routines will be obvious to children and some will need more support than others with the familiarisation process.

Disabled children

Children with disabilities within the autistic spectrum face a particular struggle to grasp the skills of social interaction and can be made very anxious by changes in routine. It is especially important that practitioners (childminder or a child's key person in a group setting) help a child to feel part of regular routines. Children with autistic spectrum disorders can be distressed by changes in routine that seem minor to adults, or which their peers manage by asking a question.

Use of photos and a visual timetable can be very helpful to support children's sense of what is happening now and what will happen next. The same visuals will be just as handy for children whose learning disabilities complicate communication or children who are fluent in a language you do not speak.

Children from asylum-seeking and refugee families

The cultural, religious and linguistic background of refugee families will, of course, vary, because they come from different parts of the world. Families may also have a home language other than English and so their children may be learning English as their second or third language. The routine and approach of an early years setting or a primary school may be anything from slightly to extremely unfamiliar to the children. The exact situation will depend on their country of origin and children's experiences prior to relocation.

SCENARIO

St Agnes Pre-school has a mix of Gypsy and Traveller children along with children of settled families. The team avoids assumptions, but has learned that the settling-in process can be harder for Gypsy and Traveller children than even the most cautious children from settled families. Some children have not previously experienced such a large indoor space, with the number of people and lively activities that are usual for a session at St Agnes.

Michelle and her team have looked at use of space and better use of their outdoor area, and have found that the changes have benefited many of the children. Not all Gypsy and Traveller children have been continuously on the road, but some of those at St Agnes had limited experience with the sinks and flush toilets that their peers took for granted.

Comments
Some Gypsy and Traveller children will have experienced an early years setting. But, for others, the early days at primary school will be their very first time in a non-home environment with many strangers. If you work in a reception class you may assume that all children will have been to nursery or pre-school, because so many now have.

Male and female carers

Some families feel strongly that females should undertake all the personal care of young children, especially girls. Such an outlook may create an impasse over male practitioners as childminders or members of a mixed-sex team. These feelings may arise from cultural tradition and habit – a belief

Many families are pleased when children learn life skills

that females are more caring or the only appropriate givers of care. The rationale may also be supported by particular religious beliefs. However, some reluctance to trust male practitioners has been fuelled in more recent years by anxiety over child protection and misrepresentations about the risk of abuse to children.

If parents express reservations over male practitioners then a team, or local adviser, has to face the dilemma arising from two equally important sources of equality practice.

1   Respect for family preference based on faith or cultural tradition means that you should listen to and understand the source of reservations about a male practitioner.

2   However, equality on gender and legal implications for equal opportunities in employment are clear that male practitioners should fulfil all responsibilities of the job, unless there is a non-discriminatory basis to creating differences in role.

As a team or a service, it is preferable that you think through this dilemma before you are faced with a real parent saying the words. You need to be clear on your policy stance and the reasons for your choice, and be able to express that simply to families. On balance, I believe that the best option, expressed honestly to parents, is that all practitioners are treated equally and expected to cover the same role (the choice made in the accompanying scenario).

SCENARIO

Darren works with Maddie in the under-twos room of Crest Road Early Years Centre. A year ago Kitty's mother objected to Darren on the grounds that, 'Everyone knows men can be abusers.' Liz, the centre manager, supported Darren as they worked through the issues with this family. The consistent message was that the problem would not be resolved by promising Darren would never change Kitty. The family decided nevertheless to accept the place and developed a friendly relationship with Darren.

Razia started with the centre this week and Darren is her key person. Today Razia's mother says to Liz that they had no idea Darren would do the personal care for their toddler. Razia's parents have strong views, based in their cultural background and Muslim faith, that only females should undertake personal care of babies. The family say they want Maddie to be Razia's key person.

Choice point: Liz has two main options here and both have consequences.

Option one

Liz decides that the faith basis of the objection to Darren is sufficient to agree that Razia will become a key child for Maddie and only female practitioners will undertake her personal care. However, this decision sets a precedent that gender equality is less important than preference based on faith, or beliefs reflecting cultural tradition. It is very likely that events will travel the parent grapevine and Kitty's parents will feel with hindsight that their concerns were not shown proper respect.

Pause, rewind to the choice point . . .

Liz takes the second way out of this dilemma.

Option two

Liz apologises that the full implications of a key person system had not come across clearly to Razia's parents. Liz explains that all practitioners share the same role. She expresses respect for the family preference, but explains that, if female care is non-negotiable for Razia, then Crest Road will not meet the family's needs. Razia's mother looks doubtful, so Liz talks about childminding as a way to ensure exclusively female care.

Questions

1 Discuss the two options outlined in the scenario. How do you feel about each possibility?

2 Explore the dilemma with colleagues or fellow students.

FOOD AND MEALTIMES

Early partnership with parents should always include a conversation about children's food preferences and full communication about any foods or drinks that need to be avoided.

- Some children have allergies, occasionally severe, to certain food or ingredients found in home-made as well as processed meals.
- Some continuing health conditions arise from, or lead to, children's inability to eat or digest certain foods or drinks.
- Some families will request that their children are not given particular food or drink, because these are unacceptable for religious or cultural reasons.
- Some families follow a particular dietary option, such as being vegetarian or vegan, out of personal choice.

Any requests from families about food and drink for their children should be handled with equal respect, whatever the reason for asking. In a group setting the requests must be communicated to all team members who will have contact with children. Good patterns of communication can be especially important in schools where teachers may have the conversation with parents but support staff supervise mealtimes.

A number of world faiths have a tradition of giving thanks for food – either at most mealtimes or on specific occasions. Childminders in their home or a group team may also have a tradition of showing appreciation for food. The form of thanks needs to be general, or enable children to express appreciation with a variety of words or gestures. It should not for instance be an exclusively Christian 'saying grace'.

Food preferences and traditions vary considerably and it would be offensive for any practitioners to take the line that their own cultural tradition is the normal way of eating and any variation is evidence of 'oddness'. Neither is it accurate to describe religious or personal food preferences as a 'restricted diet', solely because a family chooses not to eat a food that this practitioner considers to be 'normal'. Children could accurately be said to have restrictions on their diet when they are unable to eat foods, for health reasons, that would otherwise be on the family menu.

TAKE ANOTHER PERSPECTIVE

The diet of any family arises from parents' personal belief systems about food. In the UK, a diet that includes meat has long been regarded as 'normal' and some people still express concern that a vegetarian diet must lead to nutritional deficiency. Meat-eaters who pronounce that they 'eat anything', and are therefore not 'faddy', are rarely willing to eat every edible animal, bird or fish. Some mainland European countries regard the UK habit of eating lamb with much the same distaste that the lamb-eaters reserve for horse meat.

In many places now the request for a vegetarian option is no longer met by a puzzled stare, although some caterers still assume that bits of fish or ham will somehow count as vegetarian. Practitioners and any team members who are involved in meal planning should show active respect for family requests and the choices that school-age children express. A vegetarian or vegan choice does not have to be underpinned by religious faith to merit respect and an active attempt to meet the preference.

How you eat

You can show active respect for different ways of eating and still give all children the opportunity to gain dexterity with the traditional UK knife and fork method. The prospect of a proper mealtime with utensils can be a novelty to some young children, whose families would locate their ethnic group identity within the UK. The spread of fast food, takeaway and microwave meals has reduced the number of families who sit down regularly together at a table to eat, and without television. So you can be helping a range of children with mealtime skills suitable for older childhood and later adult life.

You can introduce, as appropriate, different ways of eating as you explore a range of foods with children. Some cultural traditions involve cutlery but there are different traditions for eating meals and snacks.

- Even European-style knives and forks are not used in the same way everywhere. Many people from the United States cut up the meal, transfer the fork to the right hand and use that utensil to get food into their mouths.

- Chopsticks are common utensils for eating and larger versions are used for cooking in China and Japan, and other countries in what from the European perspective is called the Far East.

- Some traditions in countries within Asia and Africa involve eating with the fingers and perhaps using different kinds of pliable food like chapattis to guide some of the food. Using bread is a long tradition in parts of the UK, although more to finish off a cooked meal, especially one with sauce or gravy.

TAKE ANOTHER PERSPECTIVE

Many adults raised in the UK were given a hard time about 'Don't eat with your fingers! It's dirty!' So they unthinkingly repeat these words to children for whom they are now the responsible adult.

If this phrase pops out of your mouth, give it some thinking time. Hygiene matters, including the habit of hand-washing before food preparation as well as eating. But washed fingers are not 'dirty'; they can be safer for health than poorly cleaned cutlery.

SCENARIO

Children learn habits about how to deal with food they do not want or like. Practitioners need to recognise that habits that are unacceptable to them may be normal practice for the child's family.

The team at St Agnes Pre-school have come to recognise that Gypsy and Traveller families are a diverse grouping. They have learned that some boys from Gypsy families, not all, throw disliked food on the ground. The boys are copying the behaviour of their father and other males, who discard food they do not like when they are working outdoors. What works fine in a field causes disruption indoors. The staff are ready to show that they understand the habit and yet they still guide children over 'What we all do here, if you really don't like your sandwich'.

On the other hand, children's behaviour at mealtimes is not always rooted in a family cultural tradition. In Crest Road Early Years Centre, staff became aware that Manisha hid unwanted bits of food under the vegetable serving dish. But a gentle conversation brought out that Manisha had developed this tactic at home to sidestep her gran, who gets very dramatic if anything is left on the plate. Manisha's behaviour had nothing to do with the family's faith or culture and everything to do with her gran's attitude towards food.

Comments

- Early years professionals need to extend their knowledge of traditions that are less familiar at the outset. However, understanding and respect can go hand in hand with kindly guidance about 'What we do here'.

- Additionally, you never switch off your skills of observation and thinking, as you make sense of the actions of individual children.

Faith and food choices

Some general guidelines follow, but please recall that there is a great deal of variety within every faith. You will always need to give time for a conversation with parents and children, when they are old enough, for clear explanations and practical detail about how a particular family operates.

- Buddhists are sometimes vegetarian, but not always. As for any children who are vegetarian, you need to get into the habit of checking the ingredients of processed and convenience foods. Unless marked as suitable for vegetarians, some products include animal-derived ingredients, such as gelatine or rennet. There are vegetarian alternatives to both these items. Some cheap ice creams include animal fat.

- Most Christians do not follow particular rules for their diet, although some make a case against vegetarianism by quoting the Bible. However, a few Christian groups avoid certain foods. Jehovah's Witnesses require that meat has been bled in the method of slaughter and avoid foods like black pudding because of the blood. Some Rastafarians follow a vegetarian diet close to vegan, avoiding dairy products. If families eat meat, they will probably avoid pork and shellfish. The Rastafarian faith is a blend of Biblical teachings and African (mainly Ethiopian) cultural traditions.

- Some Hindus are vegetarian, but those who eat meat will avoid any beef and beef products, since cows are regarded as sacred.

- In Judaism, the laws of Kashrut determine the foods that can be eaten and those that are forbidden. Meat and poultry must be obtained from kosher (meaning allowed) butchers to ensure the accepted method of killing animals and that meat has been blessed by the rabbi. Meat and dairy products have to be kept completely separate at all stages of food preparation, serving and eating and in washing-up afterwards. Unless you have a kitchen organised along kosher lines, children need to bring a packed lunch and utensils from home. Less strict Jewish families will ask that their children are not given pork and probably no shellfish.

- Muslim families avoid pork in any form. As with meals for Jewish children, you have to watch out for unexpected pork products in processed foods. Meat or poultry must be halal (meaning lawful), which is achieved by the method of slaughter similar to the kosher method, and then dedicated to Allah by the imam.

- Some Sikhs are vegetarian, but those who eat meat will probably avoid beef and pork. Families will want meat that has definitely not been bled in the halal or kosher method.

In ethnically very diverse neighbourhoods, a practical approach is to ensure that children always have a proper vegetarian option at every mealtime. This choice can also work, alongside a fish option, for children from non-vegetarian families, whose meat requirements cannot be met by your local butchers.

Fasting

Giving up foods at particular times or fasting for periods is part of religious practice in some faiths.

Fasting or giving up particular foods used to be common practice within the Christian faith. Some beliefs may continue to affect how families wish their child to be fed at particular times. Some Christians still avoid meat on Fridays (the day of the death of Christ) and some give up one or two foods for Lent (the 40 days leading up to Easter), usually a food that is more of a treat, like sugar in coffee or eating sweets. Catholics may fast on Ash Wednesday, the first day of Lent. Christians from the Orthodox Church are more likely to follow the religious tradition of avoiding meat, eggs and milk products for all of Lent.

Jewish families will fast from the evening before Yom Kippur (the Day of Atonement) until the following nightfall. Yom Kippur is the tenth day after Rosh Hashanah (the Jewish New Year that falls in September) and is an important time when the sins of the past year are recalled and forgiveness is asked.

You will encounter fasting if you work with children from Muslim families, who fast during the four weeks of Ramadan. This important part of Muslim faith lasts through the ninth month of the Muslim year, based on the lunar calendar. According to the western dating system, the exact date of Ramadan varies and is 'earlier' each year. Muslims fast from dawn until sunset as a means of focusing on spiritual standards and Ramadan is complete at Id-ul-Fitr.

Fasting during the daylight hours of Ramadan is very important for Muslims and should be respected. Families are careful about bringing children into the tradition and it is not until puberty that young people will join adults completely in fasting from food or drink. If you work in a school or after-school club, then you should be aware that children may be joining the fast for some days or for a few hours within the day. Children may be more tired than usual, because they will have risen to join their family in the pre-dawn meal. They may benefit from quieter activities and a chance to sit in the shade when Ramadan falls within the summer. Children may also need a quiet room for prayer, and not solely for this time of the year.

You need to talk with the parents, and children themselves, about peace and respect for these religious needs.

Of course, any Muslim colleagues will also be following the requirements of Ramadan. Female team members may also be busy cooking to feed their family at the very beginning and then the end of each day. The hours of daylight are very long over the years that Ramadan falls in the UK summer.

If you want to find out more:

✢ Ann-Marie McAuliffe with Jane Lane *Listening and Responding to Young Children's Views on Food*. Part of the *Listening to Young Children* series from the Early Childhood Unit. Tel: 020 7843 6064 or download from www.earlychildhood.org.uk.

✢ Jennie Lindon (1999) *Understanding World Religions in Early Years Practice*. London: Hodder & Stoughton.

When food can make children ill

Some health conditions have implications for achieving a balanced and nutritional diet.

▨ Children with coeliac disease are completely unable to process gluten. This protein is found in certain grains, so it is an ingredient in some flour and other starch products, and appears in a wide range of home-made and processed foods. The result of coeliac disease is that gluten damages the walls of the small intestine, nutrients cannot be properly absorbed and children can be malnourished despite eating sufficient food. Coeliac disease can be managed but, in partnership with parents, you need to ensure a nutritious but gluten-free diet (see www.coeliac.co.uk).

▨ Some children and their families live with the consequences of type 1 diabetes, the form that has an early onset because children's bodies are never able to produce the hormone insulin, which is needed to process glucose. Children need a nutritious diet and regular meals, but do not require you to buy 'diabetic foods'. In fact, these products can be very unbalanced (see www.diabetes.org.uk).

A relatively large proportion of children now have an adverse reaction to some ingredients. The phrase 'food intolerance' covers milder reactions. An intolerance to a particular food can cause discomfort and relatively minor symptoms. The effect on health is not life-threatening, but children and adults prefer to avoid the food.

Good practice has to be that everyone in a team is fully informed about the situation and shares the responsibility to check ingredients on packets when necessary. Practitioners need to be challenged if anyone is inclined to dismiss allergies as 'fads'. Dairy foods, for example, affect some children. The main dairy intolerance is a physical inability to digest lactose, the form of sugar in milk. Common symptoms include bloating, wind and sometimes diarrhoea. Lactose intolerance is more common in families of Asian, African, Jewish and southern European origins.

Some children have more serious allergic reactions to some foods, including dairy products. Nut allergies in particular have increased in recent years. A severe reaction can bring on closure of the breathing tubes and lead to anaphylactic shock, even from small traces of the ingredient. Children with asthma are at increased risk of anaphylaxis. Parents should provide you with relevant asthma medication and adrenalin medication if needed. Injections are now usually made using an EpiPen or Anapen: a pen-like kit that is straightforward to use once you have been shown how.

WHAT DOES IT MEAN?

Food intolerance: Noticeable but mild negative reactions to specific foods or ingredients. There are physical symptoms, so the condition is different from simply not liking a food.

Food allergy: More serious symptoms, such as itching, rash, nausea or vomiting, as the body reacts to the substance (see www.allergyfoundation.com).

Anaphylaxis and anaphylactic shock: Severe and life-threatening reactions like closing up of the throat, severe asthma, significant drop in blood pressure, shown by weakness or floppiness (see www.anaphylaxis.org.uk).

DISABILITY AND ILL HEALTH

Partnership with parents is crucial, but so is a real effort by practitioners to see the world through children's eyes. Children whom adults describe as 'having special needs', do not necessarily feel 'special' in a positive way.

■ Some children evade health routines that are crucial to their well-being because it matters more to them to reduce their apparent difference from their peers. Children who need glasses or equipment to support their hearing sometimes 'lose' their aids on a regular basis.

■ Older children and young people are sometimes resistant to taking on the necessary responsibility for their serious condition, like diabetes. The transition into older childhood and then adulthood can bring new, tough phases for families.

- Younger children may react to dismissive verbal and non-verbal communication from a practitioner who indicates, even slightly, that the child's condition demands extra time or effort. Children wish to downplay a difference that this adult is making into a troublesome problem.

- Time spent listening to children will help you to understand the troubles that can accompany disability and ill health, even when the condition seems minor to adults. Children with eczema, even mild versions, can feel very self-conscious. I did not understand this reality until my daughter explained how some children in her primary school believed eczema was a sort of contagious 'lurgy'.

Medication

Some early years settings and schools still apply a ground rule that practitioners do not administer medicine. This ruling rests on the assumption that if children are sick they should stay at home. However, this stance works in a discriminatory way if medication or other health aids are crucial for a child's continuing wellbeing. The DfES has issued guidance on managing medicines in school and early years settings (search by reference 1448-2005DCL-EN and download from www.teachernet.gov.uk/publications). This guidance applies to England, but raises many practical issues that are relevant across the UK. For some children, regular medication is part of normal daily life. Other children have medication that needs to be administered in an emergency. Pain-control medication may also be necessary for some children.

Good practice is that practitioners are informed, and when necessary trained, so that they can meet disabled children's ordinary health needs and predictable emergency help, such as using an EpiPen adrenalin-injection set or an asthma inhaler.

- Keep proper written records of parents' permission and, where appropriate, a note of each administration of medicine.
- Ensure that everyone in the team has the basic information. It is risky for children when only their key person understands what should be done and when.
- Keep bottles of medicine locked in a safe cupboard, although some medication, like a child's asthma inhaler or EpiPen, must travel with them, especially in a large primary school. Some children have been put at risk by uncompromising rules about locking up all medication.

■ Share information in the whole team, so that everyone knows, for example, what to do and what not to do when a child with epilepsy has a seizure. You can learn through partnership with parents, but can also find advice on the relevant website – in this case www.epilepsy.org.uk.

SCENARIO

At Clearwater they have worked hard in recent months to ensure shared information within and between the nursery and primary school teams. Several children who attend the nursery or school have health conditions that make them vulnerable to infection and bouts of ill health.

■ Kenny, who attends the nursery, needs regular physiotherapy. With the agreement of Kenny's family, his physiotherapist undertakes one of his sessions in the nursery. Kenny is pleased for Susan and Helena to understand what he calls 'my special 'robics' and Helena has learned to do some of the exercises designed for Kenny.

■ Winston, who has sickle cell anaemia, is more vulnerable than his friends to infections and fevers. He needs to be kept warm, especially in cold, damp weather, and the staff need to find ways to achieve his wellbeing without annoying Winston, who really likes outdoor play. Winston also experiences serious bouts of illness and has to go into hospital. Susan ensures that he receives letters, photos and drawings, so that Winston knows he is being kept in mind by his friends at nursery.

■ Partnership with parents has helped Susan and Helena to know important personal warning signs for a child. Winston's mother took them carefully through what a sickle cell crisis looks like for Winston, and under what circumstances the nursery must call the family. Joanne lives with asthma and partnership started when she joined the nursery and her father explained what kind of events tended to trigger an attack for her. The nursery was careful to pass on all it had learned to Joanne's class teacher, and to the playground staff, when she moved to the primary school.

The team aim to use their knowledge to keep children safe without over-protecting them. But it is sometimes hard to maintain this difficult balance.

What ways have you found to meet the needs that arise from disability or ill health and yet still ensure children have an enjoyable childhood?

Some conditions are life-threatening and you may experience the loss of a child who has been part of your home, or attended your nursery, school or club. Adults often have difficulty in dealing with bereavement, especially so when a baby or child has died. It is important to be honest with the children in your care; they will know something serious has happened. Children become more upset, and very confused, when adults refuse to talk about what has happened. Some adults are even tempted to lie and say that a child is still in hospital or has moved away.

People are often tempted to gloss over facts and feelings. Avoid saying or implying that a child's death, 'was for the best. She is out of her suffering now.' This 'happy release' approach does not make the child's parents feel better. The clichéd phrase can also puzzle children who know their friend had a lot of pain, but they still miss her very much, so who is happy in this situation?

If you want to find out more:

You will find useful fact-sheets and suggestions for information and story books from:

❖ *ACT*, Orchard House, Orchard Lane, Bristol BS1 5DT. Tel: 0117 922 1556; www.act.org.uk.

❖ *Cruse-Bereavement Care*, 126 Sheen Road Richmond, Surrey TW9 1UR. Tel: 020 8940 4818; www.crusebereavementcare.org.uk.

SCENARIO

The team at St Agnes Pre-school experienced the sadness of losing four-year-old Sasha, who had attended for nearly a year when she died. Michelle and her colleagues took time and care to face the situation.

- They told the other children what had happened and were ready to answer questions at that time and over the following days. A few children wanted to be reassured that disabled children do not all die and that people can be very ill and recover.

- Andrea was willing to put her sadness into words and was honest when asked by several children, saying 'Yes, I cried when I heard.' The team was careful to communicate that people show sadness in different ways.

- Michelle decided that the situation called for a letter to go to all parents, explaining simply what had happened. The letter was supplemented by conversation if necessary.

- The practitioners were ready to talk about Sasha and more general feelings about loss as they arose from the children.

They looked for low-key possibilities to support children's understanding of bereavement. But the books and puppet play that engaged some children were never used instead of conversation.

■ Sasha's paintings remained on display as did the photograph of the seaside trip when Sasha and her friends had such a good time. Sasha's mother and older brother came to talk with Michelle a few days after the funeral and were clearly pleased that important memories had not been tidied away.

■ A month after Sasha's death, some of the children suggested that they could put together a special book of 'Remembering Sasha'.

Question

1 Discuss with colleagues or fellow students the main themes that emerge from this scenario for a caring and honest approach with children. You may like to combine discussion with following-up the suggestions for finding out more on the previous page.

7 Dealing with words and actions

Equality practice with children comes alive through how you deal with everyday communication and a positive approach to guiding children's behaviour. Practitioners need to talk together about policy and discuss the many practical issues (see Part 4). Adult reflection is needed to unravel grown-up perspectives and knowledge from what children, sometimes very young, are still in the process of learning. However, conversations between adults will only get you so far. You need to deal with actual children and respond to opportunities that unfold right in front of you. So in this chapter there are many examples where I offer phrases that practitioners could say. Of course, these are not the only right words to use in this kind of situation, but I believe that practitioners can work better from actual suggestions than a general encouragement that 'you have to say something'.

> **The main sections of this chapter cover:**
>
> ✳ **respect for different ways to communicate**
>
> ✳ **learning through conversation**
>
> ✳ **when words and actions hurt**
>
> ✳ **behaviour experienced as challenging.**

RESPECT FOR DIFFERENT WAYS TO COMMUNICATE

Effective equality practice will partly be led by how you set a good example in positive communication and deal with words or actions that could undermine children's sense of self-worth.

Language and accent

Practitioners in all services for children and families need to show active respect for the language(s) that children speak and any different versions of English, including accent. Children are likely to follow the example you set through your behaviour. Experiences can also be planned in a flexible way that broaden children's horizons and build an understanding that there are languages other than their own home language.

You should step in if any children try out languages or accents in a mocking way, caricaturing speech that they do not understand. In school, children may be ridiculed for their accent, whether this arises because English is an additional language for children or because they do not speak with a local accent. If you talk and listen to the children, you may conclude that some harassment is racist and deal with the incident accordingly (see page 154). However, early years and school practitioners should recognise that any children can be tormented over their accent. Troubles between children do not stay within neat boundaries drawn up by adults.

I have certainly known some middle-class children ('white' and 'black') persistently harassed in school for having a 'posh' accent by children ('white' and 'black'), whose social background was apparently more working-class. Some tormentors were successfully hiding their social class origins by learning a different accent and way of talking, in order to gain acceptance from their preferred friendship group. Children living in England may be teased for a Welsh, Irish or Scottish accent – or not, of course. But English children, whose families have moved to other parts of the UK, have sometimes been targeted on the basis of their English accent and identity. In Scotland, for instance, some areas harbour serious anti-English prejudice.

Younger children learn the language(s) and accent spoken in their family home. Older children often adjust their words and way of speaking to merge with other groups. They may choose to speak in different ways with their friends and in the school playground from how they speak in the classroom or at home. In neighbourhoods with ethnic group diversity, some words and phrases cross over between groups through the children and teenagers.

Travelling communities vary over language(s). Roma is spoken by some Gypsies. Irish Travellers have a distinct language, known variously as Shelta, Gammon or Cant. Children from both these ethnic groups, and more recent arrivals to the nomadic way of life, may mostly share the English language with peers and practitioners, but some words may vary in usage. For instance, children may use the word 'bad' to mean 'ill', 'kushti' for 'good' or 'glaze' for glass. Irish Traveller children may share the more general Irish usage of the word 'bold' to cover what English children would recognise as 'naughty'.

TAKE ANOTHER PERSPECTIVE

Practitioners need to model respect and set a good example of courtesy that can be followed by children. The basic approach has to be, 'I'm sorry, I don't understand what you're saying' or 'I don't know what that word means. Could you please explain with some other words?' This approach avoids placing responsibility unfairly with a child through, 'You're not making sense' or 'Speak more clearly.'

Children learning more than one language

For many children around the world, it is completely normal to learn more than one language in early childhood. Children in fully bilingual families may learn two languages at the same time at home, when they are very young. Many children are introduced to an additional language in early years settings or when they go to school.

Young children do not just 'pick up' a second (or third) language, they need and benefit from adult help. Remember that over-threes, learning their second language in nursery or your family home as a childminder, are not the same individuals who learned their first language from babyhood at home. Young children have many ideas and a breadth of understanding, they just cannot yet express themselves in a language that you and they share.

- Children need to feel encouraged, but not pressured, to express themselves and not worry overmuch about correct forms, until they have plenty of the additional language on which to work. Do not worry if a child is silent initially. Some children prefer to wait until they have a fair number of words and phrases before they speak out loud.

- Children will assume that the language they hear is directly relevant to what they can see in front of them. So you help by linking your short sentences to play resources, people, objects or events that are happening right now, or are shown in a photograph or other clear visual.

- Be aware that not all languages are written from left to right in the European way; Arabic, for instance, is written from right to left. When older children have started to learn a written language, they may be familiar with one that does not use the European alphabet.

- Be ready to learn some key phrases of greeting and comfort in a child's most fluent language. Encourage the bilingual child, as well as the other children, to greet each other.

Children also need contact with child speakers of any language, because children use any language in a different way from adults. You will support bilingual children by encouraging social contact and easing the possibility of friendship. In a supportive atmosphere, young children make friendly contact across language boundaries. They are creative in using non-verbal communication by gesture and a few shared words to extend play.

Children who share the same home language can support each other and it can be a great relief to them to talk with ease to someone else. You will understand this feeling if you have ever lived or worked somewhere where few people spoke your own first language. Practitioners should never give children a hard time for speaking a language other than English to each other. You can reasonably ask children to tell or show you what is

SCENARIO

A dismissive remark can be corrected courteously, so that children feel able to behave differently next time. In Falcon Square after-school club the team picks up carefully on incidents where a child's language or accent is the butt of a joke. Josie has just heard Cameron making fun of two children he does not understand. Josie is aware that some members of Cameron's family are dismissive in this way, although they are angry if anyone is disrespectful of their own accent and origins. Josie says clearly to Cameron, 'Anna and Jan aren't speaking "rubbish". They can speak Polish as well as English. They are lucky to know two languages really well.' Josie pauses, to let her point rest with Cameron and then suggests, 'If you ask Anna or Jan, they might teach you some words in Polish.'

Comments

- In this type of situation you want a child to feel able to reflect (the four- or five-year-old version) and to choose to behave differently another time. Children, like adults, do not respond well to being made to feel in the wrong, with nowhere to go.

- Adults, like Cameron's family, can behave in ways that seem illogical and unfair to an onlooker. So it is hardly surprising that some children take on board the belief that, said *to* me, this sort of remark is rude, but said *by* me to someone else it is 'just a joke'.

absorbing them, so that you or other children can join an experience or conversation.

Disability and communication

Some children will have particular difficulties with communication – either for physical reasons or because of learning disabilities that delay language development. Specific needs in communication should be addressed in line with what this individual child needs.

For instance, Andy, who is deaf, will need children and adults to face him, so that he knows they are talking with him. He can then see gestures and signs, and use his lip-reading skills (sometimes called speech-reading). Children with variable hearing loss – for example, from glue ear – will benefit from the same attention. This approach is only an active extension of what is usual good practice in communicating with children. Young children, especially in a busy or noisy group, do not always realise that someone is talking to them, especially if their name is said at the end of the sentence, rather than at the beginning.

Children who have physical difficulties in forming their words need extra time and patience from an adult, or fellow child, so that they can express their thoughts or ideas without feeling under pressure. Children with learning disabilities may take that bit longer than their peers to understand what has been said to them and to frame their reply. A greater awareness on the part of adults about these children's needs sometimes highlights that all young children would appreciate more relaxed time to communicate and less rush within a day or session.

So long as children have vision, pictorial clues can be a valuable addition for communication – for instance, a visual timetable or other images that help a child grasp what is happening next. This resource shows respect to children, whatever the reason they need extra clues. Children who are fully fluent, but in a language you do not speak, appreciate the visual hint to make sense of what you are saying.

Using sign language

Children with physical disabilities, with or without additional learning disabilities, may need to communicate in ways other than words. Adults and peers have to be close and able to watch the child. Small gestures and sounds may communicate clear messages once you get to know a child. Some children may use, or be learning to use, sign language.

Within the UK deaf community, children and adults are likely to use British Sign Language (BSL) or Irish Sign Language (ISL). Young children and those with severe communication and learning disabilities are likely to be taught the Makaton sign system (see www.makaton.org). This approach uses speech together with a selected vocabulary from BSL and symbols. Makaton is carefully structured so that young children first learn the signs for basic needs and more complex ideas are introduced step by step.

TAKE ANOTHER PERSPECTIVE

Appropriate guidelines for communication with disabled children build on basic courtesy and add specific understanding about the individual child. The discourtesies that can enter adult communication with all children are worsened by assumptions about disabled children. Thoughtless adults assume that children do not attend to words unless they are said directly to their face. But all children are alert. They notice the dismissive adult body language of shrugs and gestures, or behaviour that implies children are interruptible.

SCENARIO

The team at Crest Road Early Years Centre is careful to consider how 'special needs' work in practice. At the outset Freddy's peers were confused and annoyed with him. Nell, his key person, explained that Freddy was as big as them in size, but his thinking brain worked more like that of a younger child (Freddy's development is affected by Down's syndrome).

The other children became confident that Freddy was not going to be allowed to grab toys because he was 'special'. Several children were keen to learn sign language, known to them as 'Freddy-talk', and were soon able to understand simple requests. There were then opportunities for practitioners to say, 'Well done, you've understood Freddy wants to come into the block corner. Thanks for making space.' This approach was more effective than a general, 'Please be nice to Freddy.'

Comments

- It is a great advantage if at least one practitioner within a large group setting has learned to sign. In a very small team, or working on your own, you may not learn the skill until an individual child needs this attention.
- Hearing children, with no disabilities affecting language development, are often enthusiastic co-learners.
- Signing definitely does not mean that you stop talking – use both methods of communication.

LOOK, LISTEN, NOTE, LEARN

Disabled children, who have limited spoken language, often communicate in ways other than speech. If you have the opportunity, build up a written record of how one child communicates without words. Alternatively, you may be able to talk with the parent of a disabled child. Explain carefully what you are doing and give the parent a copy of your written report. You might look at any of the following aspects.

- How does Louisa use sounds, perhaps a few words, facial expression or gesture to communicate?
- How does Tom show that he likes something – food, drink, a game?
- How does Louisa show that she does not like something or wants to stop?
- What kinds of fun communication does Tom like: touch and tickling, making faces, blowing raspberries or sequence games like 'Round and round the garden'?

Talking and listening

Talk directly with disabled children and ensure that the other children and parents follow your positive model.

- Talk at a normal volume and dissuade any adult or child who raises their voice to a disabled child. Shouting does not make words any clearer. In fact, raised voices can be intimidating to a child and can actually distort the words for a deaf child with partial hearing or who is trying to lip-read.

- Sometimes a child may be helped by a slower pace of communication, but not to the point where the words sound patronising. Use shorter sentences and pauses to make sure that a child has understood and to give listening space for a reply.

- You can share practical hints with children and fellow adults: 'Tell Charlotte your name. She can't see you and she hasn't got used to the sound of your voice yet.' Any explanations that you give on children's behalf should include them through your words, warm gaze or touch. Perhaps the child cannot speak for herself, because she is still very young or her disability affects her speech.

- Deal firmly, although courteously, with disrespectful comments made in front of disabled children but that ignore them. Avoid blunt criticism of a fellow adult, or a child, who asks, 'Does he understand?' or 'Will she want a drink?' Use the opportunity to model courteous behaviour with, 'Andy is deaf but he understands well. Please talk directly to him so he can see your face.' Or 'I don't know if Peter would like a drink. Why don't you ask him?' When appropriate, show how to sign a question as well as say it.

- Children can tell you in different ways about the kind of help they would appreciate and which actions are not actually helpful from their point of view. It is important to listen to how children feel, and watch so they can show you. You need to communicate questions such as 'How would you like me to help?' rather than assuming you know when a child wants help and the best kind of assistance to give.

If you want to find out more:

The websites of national organisations are often good sources of information.

- The National Deaf Children's Society offers practical guidance with *Deaf Friendly Nurseries and Pre-schools* and *Deaf Friendly Teaching*. Tel: 020 7490 8658 or download at www.ndcs.org.uk; see also www.deafnessatbirth.org.uk.

Practitioners are often creative in making their own visual timetables and other resources. You can also buy visual systems.

❖ Many teams use PECS, the Picture Exchange Communication System; find out more at www.pecs.org.uk.

❖ The Triangle project developed the resource *How it is*: *An Image Vocabulary for Feelings, Rights and Safety, Personal Care and Sexuality*; download from www.howitis.org.uk or purchase the booklet plus CD-ROM from Triangle. Tel: 01273 413141 or the NSPCC Tel: 020 7825 2775.

For general support on communication see:

❖ Dickins, Mary *Listening to Young Disabled Children*, part of the *Listening as a Way of Life* series: www.earlychildhood.org.uk.

❖ Dickins, Mary, Emerson, Sue and Gordon-Smith, Pat (2004) *Starting with Choice: Inclusive Strategies for Consulting Young Children*. London: Save the Children Fund.

LEARNING THROUGH CONVERSATION

Children are curious and interested about differences and any new experiences for them. Their comments and questions are definitely not

Conversations can arise at any time

always offensive. The best way for you to answer genuine questions is with simple and honest replies. Yet adults, who deal confidently with questions about worms or the weather, often become uneasy when children's comments touch upon skin colour, visual signs of cultural background or disability. Sometimes children bring offensive attitudes and bigotry into your time with them. See page 152 for advice on dealing with rude remarks rather than curiosity and comment.

Dealing with questions and comments

Encouraging children to develop positive attitudes goes hand in hand with a straightforward response to their questions or reaction to their comments.

- Keep your replies simple, bearing in mind the child's age. If you answer questions willingly, then children will ask you again if they want more information or are puzzled. It is best for you to pause and ask, 'Is that clear?' or 'Have you got another question?' rather than go on and on.

- Give children accurate, factual information. Sometimes, the correct answer may be along the lines of, 'Some people believe that . . .' rather than your saying that it is, or is not, the case.

- Ideally, answer children's questions at the time they ask, because this is when they are interested to know. On the rare occasions when you really cannot reply, then make sure that you find out and get back to a child.

Adults are responsible for dealing with their own emotions, so that feelings of discomfort or embarrassment do not get in the way.

- Do not dodge giving a proper answer by evasive replies such as, 'You're too young to understand' or 'We're all the same inside.'

- If you feel uneasy about the question, then resolve these feelings directly. Avoid pushing your discomfort onto the child with unfair comments like 'Don't be nosy' or 'It's rude to stare.'

- Use opportunities to help young children learn genuine courtesy, and ensure that you model polite words and actions. Unjustified accusations of discourtesy muddle the situation and often annoy children because the adult comment is unfair.

Children deserve honest and straightforward replies, and some conventional replies are not helpful. Children who ask, 'Why are some people "black"?' are often told it is because the child or adult has been in the sun, or came originally from a hot country. This inaccurate reply often leads to further, reasonable questions like, 'Can I get very dark this summer, if I stay out in the garden?' or 'Antonio is from Spain and that's a hot country, so why isn't he really dark like Rashida?' A more honest, and simpler, answer to a young

SCENARIO

Consider different ways to handle this common situation. Maria is childminder to four-year-old Nick. Last week, three-year-old Satvinder joined him. This morning, Nick asked Maria in front of Satvinder and his mother, 'Is Satvinder a girl then, cos he's got plaits?'

This is a choice point for Maria.

Suppose she goes in this direction: Maria feels embarrassed and says sharply, 'Don't be so cheeky, Nick' and adds, 'Sorry' to Paranjit (Satvinder's mother), who looks uncertain about what to do but decides to say, 'That's all right.'

What is the consequence of this choice? Nick most likely did not intend to be cheeky; he asked a fair question with four-year-old social skills. He may feel criticised and avoid asking Maria similar questions in the future. Paranjit has been placed in an awkward position, as if she believes Nick intended to be rude. Satvinder feels everybody is talking about him as if he is invisible.

Pause and rewind to the choice point . . .

But suppose Maria went in this direction: she might still feel embarrassed, since her relationship with Paranjit is new, but she does not allow that emotion to determine her response. When Nick asks his question, Maria replies, 'Satvinder is definitely a boy just like you. But you're right, his hair is different from yours' and Maria's glance now brings in Satvinder and Paranjit as she says, 'Maybe we could talk about why that is.' Maria has left it open for Paranjit to speak up, if she wishes. But Maria can easily offer a simple explanation that Satvinder's family is Sikh and Sikh people do not cut their hair (see page 112).

Comments

- Young children are accustomed to addressing information questions to an adult. So you often need to bring in other people by words or eye contact, to avoid excluding them from the conversation.
- Early in my career, I made the same mistake as Nick when talking with a day nursery colleague, who corrected my wrong assumption that a young child was a girl without making me feel uncomfortable. Then it was easy for me to ask her for more information to extend my knowledge.

child is that Rashida is dark because her parents are dark-skinned and children generally look like their parents. An older child may be ready for the explanation that everyone's skin colour depends on how much melanin you have in your body, and that skin colour, like many other physical features, is inherited from your parents.

If you do not know the answer to a question, then say so, with the promise that you will find out the information. Make sure that you get back to the child. Under some circumstances, you could suggest that a child ask another child who can answer the question. Or you might perhaps check with a parent whether they could answer a query that has puzzled you.

SCENARIO

Sometimes, of course, children will ask you questions that relate to your own identity or personal characteristics. This conversation can help adults to tune into how children are trying to make sense of how physical differences arise.

Myfanwy comes regularly to the Falcon Square after-school club. Last week her father joined group time and taught the children some songs in Welsh. Today a small group of the younger children are busy mixing paints for some large face and body portraits. Five-year-old Lucy says to Josie (one of the club team), 'You and Myfanwy – you two have brown skin.' Josie agrees and several children, including Myfanwy, stick out arms or legs to compare skin tones. Another child says to Myfanwy, 'Your daddy, he does Welsh.' Myfanwy smiles proudly and Josie recalls the fun time with, 'Yes, John taught us some Welsh songs last week.' Lucy looks thoughtfully at Josie's arm alongside Myfanwy's and asks, 'Josie, do you do Welsh too?' Josie sees the confusion in the look as well as hears Lucy's words and replies, 'No, I can't speak Welsh. I have dark brown skin like Myfanwy because my father has that same colour skin. But my daddy grew up in Kenya. That's a country in Africa.'

Comments

- Josie accepted Lucy's question as a fair attempt to work from her observation that John spoke Welsh and had a dark skin colour. But were these two characteristics linked? Josie explained simply and did not imply that Lucy was being 'silly'.
- Children have gaps in their general knowledge that only become clear, and can be courteously corrected, when they feel confident to ask you questions.
- Have you encountered any examples of this kind in your interactions with children?

So long as you have established a good basis of partnership with parents and other family carers, it should not be a problem to start a conversation with, 'Could I please ask you about . . .' and gain some reliable information about the cultural tradition or faith of this family. Of course, you have to bear in mind that there is a great deal of diversity within as well as between cultural traditions. Be careful not to assume that you can safely generalise from this family to every other family that apparently shares their faith, cultural background or country of origin.

Deal gently with words

Sometimes genuine questions may come with offhand remarks. The entire comment is not rude, but children may add words that need to be picked up in a way that leaves them able to backtrack. You will lose children's goodwill if a fair question is lost in adult criticism of single words or phrases.

Your replies can gently correct a discourteous way of asking. You can also use the chance to pass on relevant information to a child who could not be expected to have this knowledge.

- Ben looks at Rashida and asks, 'What's wrong with her?' You could answer, 'Rashida is having trouble breathing. She needs to use her inhaler.' Perhaps Ben says he will sit by Rashida, 'Until she feels better' and you add, 'That's thoughtful of you, Ben. And when Rashida can breathe easier, she'd be the best person to ask about her asthma.'

- Amrita may ask, 'Why does he dribble like a baby?' You could answer, 'Joshua has difficulty swallowing, but he's not a baby. He has cerebral palsy.' You could bring Amrita alongside Joshua, if he would like her company. But you should not make Amrita feel her question is wrong by saying, 'Ssh' or 'It's not polite to look.'

- It is not helpful to say, 'Joshua is just like you', when this is obviously untrue. Joshua has many interests and experiences in common with Amrita, but cerebral palsy changes his childhood in significant ways.

- Straightforward explanations are best and you need to think what image and words are likely to connect with children's current understanding. Joshua's peers may grasp something like, 'The part of Joshua's brain that sends messages to his muscles doesn't work properly. That's why it's hard work to move where he wants.'

Blunt questions will not always come only from children; adults can sometimes be less than courteous about disability. You will promote an inclusive approach by being ready with an honest and simple explanation of what this disability or health condition means for everyday life.

The parents of disabled children can often help you with sensible explanations; they have had plenty of experience. Support organisations for a specific disability or health condition are a good source of simple answers to questions, either through leaflets or their websites. Many of the information books designed for children are also a good starting point for adults (see page 189). Questions can, of course, arise from disabled children themselves, as well as from their peers.

Children who recycle adult comments

Children may repeat remarks that they have heard from other people in an 'Everyone knows . . .' or 'My dad says . . .' mode of sharing information. The result is offensive, but a sensitive practitioner acknowledges that the child is not being directly bigoted, nor intending to hurt.

- Sometimes you will make a reply like, 'Yes, I know some people say that about Gypsies. But I think it is a rude thing to say.' It is worth thinking beyond 'rude', because that word is not always the best choice. Consider words like 'unfair', 'thoughtless', 'untrue', 'not true of everybody' or 'wrong', depending on the context.

- Sometimes children's view of a situation is inaccurate because they have been misinformed by an adult who struggled to handle their question. Perhaps Ben announces that Amrita is dark because, 'God painted her that colour – my grandad told me.' You need to say, and include Amrita with your eyes as you speak, 'No, Amrita was born with her warm, dark skin colour. Everyone looks a lot like their parents. Skin colour has nothing to do with being painted.' Since you have contradicted a member of Ben's family, make time to explain to his mother at the end of the day.

- Children will sometimes repeat a word that is in normal usage in their family. They will therefore be puzzled about your objection and you need to acknowledge, 'I believe you that your daddy says that word. But people who use wheelchairs don't like being called "a spazz". They find it rude, so I don't want to hear you say it about Joshua.'

- Children learn the vocabulary of offence that is used by older children and adults in a neighbourhood. Young children in Northern Ireland and parts of Scotland hear, and see written in graffiti, offensive ways to refer to whether families belong to the Catholic or Protestant denomination of Christianity. Practitioners need to answer children's questions, while they do not know what the terms mean, as well as saying the words are a rude way to refer to faith.

SCENARIO

Today in Crest Road Early Years Centre Lisa and Zainub were helping Nell to lay the tables for lunch. Lisa suddenly asked, 'Why does Zainub wear that funny scarf?' Nell replied, 'I don't think Zainub's head scarf is "funny". She and her mummy wear scarves because their family follows a tradition that women and girls cover their heads.' Zainub looked up from the other table and commented that some of her peers did not cover their head. Nell acknowledged, 'You're right. Not everyone wears a scarf like you and your mummy.' There was a short pause and Zainub said firmly, 'It's bad when you don't cover your hair.' Nell judged it was important not to let this dismissal pass – any more than with Lisa's remark. Nell replied, 'Well, Zainub, some families believe it is fine for girls and women to show their hair. People have different ways of dressing what they feel is properly.'

Children will feel confident that practitioners are even-handed, because you take an equivalent approach to similar situations over time. The previous week, Jonathon had heard Lisa telling Zainub, 'But you can't be the princess. I have to be the princess. You must have yellow hair to be a princess.' Jonathon intervened to say, 'Lisa, that's not actually true, you know. There are lots of princesses around the world who look like Zainub. What makes you say princesses must have yellow hair?'

Comments

- Conversations with children might provoke you to look carefully at the information and story books on your shelf, as well as what you can borrow from the library.
- Are children able to see positive images of different ways of dressing?
- Have your story books implied a world in which princesses always look 'white' European and have long blond tresses? Perhaps you need a book like *My Very First Book of Princesses* by Caitlin Matthews (published by Barefoot Books and available from www.smilechild.co.uk).

TAKE ANOTHER PERSPECTIVE

Consider the following questions and comments from children. Use the ideas in this section to reflect on how you could best reply. Discuss your ideas with colleagues or fellow students. Some examples have brief further information to give you the context.

- 'You know how you put that cream on Nneka after we go swimming? Do you do that to stop her darkness coming off?' (Nneka needs a moisturising cream otherwise her skin gets dry and cracked.)

- 'My uncle says you have to stick with your own kind; you can't trust them who aren't a Gypsy.'

- 'Shall I tell you something sad? My grandma died this weekend. Daddy says she's gone to heaven, so we shouldn't cry. It's true, isn't it, everybody goes to heaven if they're good?'

- 'Why does Marcus's dad wear that stupid hat? My mummy says it looks like a tea cosy.' (Marcus's family are Rastafarian and his father wears a multicoloured tam over his dreadlocks.)

- 'Yvette talks funny when she's with her daddy.' (The family is French-English bilingual.)

SCENARIOS

Please consider these scenarios and ideally discuss the issues with colleagues or fellow students.

1

At Falcon Square after-school club, Cameron says to Rowshara, 'My big brother says women are never as clever as men. But you're not stupid, are you?' Rowshara is surprised by Cameron's comment, but his body language is positive and his intention seems to be to give her a compliment. So she smiles and replies, 'Well, Cameron, I'm glad you think my brain's working well. I don't agree with your brother's poor opinion of women.' Rowshara has offered a model of courteous disagreement that is fair. Her reply is appropriate, whether she thinks Cameron's brother is personally disenchanted about females, or that his beliefs are part of the family's social or cultural background. Respect for Cameron's family does not require Rowshara to accept that she is less worthy of respect because she is female.

2

Fazila has recently started teaching the youngest class at Clearwater Primary School. At the end of her first week, George strokes her hand and says, 'My dad says that blackies need a good smacking. But you're nice. I'm not going to smack you.' Fazila is taken aback but gathers her thoughts fast to say, 'Thank you, George, I'm glad you like me. I'm pleased to have you in my class this year. But I am shocked to hear that your dad feels that badly about people who look like me.' Fazila pauses, but realises that, as far as George is concerned, the conversation is over for now. Fazila takes the opportunity to talk with Philip, the head, about how she handled George's comment. Fazila plans to use stories and puppet storytelling as one way to address the hostile views that George, and some other children, hear from their families.

Comments made directly about you

This section has mainly focused on what children may say to each other. But some remarks may be directed at you and your own source of personal identity. You would use ways of responding similar to those suggested earlier in this chapter, but some other issues arise when comments are made about you.

WHEN WORDS AND ACTIONS HURT

Sometimes children's words and behaviour suggest strongly that they intended to distress specific other children on the basis of their group identity. Effective policy and practice over behaviour needs to address how you deal with these situations. However, the details of good practice for a positive approach to guiding children's behaviour do not go out the window when equality concerns come in through the door.

Guiding children's behaviour

The same basic principles continue to hold, even when practitioners feel embarrassed, anxious, shocked or stressed by what children do or say.

- Children learn ways of behaving; current habits are not fixed for ever. So it is possible to help children learn alternative ways with words and actions.

- The aim is that children learn to guide and redirect themselves. They will not manage to change if they are labelled or prevented from saving face.

- Adults need to deal with unacceptable behaviour in ways that enable children to grasp (perhaps over time) why this way of behaving is not OK.

- Children need to feel confident that the adult dislikes what they have done; their actions or words do not make them a 'bad' child.

- Adults need to consider how children will replace the unacceptable option, when they are faced with situations that typically provoke these actions or words. What are children going to do instead?

- Adults must set a good, clear example of what they would like to see and hear from the children. Sometimes that means literally modelling the words and actions of 'What we do here when . . .'.

TAKE ANOTHER PERSPECTIVE

Reflect on what really matters to children in how adults deal with boundaries and rules about behaviour. What will help children learn and, when necessary, redirect their own behaviour?

The principle of fairness is central. Young children probably develop fairness as their first philosophical concept, although initially in the negative version of 'That's so unfair!' The following five basic points have shone out from what children have said to me over the years. These fair rules about rules are not suspended because equality issues are central to a situation.

1   Rules shouldn't be so difficult that you can't help breaking them.
2   The rules apply to everyone; there must be a very good reason to let children off any rules.
3   Adults should listen when you explain why you did something.
4   If adults want you to tell about bad stuff (rather than hit people), then they mustn't make things worse when you ask for help.
5   It's only fair that adults have to obey all the rules as well.

Zero tolerance?

Written policy and team discussion need to be clear about unacceptable behaviour and words that are 'not welcome here'. However, adults have to be as clear about how they prefer children to behave, and not slip into a behaviour policy that lists only what is not allowed – whether the focus is specifically on equality or not. The phrase 'zero tolerance' became more common from the end of the 1990s and a great deal depends on what this phrase means in practice, day by day.

▦ If 'zero tolerance' means heavy criticism from adults for every minor incident (from the children's perspective), then equality initiatives over behaviour will backfire. An effective policy into practice needs to fit the 'fair rules about rules' in the 'Take another perspective' box above.

▦ On the other hand, a working definition of zero tolerance should mean that incidents are never ignored. A proportion of early years settings and schools are yet to get to this stage; some are still keen to solve the problem of offensive behaviour by denying that it exists in their setting.

Even well-intentioned 'zero tolerance' will have a disruptive effect if the policy means obligatory recording and reporting up the hierarchy for specific behaviours. Some schools already have a fast-track system for any behaviour labelled as 'racist'. I have encountered situations like the scenario on page 145, where George's remark has to be logged as a racist incident and a letter sent to the family. The emotional temperature has soared and no progress is made to turn a negative family outlook towards something more acceptable.

SCENARIO

A group of the eldest children of Clearwater Primary School have become enthused about cricket. Philip, the relatively new head, has given time to coach and support a mixed team of boys and girls. This week they played in a local primary school tournament. All went well until some children from another school started to insult the few 'black' members of the Clearwater team. Other team members pitched in with support along the lines of 'Don't talk to my friend like that' and 'That is a horrible word.' They called over the umpire, who was in hearing distance, but the reaction was, 'Just ignore it. They're winding you up.'

The children were not satisfied with this answer and told Philip immediately after that game. Philip agreed that the children were right to have spoken up and said that he would follow up the incident right now in the break. However, Philip's approach to the umpire and the teacher-coach of the other team met a dead end of 'You're over-reacting' and 'The kids see cricketers bad-mouthing each other – the sledging – so of course they copy it.'

Philip decided to be brief, yet honest, with the children. He had expected to be able to reassure them that an apology would be made, but obviously this was not going to happen. He commented about the other adults, 'I am very disappointed with their reaction. I agree with you; there is no excuse for those insults. I promise you, I'll take this further – grown-up stuff. But I want to say "very well done" to the Clearwater team – you handled it exactly right.'

Comments

- During the years of primary school, children often realise how much attitudes vary and that their own positive outlook is not shared by everyone.
- Adults help by acknowledging that reality, while holding to appropriate professional boundaries.

What behaviour do you want to encourage?

Adults can make a difference to how children's attitudes develop but you have to be realistic about how a positive outlook might work with real children in practice. Over the last few decades, the balance of discussion within anti-discriminatory practice has been much more about highlighting and stopping unacceptable actions and words. We need more reflective practice about the following questions.

- How might children with positive attitudes actually behave? How do you spot children who have really taken on board the equality message?
- Helping children towards alternative words when they are legitimately cross with someone and tempted to use the difference in group identity (sex, ethnic group, faith, disability – anything) as a verbal battering ram.

Children will not always like each other and they will choose some friends to whom they are closer than the rest of a group. Children will have disagreements and they will sometimes be rude to one another. Realistically, you cannot hope for a situation in which everybody always gets along or nobody is ever left out of the play. A more sensible goal is that children will relate to one another as individuals, so that friendships develop from shared interests. You want to create a situation in which children can focus on what they have in common, as well as acknowledging that they are not all the same. But differences are not about better or worse.

NIPPA in Belfast has worked together with the Peace Initiatives Institute in Colorado, USA, to develop support materials to help children in the early years and primary schools to find common ground with children who initially appear different. The materials, including short animated stories, approach different aspects of equality and are suited for adjustment in line with local divisions between communities and sources of conflict. The key phrase spoken by children is, 'All of us are different. It's what makes us you

LOOK, LISTEN, NOTE, LEARN

When you consider equality and anti-discriminatory practice, it may seem easier to make a list of 'what we have to stop'.

- So be alert to examples of children's behaviour that show positive attitudes about being a boy or girl, about their own ethnic group or that of friends, and about disability.
- Compare your observations with colleagues within the same setting, in a childminding network discussion or with fellow students (ensuring that individual children cannot be identified).
- Discuss whether, in your practice, you tend to focus most on unacceptable words and action. Do you notice, and acknowledge, when children behave in a fair and equitable way? What does this look and sound like?

and me.' When children experience shared concerns, their sense of natural justice can support fellow-feeling. It is not OK to hurt Erin because her family go to a different church. Nor is it all right to be nasty to Omar's daddy just because some people who look a bit like him did bad things.

The programme was evaluated by Paul Connolly in 2005 and short-term effects were promising in the sense that young children seemed to be more aware of how their peers could be excluded and were more willing to be inclusive in their play. The plan is to extend the initiative into the Republic of Ireland (Eire). Find out more from Media Initiative for Children at www.mifc-pii.org.

I offer these possibilities, based on conversations with children and practitioners and much informal observation of children at play. In a positive learning environment within childhood, it is a realistic goal that children will:

- make friendships and play alliances that sometimes bring together boys and girls, or children of different ethnic groups, when this opportunity is available
- sometimes be angry with each other but avoid resorting to insults based on other children's social or ethnic group, their sex or any disability
- change habits of action and language that they bring from elsewhere; so some children will actively defend a friend who has been insulted in ways that may be acceptable in their own family or social group
- learn open-mindedness about different traditions of dress, diet or language, rather than dismissing a different way as 'odd' or 'stupid'
- understand that courteous behaviour applies to everyone; it is no more acceptable for a 'black' African child to insult a peer with Down's syndrome than it would be for a 'white' English child
- learn to make appropriate allowances for disabled children; but thereafter it is fair that children expect their peers to follow the ground rules for the whole group (see page 163).

Avoid a 'hierarchy of hurt'

During the 1990s one strand of equality practice developed that rests on a view of power that is all about adult perspectives. You will encounter some writers and trainers who still imply that offensiveness from a 'black' child to a 'white' is less important than the reverse, because of the reality of discrimination and unequal power relations within UK society. I believe this stance is unacceptable, because it imposes consequences on children that are completely unrelated to what they have done. The unequal approach also disregards the serious risk of communicating to some children that their hurt matters less, for reasons over which they have no control.

This mistaken approach is sometimes described as working within a hierarchy of hurt, or of oppression. Children are far less likely to support their peers if they experience that some hurtful remarks seem to matter more to the adults. A 'white' girl will be very hurt by a 'black' peer who taunts, 'You're adopted. That means your real mother didn't love you!' The child who was adopted deserves equal care and concern for her feelings as her peer should experience when on the receiving end of distressing racist remarks.

Children are far more likely to appreciate social injustice towards some of their peers when their personal concerns and hurt feelings are respected within their own social world. Children develop a strong sense of natural justice and can be very annoyed when they feel unfairly treated. They also tend to dismiss adults who impose the perceived injustice.

TAKE ANOTHER PERSPECTIVE

The hierarchy of hurt approach is sometimes linked with the belief that racism is a one-way route for bigotry, where racist behaviour is defined exclusively from 'white' people to 'black' people. A similar stance over sexism claims that males cannot, by definition, be disadvantaged or offended through sexism.

It will be clear from my explanations of terms (page 12) that I disagree with this value stance. If this perspective is at odds with what you have been told, please give the matter some thought. Bear in mind that the working definitions are a matter of opinion and interpretation, not of fact.

I am not alone in my perspective. Constructive approaches in work with adults seek common ground from which to move on in a positive way. For example the approaches of:

- the National Coalition Building Institute, The Learning Exchange, Wygston's House, Applegate, Leicester LE1 5LD. Tel: 0116 222 9977; www.ncbiuk.org.uk
- the One Small Step campaign in Northern Ireland, against sectarianism: www.community-relations.org.uk/campaigns/ one_small_step/.

The team at Falcon Square after-school club strive for good relations with all their link primary schools. They are aware that Brownstone Primary has recently overhauled its behaviour policy and brought in 'a zero tolerance approach to racist bullying'.

Daniel and his colleagues have noticed that Myfanwy, who attends Brownstone, has been distressed at pick-up time all this week. Today Daniel sees that Myfanwy's bag is damp and sticky. With encouragement, she confides that three girls keep being 'really horrible' to her and they empty juice drinks into her bag. Daniel is close by as Myfanwy starts to tell her father at the end of the session.

The following week John, Myfanwy's father, asks to talk with Daniel about what happened at Brownstone. Yesterday he had spoken to his daughter's teacher, who said steps would definitely be taken; the school would not tolerate such behaviour. John recounts the frustrating conversation he had today with the class teacher, who was keen to reassure him that the bullying was not racist and had nothing to do with Myfanwy's skin colour. The teacher went on, 'It was just some girls being silly and calling Myfanwy "posh". I'm afraid children get that, if they live in the bigger houses round here.' John is dissatisfied with this response, feeling that the school has dismissed his daughter's distress and the deliberate damage to possessions. John asks for Daniel's reaction and advice about the next step.

Questions

1 **What do you think? Is it less important, from Myfanwy's perspective, to be bullied over presumed social class than skin colour?**

2 **What would you suggest if you were in Daniel's position?**

Please note: this scenario is not implying that every school with this kind of policy runs a hierarchy of hurt. But some policy into practice does slide in this direction. The issues need to be raised.

Name calling matters

Offensive comments and persistent name calling are a fact of life for many children. Some children are coping with physical attack, or the kind of rough treatment that their peers try to pass off as 'just having a laugh'. But this generation of children, like their parents, are more likely to be coping with the impact of persistent verbal attacks. There are times for careful ignoring of minor misbehaviour, but it is unwise to let offensiveness pass without comment. When a child is sure that you heard, your silence will be taken as acceptance, or even approval, of what was said.

Studies of primary school experiences – for instance, by Cecile Wright or Barry Troyna and Richard Hatcher – have described the distress and daily grind for children, when racist name calling and other verbal abuse is not effectively tackled by a school. Troyna and Hatcher also pointed to the importance of ensuring that 'white' children have strong and positive sources of identity. Otherwise, children with limited sources of self-esteem are very tempted to make themselves feel better by targeting minority ethnic groups. Children in this situation may well have strong adult models from their family and local neighbourhood that push them in this direction.

On the receiving end

Children can feel desperate if they are regularly hearing rude remarks about themselves or their family, for whatever reason. They need adults to deal with incidents in ways that will help the child on the receiving end of hurtful words, or behaviour, to feel better. They deserve and need the following responses.

- Comfort, through your words or friendly touch, if they wish. A child who has been very hurt by another's words may be close to tears and welcome a reassuring cuddle. I appreciate that many school teams, and unfortunately also some early years settings, have become highly anxious about touch. But girls, and boys too, in early childhood will not believe you really care about their hurt if contact is denied when they clearly want it.
- A clear message from you that you like these individual children and feel positive about any source of identity that has been under verbal attack. Be guided by the children's own feelings and what you have learned about their personal preferences.
- Reassurance that children do not have to tolerate physical ill-treatment or name calling in order to be accepted by their peers. The key point about a joke, or a 'bit of fun', is that everyone enjoys it, not that some children find it amusing and others are distressed.

TAKE ANOTHER PERSPECTIVE

It is worth reflecting on the reasons why it is unacceptable for children to use certain words or behave in particular ways. Wise adults have some answers for 'Why?', since children increasingly pose that question.

- Mild, non-specific reprimands are unhelpful: 'That's not a nice thing to say' does not offer children much in the way of explanation.

- The answer on words may be that the remark was 'unfair', 'untrue', 'cruel', 'unkind' or another appropriate word. You can be guided by the expressed hurt or outrage of the child on the receiving end.

- The answer about actions will need to connect with ground rules about how 'we all behave in our nursery/school/club' or, for childminders, 'what happens here in my home when we have a disagreement'.

You and your colleagues need to talk together and decide a consistent approach that will be applied when you do not have time to think. There must be consistency within a team. Children feel frustrated, even abandoned, by adults when behaviour policy is implemented fitfully and some adults do not respond appropriately when children do as they are asked and 'tell' rather than lash out with fists and feet.

However, all practitioners need to be kind to themselves. Sometimes realisation comes after the event: 'I wish I'd said that' or 'That was foolish, I shouldn't have reacted that way.' Avoid wasting energy on regret, and focus on how you will behave differently faced with a similar situation in the future.

Children who give it out

Your approach to children who have given hurt or offence needs to be consistent with a positive approach to guiding behaviour.

- Explain why a remark is unacceptable rather than trying to make children feel guilty with, 'Don't you think that was an offensive (or racist) thing to say?' Is there any way to answer this pseudo-question in a way that will satisfy an irritated adult? Honest adults need to say, if necessary, 'I find that phrase offensive because . . .'.

- Children's attitudes are in the process of forming and you have a chance to influence them. It is unacceptable adult behaviour to use sweeping labels of a child like 'racist' or 'sexist', any more than you should label them as 'lazy' or 'spiteful'. Negative labels leave a child with no space to listen and to find another way of reacting.

- Furthermore, a bad adult habit of dismissing children through labelling can be recycled by children against each other. I have encountered the results of misguided equality practice with primary and secondary pupils who have learned to attack any behaviour that annoys them by shouting 'That's racist!' or 'You're sexist!' at peers.

- Dislike the behaviour; but show you continue to like and accept the child as a person. So you say to Sally, 'I think that was a rude name to call Isaac' rather than, 'You are such a rude girl!' You might judge that it is an appropriate time to say a bit more – perhaps, 'Yes, it is true that Isaac and his family are Jewish and that is no reason for being rude to him.'

SCENARIO

The team in Clearwater nursery class used to tell children to think about the feelings of another child. But they realised that they lost the children by trying to get them to be empathetic on the spot.

Today Alice has verbally lashed out at Simon with, 'You're rubbish! All boys are completely thick. My mum says men are a waste of space.' In the past, Helena would have tried something along the lines of, 'You've made Simon really upset. He feels as bad as you would if he had been that nasty to you. How do you think you would feel if Simon said you were rubbish?' Helena has joined the nursery from time spent with seven-year-olds. She noticed that, even in middle childhood, many children still do not connect with this emotional maze, especially when feelings are running high.

So instead, Helena says, 'No, Alice, it's not OK to tell Simon he is "rubbish" and words like that. I wouldn't let him trash you because you're a girl, and you don't trash Simon just because he's a boy.' Helena has made her point that Alice's words are unacceptable and why, so she goes straight on to say, 'I can see you're really cross with Simon. So, let's hear about what made you so cross.'

As a result of their discussions, Helena and her nursery colleague, Susan, have also become more aware that their original approach, although well-intentioned, was based on guesswork about children's feelings. Many boys, and some girls, did not like being told they were 'upset', nor the 'poor Simon' impression that could accompany a sense of pity.

Questions

1 What approach do you tend to take in situations similar to that described in this scenario?

2 If you take the 'emotional maze' strategy, reflect on whether children really do follow your line of explanation. Can you make it simpler?

Listen to what happened here

Practitioners must use their skills of observation, listen to the children and avoid swift assumptions.

- Practitioners who work in an ethnically diverse neighbourhood will be very aware of the possibility of racist bullying. But it is poor practice, and unfair, if teams assume that arguments, or even fights, between children of visibly different ethnic groups are automatically racist.

- In a similar way, you should not assume that the boys are necessarily at fault, or started it, in an altercation with the girls. Nor is a disabled child necessarily always the innocent party in an affray. Good practice, as in any adult intervention in the world of children, has to be that you ask and listen, but do not leap to conclusions about the rights and wrongs of the situation.

Responsible practitioners deal with unacceptable words and actions, but also listen to children in order to understand the conflict that led to the insults or shoving. Part of an effective policy on behaviour has to be coaching even young children in the skills of conflict resolution. In any emotionally charged situation, children will take more notice of adults who are clearly listening to what has happened. You will lose them if you apply rigid rules or unfairly, from children's perspective, take one child's side over that of another.

- You can sympathise with Omar's frustration that his game has been disrupted while saying, 'It's still not OK for you to use that word about Erin's family' (an offensive term about being Catholic). After you have made the point (not gone on and on about it), show your willingness to problem-solve with the children by saying, 'Tell me about what happened here.'
- Real life in primary school playgrounds or after-school clubs is that practitioners may find themselves resolving the details of the argument that comes to light because Erin, who is 'white', has shouted a racist term at Omar. If you show you are willing to listen, it may become clear that Erin is beside herself with anger because Omar called her a 'lezzie'.

By six or seven years of age some children have learned very robust language and are disdainful of other children on the basis of their sex or a shaky grasp about sexual orientation. 'Cow', 'cissy' or 'fairy' may be the milder versions you hear. Some children have already learned to use 'homo' as a term of abuse and some boys have learned that it is all right verbally to attack girls as a 'slag' or 'bitch'. Neither sex should be allowed to bad-mouth the other and no practitioner should let themselves believe that it matters less if the girls are being offensive to the boys than the other way around.

During the primary school years, male or female practitioners may have to deal with rude remarks addressed to them. You need to reply firmly with rejoinders like, 'I don't make personal comments about your body. I expect the same respect from you.' You need to find ways to separate out parts of offensive remarks with, 'Intelligence has nothing to do with my skin colour, nor with yours. And I don't call you "stupid" just because we've disagreed. Right, I've said my bit. Go on, I want to hear your point of view about . . .'.

BEHAVIOUR EXPERIENCED AS 'CHALLENGING'

Children's behaviour is shaped, at least to some extent, by how adults react. It is possible to make a difficult situation worse, and an effective policy over children's behaviour has to include awareness of likely internal and external influences on individual children.

Social stress and violence affect children

The news media bring information about the reality of violence in many parts of the world. However, some readers will live and work in neighbourhoods in the UK where violence is a continuing possibility each week. The conflict may affect some families more than others, when violence is targeted at specific groups.

SCENARIO

The team at Crest Road Early Years Centre are aware that Clement and his family have suffered months of racist abuse from their 'white' neighbours. Liz, the manager, has offered all possible support to Clement's family and it seems possible that the other family will finally be moved by the council.

Clement's mother has done her best to protect her children from the intimidating atmosphere around their home, but Clement has been distressed and his behaviour shows how his sense of personal safety has been undermined. The Crest Road team has been ready to support Clement as he struggles to follow the ground rules on days that have started with a verbal onslaught and physical intimidation from the neighbours.

The team understands why Clement sometimes bursts out with, 'All "white" people are nasty shouters', but has found ways to address the sweeping generalisation. Sometimes they ask gently, 'Did your day start badly, Clement?' On one occasion, Clement had made a fierce remark, looked at Nell's 'white' face and burst into tears. Nell offered Clement her arms and he snuggled into her as she reassured him, 'I'm sorry your neighbours are so horrible.' Nell responded to Clement's repetition of, 'I don't mean you' with 'I know, Clement. It was your sadness speaking.'

Comments
Some children and their families have to deal with unacceptable behaviour from members of another ethnic group. It is still important that you do not ignore negative generalisations dismissing entire groups because of the bad behaviour of some individuals.

157

Anti-sectarian initiatives

In Northern Ireland, more than one generation of children has now been raised through times of violence and divisive social conflict. Equality initiatives in this part of the UK are grounded in anti-sectarianism, as well as other aspects of equality practice. However, supportive work with all types of practitioners has needed to acknowledge that these adults are also affected by the social stresses. It is that much harder to support young children if adults never get the opportunity to deal with what recent history has done to them.

If you want to find out more:

❖ Led by Rosie Burrows and Brid Keenan, *We'll Never be the Same Again* (2004) is the report of a Barnardo's project in Northern Ireland that arose from the pilot work in *Parenting in a Divided Society*. The materials extend to support for practitioners who work with children. The main project focused on parents but has strong messages for practitioners who cope with stressful conditions partly by hoping that children are unaware. Download the report at www.barnardos.org.uk.

SCENARIO

Early years, school and out-of-school practitioners cannot step aside from rejecting attitudes when they emerge right in front of them through children's language or play. However, your response needs to be holistic.

At Crest Road Early Years Centre the team wanted to develop a consistent response, as hard as they found some of the situations. Darren was ready to step in with words when Beverley tried to repeat her family's view with, 'Them Mosems are very bad. They blow people up!' Darren commented kindly but firmly, 'Are you talking about people who are Muslims, Beverley? That's an awful lot of people to call "bad". It's not true that everyone who is a Muslim wants to hurt people.'

But two weeks later Jonathon knew it was equally important to acknowledge Amir's excited call as he bashed over his building with a plane, 'Hurray! All the 'mericans are deaded now!' Jonathon sat down close to the play and said, 'Amir, I feel sad about people who are killed – not glad about it.' Amir looked puzzled, 'But it's good to kill bad people.' Jonathon continued, 'Yes, I know people are killed in wars. But I don't think it's a time to say "Hurray".'

The centre team is well aware that Beverley's family express bigoted views about local Muslim families, but it is just as relevant that, in September 2001, Amir's family kept his older siblings home on the day after the World Trade Center was attacked in New York because the family celebrated that event.

Comments

- These situations are not at all easy. But teams and individual practitioners such as childminders need to take an even-handed approach to bigotry and rejection by any family of another faith or ethnic group.
- Have you faced a similar situation? What was your response? Would you take a different approach now?

Anti-Muslim reactions

Events through the early twenty-first century have stirred anti-Muslim feeling (sometimes called Islamophobia) through an unjustified generalisation from some groups within Islam to everyone within the faith. Similar sweeping faith generalisations for Christianity did not occur through the years of IRA bombs in mainland Britain. Some useful materials have emerged to support practitioners, although it is rare for these resources to create links with the anti-sectarianism expertise from Northern Ireland.

If you want to find out more:

- Adams, Sian and Moyles, Janet (2005) *Images of Violence: Responding to Children's Representations of the Violence They See*. Husbands Bosworth: Featherstone Education.

- Community Relations Commission of Northern Ireland: www.community-relations.org.uk.

- Connolly, Paul, Smith, Alan and Kelly, Berni (2002) *Too Young to Notice: The Cultural and Political Awareness of 3–6-Year-Olds in Northern Ireland*. Belfast: Community Relations Council.

- Lane, Jane and Baig, Rashida (2003) *Building Bridges for Our Future: The Way Forward Through Times of Terror and War*. Wallasey: Early Years Equality.

- Learning and Teaching Scotland has a section, with ideas and examples, to explain anti-sectarianism; see www.ltscotland.org.uk/ antisectarian.

✤ Northern Ireland Council for Integrated Education (NICIE) (2002) *The Anti-Bias Curriculum.* Tel: 028 9023 6200; www.nicie.org.uk.

Children from refugee and asylum-seeking families

Children and their families will often need support, although this will depend a great deal on the circumstances under which they have left their country of origin. However, disorientated and distressed children will not benefit from joining busy early years settings where practitioners are already overstretched. I have encountered some groups where there is insufficient personal attention for young children whose lives are relatively stable. It does not work to place children from refugee or asylum-seeker families in such settings in the vague hope that an early educational setting must be 'a good thing'. Children react to the uncertainty through their actions and there is then a high risk that 'cries for help' are treated as behaviour problems.

Any early years setting with refugee children needs to have access to specialist advice to supplement the support you offer through daily routines and experiences. You need to be aware of the following factors.

▨ Children's experience may make them very vulnerable to what seem like overreactions to potentially aggressive situations. Some children may be very easily distressed or may hit out in self-protection. You need to offer emotional support and understanding, as well as guide children towards more appropriate reactions now they are in a safe place.

▨ Like their peers, refugee children are likely to play out their experiences: with dolls and small world figures, through pretend play themes and in drawings or stories. Bear in mind that what you assume to be violent pretend play and perhaps wish to discourage, could be a literal reworking of what this child has seen. The play may be therapeutic, although you will have to guide children in order to reduce any negative impact on peers.

▨ Some children may wish to talk about their memories or continuing worries and some may have realistic fears for family or close friends left behind in a war zone or in refugee camps.

(See page 69 for useful resources.)

Assumptions combining gender and ethnic group

Gender stereotypes can shape how practitioners react to boys and girls, leading to positive or negative interpretations of children's actions and play choices (see page 56). An even-handed approach to boys seems to be

Children will explore shared interests together

further put at risk by how some practitioners relate to boys from families of African-Caribbean origin.

Cecile Wright noted that African-Caribbean boys were among the most criticised and reprimanded in the mixed classrooms she observed. The boys were told off for the kind of behaviour that was often ignored for 'white' children. The 'black' boys were more prominent in school discipline procedures such as being sent out of the classroom and exclusions. Wright's observations are supported by national statistics on school exclusion. Later problems seem to have roots in boys' early school and pre-school experiences.

- Some practitioners have stereotypical beliefs that all African-Caribbean families use harsh, physical discipline. A linked belief is that the boys will find it hard to settle in out-of-home settings. This attitude can lead practitioners to treat the boys differently: they 'just' need to run around outdoors. This assumption is especially negative when early years teams fail to value outdoor learning.

- There are broad cultural differences in the use of spoken language and body language. The communication style of some African-Caribbean families is more forthright and boys especially may be judged by practitioners to be 'cheeky' or 'disruptive'. The usual dangers of labelling a child follow, and boys start a career as a 'troublemaker'.

- Negative judgements may be shared among a team who have not established an effective and professional policy on behaviour. Individual children have fewer and fewer options. Adults become more fearful of losing a power struggle with the boys than tackling behaviour in a positive way, including reflection on their own actions and words.

All boys need early years experience that develops positive attitudes towards learning and the school experience. Older boys and teenagers, from all ethnic group backgrounds, sometimes confide in 'safe' adults how they cultivate a tough exterior to hide an interest in study or books. Boys from an African-Caribbean background seem especially needful of positive male role models. They encounter many messages, not least from some aspects of street culture, that lead them away from valuing what they can gain from a learning environment such as school.

Behaviour that is 'normal' for children

Children learn patterns of behaviour from their families and any home will reflect the social and cultural identity of parents. Practitioners need to be aware of, and ready to learn more about, broad differences in behaviour and body language. Two examples follow, in which I suggest that the way to resolve the situation is different although still communicates respect.

Eye contact

A broadly western European cultural tradition is to encourage children to make eye contact with adults. Reduced or fleeting eye contact is often interpreted as inattention or shiftiness, and possible evidence of guilt. However, children whose family origins are from many other parts of the world are taught that it is courteous to drop their eyes when talking with adults, especially if being reprimanded.

In this situation I think the responsibility of practitioners is to flex to the comfort of children. You may find it hard to believe a child is listening to you when they have limited eye contact. Resolve your feelings by asking them to use words to indicate understanding, rather than requiring that they look directly at you.

Spitting

Generally speaking in Europe it is not accepted behaviour that children or adults spit in the street or at other people. Spitting is more acceptable in some cultures. Spitting on the hand, or pretending to spit, is sometimes an action judged to ward off bad luck – a tradition in parts of Greece, but also a superstition for some people whose European origin is the UK. I have now encountered several instances when children used spitting towards someone else to emphasise their position in an argument. Practitioners realised that the behaviour arose from the family's cultural tradition.

In this situation, I think the responsibility of practitioners is to communicate courteously to families and children that, 'We have no spitting in school'. Further explanation can follow that, 'I understand you think it is all right to spit. It is your choice what you do in your family. But many children here are upset and cross about this behaviour. We will help your children to make their point strongly with words.'

SCENARIO

Disabled children are still boys and girls who need firm but fair adult guidance over their behaviour.

- In Clearwater nursery class, the children understand that Kenny needs space for his wheelchair. Occasionally he misjudges a turn and has collided with their constructions. Today the children in the block corner are adamant that Kenny crashed into them on purpose – not least because he reversed for another go. They want to see Helena deal fairly with Kenny.

- Ciara can be very ill as the result of coping with cystic fibrosis, but her parents have been clear in discussions with Maria, her childminder, that they want their daughter to have a playful childhood and to make friends. So they ask Maria to use the same ground rules for Ciara's behaviour that apply for Nick and Satvinder.

Comments

- Some families struggle to find the balance expressed by Ciara's parents. Some parents, or other family members, may feel so saddened by their child's disability that they are unable to set and hold to boundaries suitable for any child. Supportive practitioners can be of immense help and can offer advice without the critical implication that parents are 'overprotective'.

- Of course, it is appropriate that parents and practitioners take account of the impact of a child's disability or health condition. Children's peers can be genuinely understanding that, 'Ciara sometimes feels rotten, and that's not her fault,' or that, 'Kenny sometimes makes a mistake steering his wheelchair.'

Disability and behaviour

A basis for non-discriminatory treatment is that fair and reasonable adjustments are made for behaviour that is a consequence of a child's condition. Thereafter, however, it is important that disabled children are expected to follow the same ground rules as their peers. If disabled children are seen to be 'allowed to get away with things', then their potential play companions and classmates will get annoyed (see the Scenario on the previous page.

Some children live with conditions that provoke intermittent or continuous pain. Readers who experience bouts of back trouble or migraine will understand how wearing it is to cope with pain. The situation can lead even stoic adults to be very cranky. There is good reason to suppose that being in constant pain may be an underlying cause of challenging behaviour from some disabled children or young people. (See also page 92.)

Disability campaigners express concern that different kinds of settings, like schools, have been more responsive initially around equalising opportunities arising from physical and learning disabilities. However, disability also requires practitioners to recognise issues around behaviour. For example, children with autistic spectrum disorder and Asperger's syndrome can experience severe struggles to manage the details of group life in a nursery and increasingly the more formal context of school. Partnership with parents, as well as getting to know children as individuals, will help to avoid a situation in which children are unfairly held responsible for behaviour that they cannot control without a great deal of step-by-step support.

Physical restraint can become an issue over the behaviour of any children, but is probably heightened if children have emotional and behavioural difficulties. Part of good care in early years, school and out-of-school services has to be that adults use their greater strength wisely to keep children safe. Refusal to use touch could well be seen as neglect, a failure in the duty of care by responsible adults. Practitioners need to use close physical contact when children are plunging into an unsafe situation, or because they are hurting each other and will not stop unless an adult intervenes.

Adults should use their physical abilities with care, when action has to be prompt; this care is for the wellbeing of the adults as well as the children. Children who are older are also usually larger. Practitioners need special training in safe physical handling, especially when children's disabilities mean that their behaviour may be unpredictable and challenging. Many school practitioners are fearful of using any kind of touch, but guidelines are clear that physical restraint will sometimes need to be used. The Teacher Net website (www.teachernet.gov.uk) has downloadable guidance about touch and physical restraint in schools.

If you want to find out more:

❖ Collins, Margaret (2004) *But is it Bullying? Teaching Positive Relationships to Young Children* and (2005) *Young Buddies: Teaching Peer Support Skills to Children Aged 6 to 11*. Bristol: Lucky Duck Publishing, and other titles from this source: www.luckyduck.co.uk.

❖ Connolly, Paul (1998) *Racism, Gender Identities and Young Children: Social Relations in a Multi-ethnic Inner-city School*. London: Routledge.

❖ Drifte, Collette (2004) *Encouraging Positive Behaviour in the Early Years: A Practical Guide*. London: Paul Chapman Publishing (especially relevant for supporting disabled children).

❖ Early Childhood Unit: *Listening as a Way of Life* series, including Mary Dickins *Listening to Young Disabled Children* and Nicky Road *Are Equalities an Issue: Finding Out What Young Children Think*, from 8 Wakley Street, London EC1V 7QE. Tel: 020 7843 6449 or download at www.earlychildhood.org.uk.

❖ *High/Scope UK*, The High/Scope Institute, 192 Maple Road, London SE20 8HT. Tel: 020 8676 0220; www.high-scope.org.uk. Videos and books about teaching children the skills of conflict resolution.

❖ *Kidscape*, 2 Grosvenor Gardens, London SW1W 0DH. Tel: 020 7730 3300; www.kidscape.org.uk. Information about positive approaches to behaviour and dealing with bullying in the school years.

❖ Rogers, Bill (ed.) (2004) *How to Manage Children's Challenging Behaviour*. London: Paul Chapman Publishing (any of Bill Rogers's books are useful and practical for the school situation).

❖ Save the Children (2000): *Anti-bias Approaches in the Early Years: A Guide for Practitioners in Avoiding Discrimination Among Young Children*. Save the Children Publications, c/o NBN International. Tel: 01752 202301. Useful resources like *Count Me In* and *Think of Me, Think of You* can be downloaded at www.savethechildren.org.uk.

❖ Troyna, Barry and Hatcher, Richard (1992) *Racism in Children's Lives: A Study of Mainly White Primary Schools*. London: National Children's Bureau.

❖ Wright, Cecile (1992) *Race Relations in the Primary School*. London: David Fulton.

8 Experiences and resources

Ideas about experiences and adult-initiated activities must be seen as a resource for practitioners to access. They are not a have-to-do list – certainly not targets to be completed within the early years. You have a chance to influence children's outlook now and you can sow seeds for the future – just avoid setting a goal that involves bringing in the entire harvest before middle childhood! Other people will influence the children, because raising the next generation is a long-term project. Your role is crucial over the time that you are personally responsible for the opportunities of these individual children in your setting or family home as a childminder.

> **The main sections of this chapter cover:**
>
> ☆ **an inclusive learning environment**
>
> ☆ **experiences for creativity**
>
> ☆ **imaginative play**
>
> ☆ **books, stories and storytelling**
>
> ☆ **experiences relevant to faith.**

AN INCLUSIVE LEARNING ENVIRONMENT

All children, and families, need to feel a sense of personal welcome and belonging within your setting, or when they enter your family home if you are a childminder. Children and their families absorb the messages communicated by the physical details of your environment: spaces, access, the range of resources and how you choose to use the potential of visual displays. Children need to be reassured that 'people like me' obviously have a place here.

Putting resources in context

Any experiences or resources have to make sense to young children, connecting with their existing knowledge. Children younger than three years are developmentally grounded in themselves and their familiar social world. Three- and four-year-olds still need to 'start with me'. Nothing is gained, and much can be lost, by trying to speed up children's general knowledge over equality issues.

Any policy has to come alive in the children's world

TAKE ANOTHER PERSPECTIVE

Easier travel and global communications can create a 'small world' feel, but this generation of young children still build their understanding and ethnic group identity through personal contacts, conversations and the sense that they make of experiences. Look also at the discussion on page 70 about how you developed your own sense of identity over childhood.

Helpful adults need to be grounded firmly in the child's world. Some play resources are promoted with nonsensical claims. I recall listening to the promotional spiel of one sales representative at an exhibition stand with an extensive array of books and related materials. This person was telling me, with a straight face, that the teddy that came with one kit 'teaches young children about culture'. There is no way that three- and four-year-olds, or any other age group, learn culture from a cuddly toy.

Who can I see?

Visual images, books and play resources should be a rich source of positive images in which children can see themselves and their families. But all children also need positive messages about children, and adults, who do not look immediately familiar. Displays of all different kinds, including your book resources, are a way to offer accurate images of children and families who are not represented locally, or who are in the minority. Balance in illustrations is just as important for babies and toddlers, who have not yet worked out the representational meaning of pictures – babies are busy looking and toddlers will soon notice details – but their families will be coming regularly to your setting or own family home. Images are a form of communication between adults as well as for the children.

You can create displays through photos of shared experiences enjoyed by children who are currently in your setting or family home, but do not overlook the many positive images that are available free from posters and guidance materials for each nation in the UK (see the list of websites on page 36). Appropriate photos can be cut out of magazines and catalogues, but you can also find and print images from the Internet by using a facility like searching in Google by 'Images'. Many of the organisations listed on page 200 sell good-quality visual materials and illustrated books.

A question of balance

You need to consider the balance of images you offer and be aware of what else children are likely to encounter during their time with you.

- Charity catalogues, like those from UNICEF or Oxfam, sell posters and photo cards. Yearly diaries sometimes include good-quality pictures of children and families from around the world, including European locations.

▓ Be cautious, though, about charity posters whose target is fundraising, and therefore emphasise problems and distress. If you are not careful, you can give a negative image of some parts of the world. Similar problems can arise over images of disabled and sick children. You would not extend children's knowledge about animals only from RSPCA charity appeals.

▓ Travel brochures can be a good source of pictures of many different countries. *National Geographic* magazine has stunning photographs and back copies often end up in second-hand book shops.

▓ These images need to be balanced with more everyday images of families shopping, at mealtimes or children at school. Children need to understand countries and cultures less familiar to them through shared experiences as much as the possible differences.

▓ Are the children in any photos or posters from less familiar places showing a variety of emotions: happy, excited, serious but sometimes needing comfort or looking thoughtful?

▓ The same question applies for images of disabled children or adults, who in real life are not permanently smiling. People with a disability sometimes feel sad or fed up, not necessarily because of the disability. When children have limited contact with disabled peers, then illustrations, and books, will be the main source of their views.

LOOK, LISTEN, NOTE, LEARN

It is also important to reflect on the gender balance of visual materials.

■ In your setting, or home if you are a childminder, what range of pictures or photographs are obvious to children? What messages do these illustrations give to children or parents?

■ Can they see caring men with young children as well as women? And are these ordinary-looking men – not all models or celebrity fathers?

You can create unique visual material by using photographs taken within your daily practice. These images can be especially effective when they are part of a learning story created with children themselves. Photos and scribing by you, and emergent or actual writing by children, build into a book about a continuing experience, like 'How we found out about what police officers do.' Look at Carmel Brennan's *Power of Play: A Play Curriculum in Action* (2004) IPPA, distributed in the UK by Community Insight (see page 169).

Can I move around easily?

All public buildings now have to make reasonable modifications to ease access by wheelchair, or for anyone with a disability affecting mobility. Improvements for disabled people are usually inclusive and improve facilities for many people. For instance, sloped entrances, rather than steps, and more spacious toilets are an immense help to every adult pushing a buggy. Contact with disabled children or parents can make you reassess ease of access to, and movement around, your setting.

- Perhaps you take a considered look at how Joshua, with cerebral palsy, will move around the room. It may dawn on you that creating more space for Joshua will encourage you to remove some of the clutter that is unhelpful for the existing group. Perhaps the narrow access to your book corner is the source of avoidable, minor collisions between children.

- Andy, who is deaf, may show unease at a visually over-busy nursery. Lack of clear areas mean that children cross his line of vision without warning and disrupt his play. Charlotte, who is blind, may show that you need to consider predictable routes between indoors and outdoors. However, the changes also improve the learning environment for these children's peers.

If you want to find out more:

Free booklets from Community Playthings about planning a child-friendly environment in general: *Spaces* and *Creating Places*. Contact them at Brightling Road, Robertsbridge, East Sussex TN32 5DR. Tel: 0800 387 457; www.communityplaythings.co.uk.

Inclusive play resources

People often think that disabled children will need expensive, specialist play equipment. Some additional play resources may be useful, but many of your materials will be suitable for disabled children. On the other hand, many items marketed for special needs are truly inclusive. All children want to enjoy the large sound-making boards, large wedges and ball pools. Sensory areas or rooms are often developed with disabled children in mind, but the experience is suitable for everyone.

Special programmes

Some disabled children will have special programmes of work – for instance, speech therapy, physiotherapy and directed physical exercises – or a graded

SCENARIO

Michael has cerebral palsy, but that does not stop him wanting to get stuck into the sand and water play at Crest Road Early Years Centre. His parents chose Crest Road after a short, unhappy experience in another centre where staff acted as if Michael would only be able to use 'special' equipment. Michael had also felt insulted because one practitioner in his previous nursery had given him 'baby toys', apparently on the grounds that they were easier for him to handle. Some practical reorganisation was needed at Crest Road to ensure Michael could get access for his standing frame. He is fully confident now to announce, 'I need my parking space!', if his peers have not left enough room.

Freddy has learning disabilities associated with Down's syndrome. Staff have to be aware that, long after his peers were ready to have play materials with very small parts, Freddy still sucks on little items. He has benefited from a range of resources at a similar developmental level. Freddy needs to practise his skills, but would soon become bored with the same play items.

Questions

1 Consider what changes might be necessary in your setting or family home as a childminder, if you were joined by a child like Michael, with mobility affected by cerebral palsy. Look for ideas on www.scope.org.uk.

2 Reflect on what range of play materials could be of interest to Freddy, allowing for the fact that he is four years old but behaves and thinks much more like a two-year-old. Look for ideas on www.downs-syndrome.org.uk.

learning programme. Some children in your care may have an individual programme resulting from their special educational needs assessment. Any special work appropriate for individual children should be fitted into a full and rounded day or session for them. It is a question of balance in the whole life of children and their experience in your setting. Focused experiences that will help a child's individual needs should be presented with care and shared enjoyment by the adult concerned. A child who has physiotherapy as she lies across a big coloured wedge may regard this as play, especially if these same wedges are used as play equipment at other times.

Of course, disabled children can become unhappy and frustrated if they never seem to have a choice about what they do. It is no fun at all if every activity is adult-directed with a seriousness that has nothing to do with play. Even if adults have good intentions, it is miserable for disabled children if they get treated as the object of a special educational or physical programme. All children need and want enjoyable times, company, conversation and a chance just to mess about with enjoyable resources, for no particular reason except that 'I want to!'

Unfamiliar routines or play

Children from refugee and asylum-seeker families may find early years and school routines confusing; it depends on their previous experience. All children around the world play, unless their childhood has been extremely restricted or abusive. With friendly adult support, young children who are not yet fluent in English will often establish games that do not require much shared language. In schools or after-school clubs, a buddy system can help a great deal. Uncertain children have another child who becomes a familiar face and helps with regular routines. School playground staff can be effective in ensuring playground games that can be shown, if unfamiliar, and do not require a shared language to work.

The UK early years tradition has long emphasised that children learn through play, but parents from a diversity of social and ethnic backgrounds can be puzzled by what exactly is meant by 'learning through play'. Practitioners need to be ready to explain the phrase, connecting the words with examples of what children do day by day. It is also crucial that a learning-through-play approach does not operate in a narrow way, excluding learning that does not fit a rigid early years template.

Practitioners must actively value what children learn from parents, who teach them skills they will need in adult life. For example, some Gypsy and Traveller traditions regard childhood as an apprenticeship for adulthood, not a stage apart from the rest of life. Children may be adept at skills that most of their settled peers explore only through pretend play, such as looking after animals or household tasks. However, families from a range of cultural backgrounds value sharing daily life skills with their children – I feel strongly about it myself.

Outdoor learning and physical activity

Many early years settings and schools have rediscovered the outdoor environment as offering rich potential for learning. Social learning probably means girls may be more concerned than boys about getting wet or muddy. Of course, you do not insist that any children plunge into activities about which they are wary. However, a generous amount of outdoor time, ideally free flow between inside and outside, leads to full engagement of both sexes. In primary school, the adults who supervise playtimes are very important, but they are often undervalued as team members (see also page 219). The school playground can be a lonely place for any child if adults do not take care.

SCENARIO

The team at St Agnes have reflected on possible assumptions about girls and boys as part of their effort to make better use of the outdoor space and new clambering possibilities. Here are some recent examples raised in team meetings.

- Three-year-old Angela is uncertain and today said, 'I can't go up there. My mum says girls are no good at climbing. I'll fall and hurt myself.' Andrea avoided saying bluntly that Angela or her mother were wrong. She replied, 'Well, I've known a lot of girls who are really good climbers. You could try climbing just as far as you're comfortable with. I'll be standing right here.'

- Some of the boys in the pre-school were confident with the new hockey set. But some boys, Jed and Ricky in particular, were anxious about being hit by a ball or stick. Staff acknowledged the boys' concern, and let them handle the soft balls and watch the play before opting to join in. A clear rule was also made that hockey sticks were to be lifted no higher than waist level.

The pre-school had supplemented its limited store of simple games equipment. The team has used the opportunity of Tim's work-placement period with them to show adults crossing possible gender boundaries. Andrea often leads the hockey game and soft football. Tim has been enthusiastic to learn skipping rope skills.

Questions

1 Many practitioners hold unchecked assumptions about girls and boys in play. Ideas have probably been established within your own childhood.

2 Reflect on whether you tend to wait longer with boys on a climbing frame to say, 'Isn't that a bit high?' Or do you assume girls will be more concerned about getting grubby outdoors? Do boys who are uneasy get less support or a surprised adult expression?

Barriers that block access for disabled children are often not physical; attitudes and anxiety can get in the way. You may be aware of the extra help needed by children whose physical disability makes them wobble or whose learning disability means they cannot judge risk as effectively as their peers. Disabled children may need kind guidance (just like their peers) and will benefit from sensible adjustment of their playing space or equipment. But then children just want to get on with their play and grow in competence like their peers. Children want to have some adventures and will accept some bumps or bruises. Disabled children are not helped by excessive protection, however well-intentioned.

TAKE ANOTHER PERSPECTIVE

The Play Inclusive (P.inc) project in Edinburgh has shown how much inclusive practice actually created a good time for all the children, in this case within an adventure playground. Theresa Casey describes how disabled children might need additional adult support to join in play. But her descriptions are consistent for supportive adult behaviour for all children: enabling children to leave as well as join play, helping a confused child by making a complex game more transparent so a child can keep pace, and adult modelling of how to play in this game.

The example of eight-year-old Milly shows how the interests and concerns of individual children are noticed and extended. Milly, whose behaviour is affected by autistic spectrum disorder, needed to follow her own routine of checking out the adventure playground on each visit. The playworkers observed her regular route and each day put something of special interest at her favourite lookout point – a floaty scarf or a mirror.

- Casey, Theresa (2005) *Inclusive Play: Practical Strategies for Working With Children 3–8*. London: Paul Chapman Publishing.
- Casey, Theresa with Hooper, Ivan and McIntyre, Susan (2004) *Play Inclusive Handbook: A Practical Guide to Supporting Inclusive Play for Children of Primary School Age*. The Yard (Scotland Yard Adventure Centre. Tel: 0131 476 4505).

The organisation Kidsactive has many years of experience in creating adventure playgrounds for disabled children and their siblings. Their approach has been to use risk assessment to enable children to get involved, rather than find excuses for why they cannot join lively play. Any practitioner needs to evaluate genuine potential risk for individual disabled children and take necessary steps for sensible protection. Some children may need special equipment, but more often the answer is appropriate adult support, in some cases a consistent adult companion.

If you want to find out more:

- *Action for Leisure*, PO Box 9, West Molesey KT8 1WT. Tel: 020 8783 0173; www.actionforleisure.org.uk.

- Barbarash, Lorraine (1997) *Multicultural Games*. Champaign, IL: Human Kinetics.

- Dunn, Opal (2001) *Acker Backa Boo! Games to Say and Play from Around the World*. London: Frances Lincoln.

- *Kidsactive* has merged with *Kids,* 49 Mecklenburgh Square, London WC1N 2NY. Tel: 020 7520 0405; www.kids.org.uk. The website has details about the National Inclusive Play Network and the Playwork Inclusion Project (PIP).

- Lear, Roma (1996) *Play Helps: Toys and Activities for Children with Special Needs.* Oxford: Butterworth Heinemann.

- Lindon, Jennie (2003) *Too Safe for their Own Good? Helping Children Learn About Risk and Life Skills.* London: National Children's Bureau.

- Marl, Katie (1996) *The Accessible Games Book.* London: Jessica Kingsley.

- *Positive Press,* 28A Gloucester Road, Trowbridge, Wiltshire BA14 0AA. Tel: 01225 719204; www.circle-time.co.uk. Has many books about enjoyable school playtimes and games to play with children.

EXPERIENCES FOR CREATIVITY

A well-rounded week for children in early years, school and out-of-school facilities should offer a wide range of resources that can extend their creative skills and interests. Some of these experiences can be genuinely self-chosen by children because you have organised a well-resourced box or corner. Some enjoyable activities will be adult-initiated, in that you have pre-planned to an extent, but then genuinely creative experiences of any kind have considerable scope for choices and decisions to be made by the children.

Music, songs and dance

Music and dance offer many possibilities and you can guide children to try a wide range. Notice who joins in and who stands on the sidelines. You could also watch out for unnecessary patterns such as the boys usually playing the noisier instruments like drums and the girls taking the triangles or tambourines.

Children enjoy songs and rhymes, with or without hand movements. Awareness of sound and sound patterns is helped by participation in a group, or when an individual child enjoys standing up to deliver a chosen song or rhyme. Ensure that the children's repertoire includes songs from different cultural traditions, starting with those represented in the group and local neighbourhood. You may be fortunate in having parents who could sing for children in languages additional to English. Audio tapes are also available that can supplement live singing sessions. Tapes are often sold with written song books and short explanatory leaflets giving the background to the songs.

Most musical traditions have at least some simple instruments that can be used by even young children. You can choose from a wide range of small drums, single-stringed instruments, flutes and simple whistles, xylophones, many different kinds of shakers, bells that may be shaken or small sets of bells (like gungroos) that are worn on the wrists or ankles and make music as children dance, cymbals and tambourines. See, for instance, the possibilities on offer from Music Education Supplies, 101 Banstead Road South, Sutton SM2 5LH (Tel: 020 8770 3866).

Musical activities need to be presented positively.

- Children enjoy learning to use sound makers in particular rhythms – for instance, light Caribbean calypso rhythms or the steady thump of an English marching band.

- It is important that all instruments are given equal interest and respect. The same applies when you listen to different kinds of music with the children, on tape or CD.

- Use the correct name for any instrument and talk a little with children about each one, even those that you expect will be familiar. Some musical instruments will be unfamiliar, but you can usually find information in the catalogue or leaflets sent with instruments.

- Avoid using the phrase 'ethnic instruments'. This weird term creates a negative division between 'our music' or even 'proper music', in contrast with everything else. Caribbean steel pans are no more an 'ethnic instrument' than the violin, which has a central place in English country dancing and Irish Celtic music – probably known as a fiddle.

When you listen to music, there may be a slight delay as children and adults adjust to unfamiliar musical forms. Some instruments, like bagpipes, can make an unsettling sound until the musician moves into the tune. Children do not have to like all forms of music, although they are very likely to be keen on some of the styles you introduce. Much like encouraging children to try different kinds of food, you should establish a ground rule that, after proper listening, anyone can say they do not particularly like the music, but it is not acceptable for anyone – child or adult – to dismiss the unfamiliar as 'stupid' or 'not real music'.

You may be lucky in your local resources and be able to invite to your setting a musical or dance group, or take the children to a display. Otherwise, you can be creative and use video and tapes of music, dance and song from a range of cultural traditions.

TAKE ANOTHER PERSPECTIVE

Some early years settings and schools organise a long-term creative project with the support of an in-house artist or poet. Maybe you could try this idea.

Marie Charlton has described ('Arts in action', *Nursery World*, 31 March 2005) several linked creative projects, in a largely 'white' area of St Helens in Merseyside, England, when the aim was also to stretch children's horizons beyond their immediate cultural experience. The account highlights children's enthusiasm for the opportunities to explore poetry, drumming and other creative endeavours. The project also shows that you need to invite creative adults who are at ease with young children. Levi Tafari, a poet, was able to take in his stride that some infant children were initially nervous of him. He was comfortable to answer direct questions from children unfamiliar with his dark skin colour and dreadlocks.

Nursery World subscribers can access the article at www. nurseryworld. com.

Enthusiasm for arts and crafts

The very wide range of arts and crafts, drawing from many cultural traditions, can be a source of adult-initiated experiences for children, of displays and of visits when local exhibitions are suitable. Offer possibilities, then be guided by children's specific interests and how long they want these resources out on the table or accessible in the garden. Children should be enabled to return easily to art and craft forms that have engaged their enthusiasm.

There is a tremendous range of possibilities within this area of play and learning. Some crafts are technically too difficult for younger children, but will be possibilities if you spend time with children of primary school age. More challenging crafts might still be suitable for a striking display of photos or ready-made items.

Different kinds of painting, drawing and collage offer children the chance of self-expression. Children can use the skills within pretend play themes: can they portray their favourite character or even develop an illustrated story? Children also want to draw themselves and other familiar figures such as family. Any setting needs a supply of skin colour-toned paints and crayons, then children can achieve subtle differences in skin colour – for themselves and their friends. It soon becomes obvious how 'black' and 'white' are inaccurate words for the subtleties of everyone's skin colour.

SCENARIO

The staff of Clearwater Nursery and Primary School are keen to give children time to explore different art and craft forms, and for children to return to activities like printing or weaving as their physical skills and ideas develop. The team is aware that, regardless of what practitioners say, some children learn fixed views from home about gender-appropriate activities.

- Some boys, not all, view needlework and other skills with cloth as 'just for girls'. Susan and Helena, the nursery team, have welcomed Kenny's father, who works in the fashion industry. He is pleased to show his skills in practical ways, such as mending the torn superhero cloak and joining in what soon becomes a major patchwork project determined by the children.

- Philip, the primary school head, has reinstated the woodwork tables and addressed the safety issues with families that led to their removal by his predecessor. From the nursery into the later school years, the team ensures that female practitioners are fully involved with this experience and, if in doubt of their own sawing or hammering skills, they ask to be shown good technique in front of the children.

- Consultation with children over better use of outdoor space has opened the possibility of a mural – to be planned and created jointly by children and Rachel's mother, who is an artist.

Questions

1 Are you using the simple possibilities of adult role-modelling to stretch children's horizons?

2 Your aim is not to confront families over their views about gender, but you have a responsibility to offer possibilities beyond very narrow confines.

Printing and dyeing can stretch from basic techniques and use of stencils to tie-dyeing, with origins in Indian craft techniques and much more complex techniques like batik, an Indonesian word describing printing on material when hot wax is used to resist a dye. Different styles in patchwork and appliqué have a strong artistic tradition and origins in thrift for communities who could afford to waste nothing. Patchwork has a long history in Europe, parts of India and the Far East, including Indonesia. Young children will find the technique of knitting too difficult, but are often interested in using wool for other purposes. School-age children can manage the dexterity and some boys, as well as girls, find

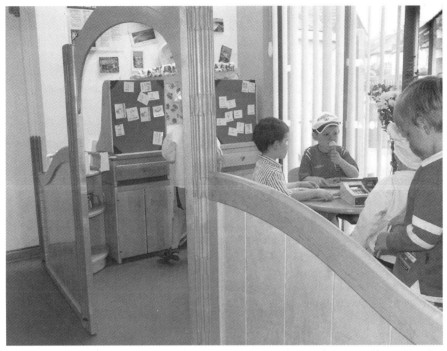

A pretend café gives plenty of scope for play

the physical movements therapeutic, as well as sometimes promoting concentration.

Weaving is an important craft in many countries around the world. Cloth is woven and rugs or carpets are produced by different methods. Weaving can be made very simple, even for under-threes, with large rug hole canvas and outdoor weaving on trellis work. Slightly older children can learn simple weaving techniques on a card or small wooden loom. Star weaving, found in Latin America and parts of Africa, uses a technique of winding wool or other thread around two crossed sticks to produce star designs that vary in colour, texture and size.

The craft of cooking

You can explore different kinds of food and drink, even if you work in a setting without a kitchen or you do not give children a full meal. Snack time offers plenty of possibilities. You could try, perhaps after a shopping trip with the children, different kinds of bread – leavened and unleavened – fruit or raw vegetables that are unfamiliar to some children, and cakes from different cultural traditions. Any food-tasting or cooking experiences should, of course, respect dietary needs in the group, whether these are food allergies or religious and cultural traditions (see page 120).

SCENARIO

Falcon Square after-school club is situated in an ethnically diverse area, yet Daniel and his team have realised that most children do not visit the full range of local food shops. They decide to extend the pick-up walk from three primary schools to buy a few supplies in different food stores. Daniel explains to each shopkeeper, in advance, what they would like to do. Over several weeks, the group has regular visits to the specialist Polish grocery recommended by Jan's mother, the small Indian supermarket run by Gayatri's uncle, the greengrocery run by Marcus's family and the local delicatessen with a range of European foods.

The aim of the trip is to look at what is available, savour the sights and aromas, and make some purchases to supplement the afternoon snack. Daniel and his colleagues are frequently surprised by the gaps in some children's general knowledge. Lucy votes to buy a coconut at the greengrocer's and is ready to explain what you have to do with it, but some of her peers are perplexed by this strange hairy item. Practitioners are also ready to deal with thoughtless or rude remarks. Here are some examples.

- Daniel converts an announcement of, 'This shop smells funny!' to 'Are the smells unfamiliar to you, Myfanwy? Maybe your family don't use the spices that Gayatri's uncle sells here. Let's see if we can work out which spice you can smell.'

- Cameron looks closely at one counter and says, 'That's very funny-looking stuff. Is it proper ham?' Rowshara comments, 'I guess Polish sausage looks unusual to you, Cameron. Let's buy a couple of slices and we can have a tasting session back at club.'

Questions

1 What local resources could you use to extend children's tastes and knowledge?

2 Think ahead about how you will explain unfamiliar foodstuffs or aromas, and deal with any less courteous remarks.

Within any cultural tradition there are variations from area to area. For instance, every family whose country of origin is India certainly does not eat very spicy food. Southern Indian food is generally more highly spiced than northern traditions. Some Indians are vegetarians, whereas others eat meat and poultry. In the same way, all English families do not sit down every Sunday to roast beef and Yorkshire pudding. So make sure you avoid giving children the impression that everyone from a given, less familiar group eats particular food. Likewise, most urban areas of the UK now offer at least some variety in types of food. Families whose ethnic group identity is English may regularly eat Indian or Thai curries.

Families who would describe themselves as Indian may opt sometimes to enjoy fish and chips or a pie.

If you can organise some simple cooking or food preparation with the children, then bear in mind that key techniques can then be used to make different kinds of food. For instance, once children learn to make a basic bread dough, the group can then produce different shapes of bread or buns. Slight variations in the basic recipe can produce Irish soda bread or unleavened kinds of bread like chapattis and puris, Jewish matzo bread and Mexican tortillas. Breads like puris, which have to be fried, could be handed over to the nursery or school cook for finishing. A basic batter mixture can, with slight variations, lead to thin English-style pancakes or French crêpes. But you can also create the thicker Scotch pancakes (also known as pikelets) and Welsh drop scones, and make tempura (Japanese fritters).

SCENARIO

St Agnes Pre-school is located in an area with limited ethnic group diversity and the team has become aware that accurate information is especially important when children may have few other sources.

The team was part-way through planning a topic on 'Africa', including ideas from crafts and cooking, when Tim joined them on his work placement. Tim was hesitant to appear to criticise but, when encouraged by Michelle, he drew on his experience of family holidays to point out that Africa was a huge continent. The magazine and topic-book resources gathered by the pre-school team were a mixed collection from different countries within the continent of Africa. Some were very non-specific, referring to 'life in an African village' or alphabet links of 'A is for Africa', but never 'E is for Europe'.

Tim's comments led Andrea to lay out a world map in a team meeting. The visual impact led to rethinking the details of planned experiences for the children. Many of the resources were good quality but needed to be grounded in the same way that the practitioners would have done for something vaguely 'European'. Michelle made a note to call and get more appropriate detail about the 'African drummer' whom they had booked to visit.

Comments

- Do you check your assumptions and general knowledge? Have you looked at a map recently? Europe is one of the smallest continents; Australia is the smallest.

- Africa, Asia and South America are all substantial and include many different countries, with human variety in language, ethnic group and faith. The landscapes are also very diverse – for example, Africa is not all 'jungle', South America is not all 'Amazonian rainforest'.

- ■ Be ready to reflect on planned experiences for children that are from parts of the world less familiar to you. Some well-intentioned topics on 'Africa' are the equivalent of doing 'Europe' by dressing in clogs as a Dutch girl, tasting some baklava and dancing the Flamenco – all to the backdrop of the Scottish Highlands.

- ■ Flexible topic planning for younger children might include 'visiting' less familiar parts of the world, but the information must be accurate and avoid stereotypes.

IMAGINATIVE PLAY

Most young children start to show imagination in their play some time in their toddler year. Their first pretend actions are very fleeting but their power of imagination grows until three- and four-year-olds are able to sustain lengthy imaginative sequences, and they often return to self-chosen themes with friends over and over again. The supportive adult role is to provide flexible resources and space for play to spread out, and to be willing to be drawn in as a playful adult, who does not then take over the play.

The home corner

Children's play will reflect their experience to date, much of it from their family life. So it is important to show respect for their views, even when you do not agree with them. For instance, a group of girls may be pretend-cooking and two boys are sitting waiting to be served. Carline's explanation that 'Men can't cook' might be met with 'Some men can't cook but I know a lot who can. How about next time Benjie does the cooking and you fix the wheels on the buggy?'

Some children will come from families where both sexes feel strongly that cooking is women's work, and possibly less to be respected for that reason. It is the choice of a family what they do in their own kitchen or dining area, but you can gently shift possibilities in your nursery, club or your own home as a childminder. You may be able to help this process if you become involved in the pretend play. Perhaps you respond to Benjie's peremptory, 'Tea, now!' with a firm but kindly, 'Well, who made you big king? Tell you what, I'll make you a nice pot of tea and then you can make me a cheese sandwich.'

Children will use the home corner to explore and play out everyday events and relationships. It is not the only focus of their pretend play, but can be a rich source of ideas and props. It is possible to obtain child-sized cooking equipment and different utensils that reflect different styles of cooking and eating. As well as pots and pans, you can have bowls, woks, ladles, large chopsticks or a steaming basket.

TAKE ANOTHER PERSPECTIVE

This area of play and learning is one in which adults have to be wary of their own assumptions.

- For instance, many UK families have a kettle in the kitchen, but in many other European countries people boil water in a small saucepan.
- Colleagues whose country of origin is within Asia may assume everyone makes tea in a saucepan and might be puzzled by a teapot.
- In various parts of the Mediterranean, or countries in northern Africa, proper coffee is made in a small heat-proof container and not with granules or powder.
- If you are unfamiliar with any cooking implements, then you need to check how they are used. You may be able to ask colleagues or parents. Suppliers may include a leaflet, or the pictures in the catalogue can help.

Dressing-up clothes

Children, both boys and girls, like to dress up because they are trying out how to be adults, as well as creating characters in their play. A range of materials and clothing will help them to explore relationships, familiar or unfamiliar. The dressing-up basket or corner needs to provide clothing that is familiar, as well as styles that are less well-known, at least to some children. A full range includes the possibility for children to create everyday clothing, as well as special-occasion clothes.

A good dressing-up resource has a range of skirts, tops and tunics, trousers, wraps, hats and other head coverings. If you work in an ethnically diverse neighbourhood, the children's families can contribute to this resource. You may choose to supplement from some of the suppliers listed on page 200. As well as different kinds of European-style dress, you can have shalwar kameez: the tunic and full trousers worn by some Asian girls and women. Lengths of uncut fabric can be draped around children to make an Indian-style sari or the wrap-around clothing styles of men and women in parts of Africa and Indonesia. Headgear can include hats and flat caps, head scarves, skull caps and turbans – worn not only by Sikh men but also by some ethnic groups in North Africa.

It is unnecessary to buy lots of ready-made 'outfits' – such an approach will also drain even a robust budget. You may need to use this source, to an extent, if you work in a neighbourhood with limited ethnic group diversity. However, a good choice of lengths of material can become anything children wish: a wrap-around sarong or a swishing cloak, the wings of a butterfly or an aeroplane. Children will have space for their creativity if you provide photos and illustrations of different styles of dress.

LOOK, LISTEN, NOTE, LEARN

Everyone will need to extend their own general knowledge in order to share accurate information with children.

- You may not know for cultures unfamiliar to you whether a set of clothes is special or ordinary wear. For instance, Japanese women do not wear kimonos as everyday wear on the streets of Tokyo, but they are more common for special occasions such as weddings.

- In a similar way, men in the UK wear top hats and tails for very formal occasions. This outfit is not usual street wear, nor are the huge hats and floaty dresses worn by women at Ascot. You may see morris dancing outfits on a village green, but these clothes are special to the occasion. English adults do not walk around the street waving handkerchiefs and tinkling bells.

- The phrase 'traditional dress' applied to some outfits will describe clothing that follows a long cultural tradition and is still in regular usage. An example could be the fabrics with striking patterns that are worn by women from some countries within Africa. However, Welsh traditional women's dress (the shawl, long skirt and large dark hat) will be worn only at cultural events or where people dress up for historical reasons.

- On the other hand, it is rather odd to describe children from families whose country of origin is India as coming into school in 'their traditional dress' – as I have seen in some articles. Are 'white' children, of UK family origin, described in this way?

Understanding and respect

Children may need some further background to make sense of what you are providing, especially if the clothes are not seen on your local streets. Displays, books and photographs can supplement children's everyday experience to show that ordinary people, adults and children, wear this style of clothing in other parts of the UK, not exclusively in 'faraway lands'.

Children, and practitioners too, need to extend their understanding of different kinds of dress, especially when unfamiliar forms are initially confusing. For instance, Scotsmen who wear a kilt are not dressing up as women, any more than an Indian man in a dhoti or a Nigerian in a wrappa. Watch out also that you do not inadvertently include for pretend play an item that has serious cultural or religious significance. For instance, the small head covering, or kippah, worn by Jewish boys is not just another hat.

Careful intervention will be necessary if children use the clothes as funny disguises, since their play could then reinforce stereotypes about ethnic groups – whether they are, or are not, represented in the setting. Dressing up should be enjoyable, but not a vehicle for making fun of other people. You should discourage any joke Indian accents when children put on a sari, as much as any mock Scots ones if they experiment with kilts.

Male–female balance

Some dressing-up boxes are weighted towards female clothing, which perhaps reflects the main source of free clothing for this activity, yet boys may find less to attract their attention.

- Make sure that your range of hats or wigs definitely has items for males as well as females. Have you got a range of waistcoats or tabards? Plenty of hats are valuable, because a suitable hat is often enough to enable a child to become a firefighter, bus conductor or doctor/nurse.

- Add some props to your collection so that children can create their own superhero outfit, knight's armour or space gear. You do not need to buy entire costumes, and children's imagination is not well-supported when there is no scope for them to add.

- Watch and listen to the children; they will let you know the key items they need for different pretend characters.

TAKE ANOTHER PERSPECTIVE

Parents do not usually mind their daughters dressing up in male attire during childhood. However, some are genuinely anxious that letting their sons dress up in female clothing will turn the boys gay or transvestite. It is necessary to respect parents' concerns, while reassuring them that dressing up in a feather boa or wig will not affect their son's future sexual orientation one way or another. The activity is much more within the English cultural tradition of pantomime dames. Male transvestites are often heterosexual, although this may not be much comfort to parents with conservative views.

You need to deal with offensiveness between the children built around sexual orientation or presumed orientation. Playground insults from the primary level include name-calling and ridicule on this basis. You need to establish ground rules about what does and does not happen within the bounds of your home or setting. Partnership with parents on equality issues around sexual orientation will need to acknowledge the starting point for these fellow adults. Families from a range of social and cultural backgrounds still feel anything from regret to outright hostility about the prospect of a son, or daughter, who strays from the heterosexual fold.

Dolls, puppets and play figures

These resources are important because they represent real babies, children or adults, and girls and boys use them in a broad range of play. Children need easy access to dolls and play people that offer an accurate representation of both sexes and ethnic group features including skin colour. It is possible now to buy dolls that look like someone whose country of origin is India or Jamaica, rather than dolls with darkened 'white' European features. Dolls should be realistically dark over their whole body – not just the faces – whether these are firm or soft dolls. Children love caring for dolls' hair and dolls who look of African or Caribbean origin give any child the chance to braid hair.

Some companies also sell different styles of baby and child clothing to fit their dolls. Suppliers also produce dolls and small-world play families that encompass some visible physical disabilities. It is an advantage if play-family figures show people who clearly differ in age as well. Childminders can supplement their home-based resources by borrowing from a toy library or attending drop-in sessions.

SCENARIO

Good suppliers offer male and female dolls, sometimes anatomically correct as well. Yet if you look in high-street toy stores, you will still find many more female than male dolls – unless the doll has become a military figure. So the message is still strong that dolls are girls' toys. However, in a welcoming home corner in a nursery, or with domestic play resources in your home as a childminder, you will encounter boys who express an interest in family pretend play with dolls. You can also deal carefully with comments.

■ At St Agnes Pre-school, Ricky has said doubtfully, 'I shouldn't play with the dolls, my dad says that's for cissies'. Tim replies, 'Hmm, I know some people feel the same way as your dad, but I don't agree. I think you can enjoy playing with dolls and still be a proper boy.' Looking at Ricky's current play, Tim adds, 'And you do need a patient for your ambulance.'

■ At Crest Road Early Years Centre practitioners are ready with gentle corrections to help children think about contradictions in what they have said. Chloe has announced to Nell, 'Men don't cuddle babies, that's mummy stuff.' Nell counters with, 'Hold on, I've seen your daddy with baby Jessica and he cuddles her a lot.'

Comments

■ Perhaps a boy in your care has a new baby sister or brother. Can he demonstrate how to hold a little baby by using the baby doll?

■ Boys who feel that dolls are not for them are often keen to use puppets. Or they weave play around figures who fit with construction materials or pretend settings such as a farm, garage or castle.

These resources are for all the children. Dolls of different ethnic backgrounds need to reflect the diversity of children in your care, but are also a contribution to extending children's horizons. You do not wait until a 'black' child joins you to buy a doll who has features other than 'white European' (nor finally get such a doll out of the cupboard!). It would be equally foolish to suggest you postpone buying curly-haired dolls because the children currently in your care have straight hair. Likewise, dolls or play people with visible disabilities are not exclusively for disabled children themselves.

TAKE ANOTHER PERSPECTIVE

Discussion about dolls for young children often leads to a conversation, or argument, about golliwogs. Some 'white' adults, probably now middle-aged or older, had a cherished golliwog in their own childhood and may have collected the badges when Robertson's Jams gave out paper cut-outs and metal badges.

Everyone deserves respect for their own childhood memories, but this situation requires sceptical 'white' practitioners to show empathy for the views of 'black' colleagues or parents. Emotional literacy also extends to making the effort to look through the eyes of all 'black' children. How are children likely to feel if a caricature is all that is available to support their own self-image?

If you are a 'white' reader, imagine that almost all the characters in the books of your childhood were 'black'. In your nursery or school there was a much-loved book that had a 'white' character, Pinocchio. This little boy was also produced as a doll and was the only doll in nursery or toy shops that had a 'white' face. The other children called you and the few other 'white' boys and girls 'Noky'. They made offensive remarks about the length of your nose and claimed that it grew because you told lies. The 'black' adults knew you were upset but would not take your distress seriously. Your parents were told, 'Noky dolls are part of everyone's childhood. It's nothing personal, it's just a doll. Anyway, children don't notice things like that.'

- How would you have felt as a child? Try hard to put yourself into this imagined situation.

- How might you feel as an adult looking back, especially one who is now being told 'You're making a fuss about nothing'?

BOOKS, STORIES AND STORYTELLING

Many books have now been published that support a positive approach to all aspects of equality. But you could be forgiven for thinking there was little available if you restrict your search to high-street toy and book shops. Use some of the mail-order companies listed on page 200 instead. The examples in this section are only a small selection of available good-quality books.

There is a difference between books that tell a story (fiction) and books that inform (non-fiction). You need to check that some groups of children or adults do not appear exclusively, or mainly, in the non-fiction type. Information books are just as important as story books within a range of resources. Some children, perhaps more often boys, can best be encouraged into valuing books, and the future possibility of being a reader, because they have plenty of information books to look at and to fuel conversation with you.

Information books

Some books about 'children from other lands' can extend children's general knowledge in a reliable way, but ensure that you are not giving children, especially in a mainly 'white' area, the inaccurate idea that the UK is all 'white'. You also need books that feature children and their families from the different towns and cities and the countryside of the UK. Look carefully at any books on children 'around the world' to ensure that they do not give an unbalanced image – perhaps that 'Asian children' live only in rural areas, when the truth is that many live in towns and cities. It is valuable to have, or borrow, information books showing common child and family experiences within the images of diversity. Here are a few examples.

- The *Small World* series from Milet Limited illustrates shared experiences such as eating, smiling and carrying.
- The *From Dawn to Dusk* series, published by Frances Lincoln, has different titles that show the day of a child in different parts of the world.
- Or try *A Life Like Mine: How Children Live Around the World*, a joint publication from UNICEF and Dorling Kindersley (London, 2002).
- School-age children could well relate to *If the World Were a Village* by David Smith and Shelagh Armstrong (London: A&C Black, 2003), a book that creatively explains the daily lives of families around the world by reducing huge population numbers into a 'village' of 100 people.
- Some books are an effective blend of information and story. For example, *That's my Mum* by Henriette Barkow and Derek Brazell (London: Mantra, 2001) shows two friends of mixed ethnic group heritage through their daily lives. The storyline also addresses how the two children deal with the fact that, by skin colour, each child looks more like their father than their mother.

There are some good series that aim to inform children about specific disabilities or chronic health conditions. These books provide straightforward information, usually with illustrations of real children. They can also be a good start for practitioners who need to extend their own knowledge. Some possibilities include the *Events* series, published by Hamish Hamilton, or the *One World* series, published by Franklin Watts. Organisations supporting a specific disability or health condition often give ideas about relevant information books.

Good stories

Some story books will feature non-human characters: animals, monsters or outer-space aliens. Some equality issues still arise: does mummy fox ever take off her apron and go boldly, and what happens if you look different from the rest of the little aliens? However, the following questions for reflection are aimed more at the balance of human characters.

- Can all the children in your care see themselves in the books on your shelves, that you read to them and that you borrow from your local library?
- Also, to what extent are your books, along with other play materials, stretching children's understanding of the world beyond their immediate neighbourhood?

- Across the range of books are there children of visibly different ethnic groups, children and adults of mixed heritage, Traveller and Gypsy as well as settled families?

- These stories are not 'multicultural books', they are just books. You should offer children a selection that ranges across a diversity of cultures. A story about a Chinese family is no more 'multicultural' in itself than a tale spun around their 'white' European neighbours.

- Are there some characters who have a disability or chronic health condition but who are just getting on with their lives through the story? Alric, who has epilepsy, deserves to see children like himself as characters in a story, not exclusively through an information book about the condition.

Shaking off stereotypes in fiction of any kind can take some time. In terms of ethnic group identity, characters of a non-European background have moved from being a faithful servant or sinister foreigner. Over the 1960s and 1970s there was a phase when, once a 'black' character was included in a book, television drama or film, there almost always had to be a skin colour-related plot line or problem. Now we seem to have moved to a point where it is much more possible that characters from a diversity of 'black' ethnic groups can be a family man or a villain, the caring mother or nightmare female boss.

Many story books now show positive images in terms of gender and ethnic group identity for children and adults. Fiction featuring disabled characters is still emerging from a similar struggle to reach some balance. If you browse the shelves of a local book shop or the library, to what extent are disabled children or adults featured in stories? Good books definitely exist – for example, two books by Verna Wilkins: *Boots for a Bridesmaid* and *Are We There Yet?* (Tamarind).

If you want to find out more:

The quality of newly-published books can still vary and, of course, some written years ago may still be on the shelves. Look carefully through any materials.

- Working Group Against Racism in Children's Resources: *Guidelines to Support Practitioners in Evaluating Books and Other Resource Materials*, WGARCR, Unit 34, Eurolink Business Centre, 49 Effra Road, London SW2 1BZ. Tel: 020 7501 9992; www.wgarcr.org.uk.

- Saunders, Kathy (2000) *Happy Ever Afters: A Storybook Guide to Teaching Children About Disability*. Stoke-on-Trent: Trentham Books.

When I wrote the first edition of this book during 1997 I found only a small number of books that featured Traveller or Gypsy families. Some were already out of print, although available to borrow from libraries. *The Way We Live* series published by Hamish Hamilton includes *A Traveller Child* and *A Circus Child*. The A&C Black *Strands* series includes *Gypsy Family*. Rumer Godden's *The Diddakoi* (London: Puffin) is a story for older readers, but works well to be read in episodes to younger children. The situation has now improved, mainly because many local authorities have produced their own materials. Your local team may be called the Traveller and Gypsy Education Team or the Minority Ethnic Education Service. Otherwise, do an Internet search. I found many sources by Googling 'Traveller Education Service' for the UK.

Character and plot matter

Any stories for children still need good basics in characters and an absorbing plotline. Balance can be lost if writers and illustrators try always to present counter-stereotypes. For instance, disabled children are not always brave and happy; sometimes they are mean and horrible, just like their peers. There is nothing the matter with some stories featuring caring mothers or girls absorbed in traditional female activities; Janet should not always have to make the sandwiches, but neither should she be forever wielding a large mole wrench. Overall your books should reflect the ethnic group diversity of the UK, but the range can include stories where the family is 'white' and so is most, perhaps all, of the immediate neighbourhood. This situation is real life in many parts of the UK.

Stories also have to work as an engaging tale and have characters that provoke children's interest. It is most effective to show through the good storyline that Tammy's wheelchair does not stop her having adventures with her friends. Whether listening, or reading to themselves, children abandon a weak plot which is overwhelmed by a wish to challenge stereotypes. Furthermore, you cannot predict that the obvious message, from an adult perspective, will be what most strikes children. Enjoying books and storytelling with children should include opportunities to chat around the storyline and the characters.

TAKE ANOTHER PERSPECTIVE

Children need a wide range of browsing and reading materials. Once children are able to choose books as independent readers, girls seem to select a wider range than boys. In terms of fiction, girls seem to be ready to read 'boys' books', whereas their male peers are more likely to avoid books they see as being pitched towards girls. Girls are not usually put off a book by a male main character but the reverse happens more often: boys are less interested in a book with a heroine.

- Why do you think this happens?
- Share and discuss your thoughts with colleagues, fellow students or friends outside your profession – ideally male as well as female.

Bear in mind that some story books written for independent readers work well for an adult to read aloud in episodes. This way of sharing a book is enjoyable for children who cannot yet read to themselves, but is equally engaging for older children in school or an after-school club. Listening to a good story in episodes will sometimes provoke the interest of boys and girls who can read but have yet to see the personal value of this skill.

Traditional tales of different kinds

Children enjoy folk tales, myths and legends, and available books draw from a wide range of cultural traditions. Always read any tales to yourself before reading them aloud to children – some are too scary for younger children. You will find possibilities from series such as *Myths and Legends* (Heinemann) or *Landscapes of Legend* and *The Best Stories Ever Told* (Franklin Watts).

Each major world faith has significant narratives that highlight beliefs or are central to a particular celebration (see also page 195). You may choose to explore a story as part of a celebration with children, but some stand alone as excellent accounts in their own right.

- Be ready to explain the context of any story to all the children. Do not assume that children whose families are nominally of the faith necessarily know much about the story or the celebration.
- Treat all stories with equal respect. Depending on your own religious affiliation, or the faith in which you were raised, do not imply that some accounts are the factual truth and others are simply nice stories.

Several mainstream publishers offer books to support this kind of learning through narratives. I especially like the style and illustrations of the series *Tales of Heaven and Earth* from Moonlight Publishing (Tel: 01235 821821), distributed through Ragged Bears (Tel: 020 8804 0400).

Dual-language books

There is a wide choice in dual-language books, which can be supportive for bilingual children but equally valuable for monolingual children who are discovering that the whole world does not share their spoken and written language. You can buy tapes of stories, songs and rhymes in different languages, or you may be fortunate in having bilingual practitioners or parents who could make a tape for your setting or childminders' drop-in session.

Even in an apparently non-diverse area, there will be practitioners, parents or grandparents who have a second language. In mainly 'white' areas, there may well be families whose origins are Irish, Polish, German or some other mainland European country. Children may giggle at first, especially if the unknown language is spoken by someone from whom they have previously heard only English. You can acknowledge that hearing a new language from a known adult seems odd at the start, but you need to model respect for any language and perhaps acknowledge that Somali or Italian children might find English amusing at the first time of hearing.

You could alert children to different written forms of language. Some bilingual families may be able to help you in displays of languages that use different alphabets and forms of writing. In school, you may be fortunate that some children can actually demonstrate writing in their home language. You can buy multilingual 'Welcome' notices. However, ideally, it would be worth developing one of your own, that draws on the languages spoken or understood by the families who actually attend your setting.

Storytelling

Storytelling can be an enjoyable supplement to reading story books. Many cultures around the world had, or still retain, strong traditions of oral storytelling. You may be fortunate to have someone local who is a skilled storyteller. But you can become an engaging storyteller using books that you know by heart and simple props. You need to develop your skills by drawing from a range of cultural traditions represented by the stories. If at all possible, offer some storytelling supplemented with signing.

Children are often keen to become involved directly in the storytelling. Helen Bromley describes how she first came to her creative idea for story boxes. In her reception class she had a group of boys who did not seem to be engaged by books or telling stories. Then one day she made available a number of shoe boxes and flexible materials, including some animal figures. She listened, watched and realised that all the boys had many ideas for stories, and the plotlines and characters were emerging round materials that they could get their hands on.

Storytelling to support empathy

It is possible to build on children's power of imagination through storytelling as well as story reading. You can use puppets and special dolls that take on a consistent character and personal history. The overall aim of any of these approaches for equality is twofold – to:

1   support children towards empathy – a sense of fellow-feeling for others and a willingness to consider how someone may feel; empathy is about finding common ground, as well as grasping differences of perspective and priority

2   extend children's knowledge and understanding beyond their personal experience and immediate neighbourhood.

It will be important that no child feels that a story or puppet play is directly linked with a recent altercation between individual children. The aim must be to support and certainly not that children are being criticised yet again for an incident that was supposed to be finished.

Persona Dolls are one example of harnessing children's ability to enter a world of pretend. Babette Brown has been active in bringing the idea of Persona Dolls to the UK. These special dolls, who are given names and

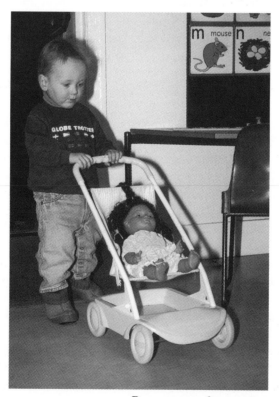

Resources are for everyone

personal histories, can be used in a gentle way with children to help them explore the perspectives of people who appear different from themselves. These dolls, and similar resources, have the potential to support positive attitudes on any aspect of difference and are often introduced within a regular, short circle time. However, practitioners need to reflect on the balance of any story that is woven around a doll or puppet. You may wish to alert children to sources of social inequality and unfairness, but it will be unhelpful if the story evokes more pity than fellow-feeling.

Like any experiences offered to children, these resources cannot work alone. They are effective against a backdrop of daily experiences around conversation and how adults deal with behaviour (see page 142). There is little point in practitioners recounting a story with the (written paper) aim of promoting understanding of physical disability if nobody deals with Leanna's daily experiences of being rejected for play 'because she keeps dropping things'. In fact, Leanna may feel even worse because she has noticed the inconsistency in practitioners' approach. Children are sharp observers and, certainly by primary school age, very able to voice their grasp of, 'Well they [the adults] say . . . but they can't be bothered when . . .'.

If you want to find out more:

- ❖ Bromley, Helen (2002) *50 Exciting Ideas for Story Boxes to Make*. Walsall: Lawrence Educational.

- ❖ MacDonald, Simon (2005) *The Little Book of Puppets in Stories*. Husbands Bosworth: Featherstone Education Ltd.

- ❖ Medlicott, Mary (2003) *The Little Book of Storytelling*. Husbands Bosworth: Featherstone Education Ltd.

- ❖ Persona Doll Training, *Persona Dolls in Action* video and book, 51 Granville Road, London N12 0JH. Tel: 020 8446 7056; for other materials and examples of using Persona Dolls, see www.persona-doll-training.org/.

- ❖ Portsmouth Ethnic Minority Achievement Service offers a useful case study on www.blss.portsmouth.sch.uk/earlyears/eypdolls_tr.shtml.

EXPERIENCES RELEVANT TO FAITH

If you work in a diverse area, you may have children attending your setting whose families follow a number of different world faiths. Families may be able and willing to support experiences in the setting. You should not restrict yourself only to those faiths that are represented in your current setting or neighbourhood. Your aim is to extend the learning of all the children but you need to be realistic about how much you try to cover, especially within the early years. You have plenty of time over childhood; early years practitioners must not feel responsible for covering significant amounts of ground.

LOOK, LISTEN, NOTE, LEARN

Even if you are not based in England, please discuss this example from the Foundation Stage. These are two related early learning goals from 'Personal, social and emotional development' (page 42), that children (five-year-olds, by the end of the stage) will:

■ understand that people have different needs, views, cultures and beliefs, which need to be treated with respect

■ understand that they can expect others to treat their needs, views, cultures and beliefs with respect.

Notice that respect is defined clearly as a two-way process. The related stepping stones emphasise that experiences cannot work effectively if there is an imbalance away from 'own culture' and a premature push to understand 'other cultures'.

■ Three-year-old: 'Make connections between different parts of their life experience'.

■ Four-year-old: 'Show a strong sense of self as a member of different communities, such as their family or setting'.

■ Five-year-old: 'Have an awareness of and show interest and enjoyment in cultural and religious differences' and 'Have a positive self-image and show that they are comfortable with themselves'.

Reflect and discuss with colleagues or fellow students how you need to behave as a supportive early years practitioner.

■ What would it be helpful for you to do or say?

■ How might you build on experiences and opportunities that arise spontaneously through children's conversation or their play?

■ Finally, if you are going to plan adult-initiated experiences, what could be helpful and why?

Awareness of attitudes

Young children are in the process of developing their views on moral and spiritual issues, just as they are learning attitudes about social relationships and how people should behave. Practitioners should not tell children what they should believe. However, making information available to children is not the same as 'indoctrinating them'. Children will learn attitudes towards different faiths and religious practices even when adults claim they have said and done nothing. Practitioners who make no effort beyond celebrating what the team view as the 'normal' festivals, from only one faith, effectively tell the children that this faith is the only one that matters. The same proviso applies to childminders.

Some children live in neighbourhoods where adults express bigoted views against faiths other than their own or denominations of the same world faith. Equality practice in Northern Ireland and parts of Scotland has to address the strong sectarian views expressed by adults of the Protestant and Catholic denominations of Christianity. Children easily absorb these negative and rejecting attitudes. Some early years settings and the integrated schools movement have made great efforts to address the development of attitudes. (See also page 149.)

Sometimes practitioners are anxious or uncertain, asking: 'Are we expected to tell young children all about religion?' The answer to this question has to be 'No.' You start a process of knowledge and understanding that will continue. You open possibilities for children by introducing a few ideas and providing a realistic range of experiences. This approach has much in common with other areas of your work with children. For instance, early years practitioners are not trying to show a four-year-old everything there is to know about mathematical understanding, or tell every last detail about scientific investigations. You introduce basic ideas, and encourage children to explore through doing and asking questions. If you work in a school, then your approach to religious education will be guided by the relevant educational legislation for your part of the UK.

Festivals and celebrations

This kind of experience is not the only way in which you can show respect and steadily extend children's knowledge. Faith is often interwoven with cultural tradition. So other aspects of good practice will support equality relevant to faith – for example, use of books (page 192), food and cooking (page 123) or respect for personal care (page 109).

You need to bear in mind that families who follow a particular world faith are not Hindus only at Divali, nor Christians just over Easter. People follow the tenets of a faith and worship throughout the year. It can be more effective to reflect on ways to show daily life and common ground between groups that look different at the outset. Commonalities in daily family life also make most sense to children younger than five or six years – for instance, how families greet a new baby or celebrate marriage. This section discusses good practice over celebrations because this kind of adult-initiated experience is so common in early years and schools. However, it would be poor equality practice if practitioners used celebrations as a simple way to tick off their responsibility.

Make a limited selection

You cannot celebrate all possible festivals and, if you tried, children and adults would become dazed and confused as one celebration followed another. You could celebrate the key festivals of families whose children attend your setting. So it is very likely the selection will include some celebrations with roots in long-standing traditions within the UK. When children are well-grounded in their own cultural background, you could add one or two other festivals that will be a source of learning for everyone. Take your time and be realistic – no celebration will mean much to under-threes, although cake and gifts are always welcome!

Involve parents and the local community

You can look beyond your immediate setting for support and information. Some of the children's parents, as well as local people, may be pleased to explain their faith or particular secular celebrations to you. Some may be happy to speak to the children in a group setting or to act as guide in a visit by school-age children to a local place of worship. Practitioners working in city areas are likely to have a wider range of opportunities of this kind.

Be sure that you brief a parent, or local person, who speaks to the group or whom you invite to a school assembly. It is important that their approach is one of 'I believe . . .' or 'We believe that . . .' rather than 'What I am telling you is the only truth.' You need to exercise the same care in learning about world faiths as the consequences of ethnic group and cultural background. Avoid assuming that the few people with whom you speak about a faith that is unfamiliar have told you everything that there is to know.

Respect parents' wishes

Some parents will be open to their children's celebrating a range of festivals, but it is parents' responsibility to raise children within a given religious faith if they so wish. Some parents may be uneasy about celebrations other than in their own faith, although some may be reassured by your explanation that children are learning respect, not allegiance. If parents feel strongly, then it cannot be good practice to insist.

Families who are Jehovah's Witnesses hold a memorial service on the day of Christ's death (a week before the Jewish Passover) but they do not celebrate Christmas, Easter, birthdays and a number of other celebrations because the main origins of these festivals are judged to be non-Christian. Families from a range of backgrounds have serious reservations about Halloween.

Generally speaking, families or colleagues will not take offence at a celebration, religious symbol or story that comes from a faith to which they do not subscribe. An effective equality policy into practice should ensure respect and even-handedness. You need to be aware if any kind of symbolism carries greater significance locally – for example, the issues raised on page 84 about anti-sectarianism in Northern Ireland in particular.

Show equal respect

Once children are genuinely old enough to understand some of the ideas, then you can give them experiences of a small number of celebrations through the year. It is essential for equality practice that equal respect is shown to each celebration in terms of amount of time and attention to detail.

- Definitely do not explain one celebration in terms of the beliefs or events of a religion more familiar to you. Some festivals share a focus on light or the exchange of presents, but there will be differences as well as shared themes. So do not describe Divali as 'a kind of Christmas' (or the other way around). And do not let it pass if children make this comment. You might say that there are some similarities, but the two are different.

- You need to avoid any implication that 'Other people have colourful festivals' but 'We have serious religious events'. Unfamiliar celebrations, or those from faiths that are not represented in the group, should not be treated as 'exotic' or 'just a bit of fun', in contrast to familiar festivals, which are treated as 'normal' and 'serious'.

- Consider how much time you spend on different celebrations. If you spend all of December on Christmas and only one or two days on any non-Christian festival, then your actions are saying as loudly as words that you value Christianity most highly.

- Any adult-initiated activities must leave children with genuine choice. You undermine the aim of extending children's learning about a faith and/or a celebration, when the main message for them is, 'I have to make a Hanukkah card before I'm allowed to go back to play.'

- Celebrations with a long religious and cultural tradition should be respected in their own right and not absorbed as handy source material for your early years or primary curriculum. In my view, some topic books border on disrespectful for the enthusiasm with which significant cultural or faith events are slotted into curriculum headings.

■ Make sure that any activities with religious meaning are treated with respect. Children should never pretend to pray, nor do joke meditation or obeisance. If you work in a primary school, you may introduce children to some artefacts with religious meaning – for instance, the rosary used by Catholic Christians or the Seder plate used to celebrate Pesach (the Jewish Passover).

If you want to find out more:

❖ *Child's Eye Media*, Mauldeth House, Nell Lane, Manchester M21 7RL. Tel: 0161 374 5509; www.childseyemedia.com. Has *Festivals* videos that offer a suitable child and family perspective.

❖ Lindon, Jennie (1999) *Understanding World Religions in Early Years Practice*. London: Hodder & Stoughton.

❖ *Support 4 Learning*: www.support4learning.org.uk. Information online about yearly calendars relevant to different world faiths and celebrations, also Internet links to other information sites.

❖ *Teacher Net*: www.teachernet.gov.uk/teachingandlearning/subjects/re. The RE section of the website offers information and website links.

❖ Magazines like *Nursery World* and *Practical Pre-School* are a good source of ideas and information; however, the features often work best as part of your resource file as ideas to use over time and ways to ensure you are well-informed – the aim is not to try to do every possible variation on a celebration this time around, nor to impart all the information to children, especially under-fives.

Resources by mail order

❖ *Articles of Faith*, Resource House, Kay Street, Bury BL9 6BU. Tel: 0161 763 6232; www.articlesoffaith.co.uk. Books and other materials to support understanding of different world faiths.

❖ *Books Education*, 8 Park View Gardens, Hendon, London NW4 2PN. Tel: 020 8202 6776; www.bookseducation.com. Wide range of books, stretching well into the school years.

❖ *Christian Aid*, PO Box 100, London SE1 7RT. Tel: 020 7620 4444; www.christian.aid.org.uk. Its education catalogue can be a good source of pictures.

❖ *Community Insight*, The Pembroke Centre, Cheney Manor, Swindon SN2 2PQ. Tel: 01793 512612; www.communityinsight.co.uk. Publications for early years and playwork practitioners, and books for children.

❖ *Early Education*, 136 Cavell Street, London E1 2JA. Tel: 020 7539 5400; www.early-education.org.uk. Cards and posters.

❖ *East-West Education* (EWE), 3 Keymer Gardens, Burgess Hill, West Sussex RH15 0AF. Tel: 01444 236322; www.eastwesteducation.org. Children's dressing-up clothes, dolls and dolls' clothing.

❖ *Eduzone*, 29 Friern Barnet Road, London N11 1NE. Tel: 08456 445556; www.eduzone.co.uk. Supplies dolls, play figures and puzzles.

❖ *Galt Educational and Pre School*, Culvert Street, Oldham, Lancashire OL4 2GE. Tel: 0870 2424477; www.galt-educational.co.uk. Play materials and equipment.

❖ *Letterbox Library*, 71 Allen Road, London N16 8RY. Tel: 020 7503 4801; www.letterboxlibrary.com. Mail-order children's books, specialising in a non-sexist and multicultural list; dual-language books and posters.

❖ *Little Tiger Press*, 1 The Coda Centre, 189 Munster Road, London SW6 6AW. Tel: 020 7385 6333; www.littletigerpress.com. Children's books in different languages and some dual-language books.

❖ *Mantra Lingua*, Global House, 303 Ballards Lane, London N12 8NP. Tel: 020 8445 5123; www.mantralingua.com. A wide range of books in different languages, tape and story packs, song collections, poster and wall friezes.

❖ *NES Arnold Ltd*, Ludlow Hill Road, West Bridgford, Nottingham NG2 6HD. Tel: 015304 18901; www.nesarnold.co.uk. Dressing-up clothes, dolls, posters and display cards.

❖ *Oxfam*, c/o BEBC Distribution, PO Box 1496, Parkstone, Poole, Dorset BH12 3YD. Tel: 01202 712033; www.oxfam.org.uk/coolplanet. Resources for children and website materials for school age, illustrations and publications.

❖ *Pre-school Learning Alliance* through PPA Promotion, 45–49 Union Road, Croydon CR0 2XU. Tel: 020 8684 9542; www.pre-school.org.uk. Wide range of books, booklets and friezes.

❖ *Save the Children*, 17 Grove Lane, London SE5 8RD. Tel: 020 7703 5400; www.savethechildren.org.uk. Booklets and posters.

* *Shining Star*, c/o 4 Hilldown Road, Highfield, Southampton, Hampshire SO17 1SX. Tel: 023 8048 3633; www.shining star.info. Wide range of books and play resources.

* *Smile Child*, Unit 3, Callington Business Park, Tinners Way, Moss Side Industrial Estate, Callington PL17 7SH. Tel: 01579 383050; www.smilechild.co.uk. Selection of play resources, music and books.

* *Tamarind Ltd*, PO Box 52, Northwood, Middlesex HA6 1UN. Tel: 020 8866 8808; www.tamarindbooks.co.uk. Books, puzzles and posters.

* *The Festival Shop*, 56 Popular Road, Kings Heath, Birmingham B14 7AG. Tel: 0121 444 0444; www.festivalshop.co.uk. Books and other materials about different world faiths and cultures.

* *UNICEF*, 55–56 Lincoln's Inn Fields, London WC2A 3NB. Tel: 020 7405 5592; www.unicef.org.uk. Pictures, some play resources and music.

* *Winslow*, Goyt Side Road, Chesterfield, Derbyshire S40 2PH. Tel: 0845 230 2777; www.winslow-cat.com. Resources for supporting disabled children.

Part 4

Working well with other adults

This part of the book homes in on the significant strand of friendly, working relationships between adults, within the visual image of Celtic knotwork. What happens between fellow practitioners, and the communication between home and early years or school-age provision, is interwoven day by day for a holistic approach to equality practice for children.

Chapter 9 focuses on practitioners working well together: in the team of a group setting, or as childminders who are part of the local childminding service and may also be accredited to a childminding network. The values of your practice should be clear through your written policy on equality issues. Your policy should demonstrate your commitment, or that of the whole team. But the implications of policy will not always be absolutely clear. Discussion within a team and between fellow professionals will be necessary to resolve different interpretations, misunderstandings and maybe outright disagreement.

Partnership with parents and other family carers is central to effective and courteous early years, school and out-of-school practice. Chapter 10 focuses on how equality practice should go hand in hand with partnership, as well as situations in which agreement or compromise may be difficult. An equality policy is not a value-free zone. This part of the book, like other chapters, offers examples where practitioners have to be clear about the priorities underpinning their equality practice.

9 Working well with fellow practitioners

Early years, school and playwork practitioners need to establish and maintain good communication with a network of professionals, many of whom will be based locally. Some practitioners additionally work on a daily basis with the same set of colleagues in a team. Childminders most often work alone in their own home, although many now have an assistant or work as couples who have registered jointly. Many childminders have now chosen to join their local childminding network and benefit from the opportunities for professional discussion and support.

> **The main sections covered by this chapter are:**
>
> ✶ **discussion and reflection**
>
> ✶ **diversity in the team**
>
> ✶ **professional behaviour and social learning.**

DISCUSSION AND REFLECTION

When you work in a team, whether with one other person, five or twenty, it does not mean that everyone has exactly the same tasks, nor are they expected to fulfil their role in an identical way. Effective teamwork, supported by good leadership in a group setting, leaves scope for individual style and interests. However, individuality needs to be expressed through the filter of a shared commitment to common values and priorities.

Individual practitioners within a team, even one composed of a childminder and assistant, are interdependent: what one individual does in his or her work affects colleagues, because they are all part of the same service. This quality of interdependence is positive when everyone remains aware of how their areas of responsibility dovetail with those of their colleagues. If one or two practitioners behave as if their actions and views are just a matter of personal choice, colleagues soon realise the potential negative consequences of interdependence. Good teamworking is crucial for equality practice, just as much as for other professional responsibilities.

Share with colleagues what you learn from individual children

SCENARIO

Michelle, the leader of St Agnes Pre-school has been relieved to see the back of Sophie, a practitioner who left of her own accord last term. Sophie was noticeably friendlier to parents who attended St Agnes church, where she herself worshipped. Sophie's biased approach to partnership would be unacceptable in any case, but additionally the pre-school only rents the hall from the church council, the setting is not affiliated with the church.

Michelle had worked hard to address Sophie's unprofessional behaviour, through supervision and clear goal-setting for change, but the next step would have been formal disciplinary procedures. Sophie had been offhand about activities during the exploration of Divali. She also insisted on saying a very Christian style of grace at snack time, despite a clear policy that any form of appreciation had to be more inclusive.

Sophie's words and actions had hurt Jamal's grandmother, who was the first person to raise the matter tentatively with Michelle. Ricky's father had been clearly annoyed that Sophie 'has been trying to brainwash my son' and asked that Sophie no longer be Ricky's key person. Even those parents who were favoured by Sophie's smiles and friendlier conversation, looked uncomfortable about the unequal treatment.

Michelle was aware that it was increasingly difficult for parents to separate Sophie as an individual from her role as a team member. Ricky's father had summed it up with, 'Michelle, I know you don't agree with how Sophie behaves, but she works in your pre-school. If you don't sort her out, it looks like you don't care about her disrespect to some of us.'

Questions

1 St Agnes Pre-school has to have a consistent approach on equality across the team, as with any practice issue. What were the main problems with Sophie's behaviour? Why was it unacceptable?

2 If Sophie had not left voluntarily, what would have been appropriate next steps for Michelle?

3 Suppose that Michelle receives a request for a job reference for Sophie. How should she communicate her serious reservations about her ex-colleague?

Shared values and priorities

Individuals can work together as a team, or a pair, when they are enthusiastic about what they are doing and feel that the work matters. With a shared commitment to values and an understanding of priorities, individuals can pull in the same direction. Good and effective equality practice, like any other aspects of your work, depends on a continuing experience of trust in your colleagues. Trust over equality is created from experience that colleagues are:

- reliable – they follow the pattern that has been agreed in response to children's questions and comments; they do not assume words are intentionally offensive without good cause

- consistent – they offer the same standard of courtesy to parents, and kind attention to children's personal-care needs, regardless of how they may feel today, or whether their relationship with that family or child is, overall, 'easy' or 'more difficult'

- honest – they express openly in the team any doubts or uncertainties about policy and implementation; they admit if they do not know something and are ready to check out assumptions.

Taking a constructive approach

Staff teams, or groups like childminding networks, need a constructive approach to discussion and disagreement. Senior practitioners, team leaders and group facilitators need to encourage colleagues and network members to consider unchecked assumptions and reflect on their use of language. However, this interaction must be supportive, so practitioners feel they have the chance to save face and make an alternative choice. Highlighting only the 'wrong' words or phrases can seriously undermine morale within a team or any sense of group support. A serious negative consequence is that practitioners then become much more concerned with 'what we're not allowed to say' than with considering the views that underlie the words.

Some team leaders, or group facilitators, are tempted to ignore conflict over equality issues, rather than resolve matters by bringing the sources of dispute or misunderstanding out into the open. Doubts and disagreements about equality practice, just like any other aspect of the work, do not go away. They bubble under the surface; some practitioners will feel resentful, some may feel disrespected, and those emotions will affect their daily practice in one way or another.

TAKE ANOTHER PERSPECTIVE

It is well worth establishing some ground rules for team or network group discussion. The circle time rules you set with children are a good place to start. Open discussion, especially of the sensitive issues that can arise with equality practice, will be supported by:

- we listen to each other
- we don't interrupt
- we can disagree with someone else, but there are no put-downs
- we can pass, and say nothing this time, if we need to think.

Adults benefit from another ground rule:

- we are ready to give an example of what we mean.

Further options support principles of constructive discussion. Here are some examples.

- Groups that have some keen interrupters may benefit from a talking stick, or other object, even if not for entire meetings.
- An alternative is to have a ground rule (or option to invoke the rule) that everyone has to summarise what their colleague has just said before they contribute their comment.
- Speakers should take personal ownership of their comments with, 'I can't see how you reach that conclusion . . .', 'I feel uncomfortable when you say . . .' or 'I have real trouble with how you . . .'.

A ground rule that emphasises an honest use of 'I' moves discussion away from 'You're rude': a guess about the speaker's intention or an interpretation about personality. As a listener, you do not know what the speaker intended; you have direct knowledge only of your reaction.

Given a chance to reflect, rather than turn to verbal self-defence, responsible practitioners will choose to change habits of language and assumptions that underpin their thinking. Many such habits have been established when practitioners were young, including early childhood when they were not in the position to make an informed decision. The overall aim should be to help people to change – not to score points and feel self-righteous about 'winning'.

Practitioners need to consider the following positive guidelines. Team leaders and group facilitators need to keep them well in mind, as they guide discussion or outright disagreement.

- Avoid simple criticisms along the lines of 'How on earth can you say that?!' or 'That's such a racist thing to say!' It is unhelpful and unprofessional to label a colleague as 'sexist' or 'anti-Semitic'.
- Labels leave people with no room to manoeuvre and risk pushing them towards a defensive reply, rather than a willingness to think about their views. This pattern of communication between the adults can set a poor model for children. You do not want them to learn to deal with each other mainly through blunt accusations and labelling (see also page 154).
- It is a positive shift to 'What makes you say that?' rather than 'You mustn't say that!' However, colleagues and team leaders may need to explain that particular words or forms of expression are not acceptable because they are dismissive or disrespectful in tone.

It is neither appropriate professional practice nor good for team atmosphere if someone just buckles under an accusation. However uncomfortable the situation, it is important to reply.

- You might say something like, 'I take your allegation very seriously. I need to hear what you believe is "racist" about what I've just said.'
- On other occasions suitable words might be 'What is sexist about my decision over . . .?' or 'How does our handling of the situation with . . . give a poor message about inclusion?'
- General throwaway lines can be met with, 'I find that rough – to be told I'm "never on the boys' side when I sort out children's disputes". Please give me an example: how I handled a situation or a decision I've made recently.'

You need to be prepared to explain what you find problematic, or offensive, in what someone has said, or how it was said.

- Move towards honest comments such as, 'I find it hard to hear you describe Sunita as "gabbling away in her own language". Do you gabble? Do I?'
- Discussion can be provoked in a positive way with an open-ended question like, 'What does it say about us that we keep talking about "ethnic food"? Why aren't fish and chips "ethnic food"?'
- Or 'When we were talking about religion, you said that most of the families around here are "just normal C of E". Can you say a bit more; what do you mean by that?'

A team leader, or practitioner who is chairing a meeting, needs to act in a fair and firm way to ensure that explanations and examples are forthcoming.

- If you are in this role, you need phrases like, 'Brian, remember our ground rule in meetings: we say more if asked to explain. Dolan asked your reasons for saying she is "over-protective of disabled children".'
- Perhaps a colleague can give no examples to support words like 'you always/never . . .'. A team leader will need to follow up with practitioners, through personal conversation or supervision, so that they can reflect on how they feel able to make such confident pronouncements.
- It is not sufficient as explanation for one person to point to their own group identity – sex, ethnic group, personal experience of disability – as a message of, 'I just know – don't challenge me!'
- A team or discussion group leader might also judge it is time to offer direct support to a practitioner who has already been very patient. You might say, 'Jayne, I've heard Asha ask you three times not to raise your voice when you speak to her. Asha's headscarf does not reduce her ability to hear. Please do as she has asked, and talk at normal volume. Thank you.'

TAKE ANOTHER PERSPECTIVE

Consider the following comments.

1 'I don't see why we have to have all this race stuff. It's not like we're living in an inner-city area. Thank goodness, we don't have those kind of problems round here.'

2 'This inclusion business is all very well. But how many disabled children do we have to accept before we can say "enough is enough"?'

3 'You shouldn't say "mixed parentage"; it's racist. Don't look at me like that. I read it in that book you've just bought for the resource shelf.'

4 'But surely the whole point about gender equality is to even things up for the girls. I don't agree with all this "poor boys" approach now. Society is still dominated by men. Boys don't need any extra help – far from it.'

5 'We live in a multicultural society – [quieter tone of voice] we may not like it – but of course I wouldn't treat any child unkindly.'

6 'We can't have Lee all obsessed with wheels and circly things. I know you said he's autistic but how is he going to learn anything like this?'

7 'But Piya's mum wants him to speak English properly, not with this strong accent. Anyway, children don't like to stand out; nobody round here speaks Chinese – or whatever it is they talk in that family.'

8 'I can't see how this group exercise is going to involve Keith. We have to share personal experiences of discrimination. He'll be left out; what can a man possibly know about being put down?'

9 'My mother-in-law's visits are a nightmare; she won't understand how things are here in Ulster. She insists on chatting with just anybody, and says, "What's the difference?" Why can't she see? It's obvious.'

- If you were these speakers' colleague, or team leader, what could be the first steps in tackling the views expressed?

- Think about actual words you might say. Of course, when life rolls along at normal pace, sometimes you will think later, 'I should have said . . .'. Avoid being hard on yourself, but do take time to reflect and be more ready for next time.

Problem solving

The aim is to be thoughtful about what you say, to talk about what lies underneath the words and how everyone might take an approach that is likely to open up children's opportunities rather than close them down. A team that has become very aware of these issues may need to alert volunteers or parent helpers to the main lessons for daily practice.

Constructive discussion between colleagues in one-to-one conversations, or in team meetings and network groups, will give people room to manoeuvre. Nobody should be pushed into a position where they are too busy defending themselves to reflect on issues and practice. Positive approaches include taking an issue beyond the surface, as shown in the following examples.

▨ 'Yes, we agreed that the babies don't understand about Divali or Christmas. And of course it's important that we don't put them – or any of the other children for that matter – onto some kind of card-making treadmill. But equality does matter for our under-threes. I don't think we've had a proper discussion yet about what does work for them.'

▨ 'I know that Stefan and Ben have staked a claim to the bikes. But are we being fair to say that there's a problem because boys won't share? What about Alric or Terry? They seem to be willing to take their

LOOK, LISTEN, NOTE, LEARN

Responsible practitioners are reflective. They are ready to use their observation skills to understand what is really happening in the garden, during circle time or between the two children who regularly argue. Informal, alert observation and willingness to discuss practice can lead to changes that are positive for the children. Look at the following two examples of reflective practice.

1: Everyday Stories

■ This resource provides descriptions and commentaries of nursery life for babies and toddlers. Among many other ideas, you will find food for thought on equality issues as they affect under-threes – for example, in the stories of Amy and Angelina. Access this resource on www.ncb.org.uk/feature/eds/appendix.asp. The research, undertaken by Peter Elfer and Dorothy Selleck, is also reported in Anna Gillespie Edwards *Relationships and Learning: Caring for Children Birth to Three* (London: National Children's Bureau, 2002).

2: Windham Nursery School and the 'boy year'

■ This nursery team, within the Windham Partnership in south London, were faced in the year of 2003/04 with a group that was 75 per cent boys. The team recognised that such a bias towards very young males was going to affect the dynamics of the whole group. This situation was approached constructively as an impetus to reflection and possible adjustment, not as a negative problem.

■ You can read an account of what the team managed and how in *Male Agenda*, a report by Karen Faux (*Nursery World*, 2 June 2005; *Nursery World* subscribers can access this on www.nursery-world.com). The Windham team discussed use of space(s) in a flexible way, making the most of outdoor learning (already a strong value in the setting) and recognising a range of possible experiences that could support different skills, such as fine motor control and building a firm basis for early literacy.

turns. And I don't think we ought to sort this problem by taking the bikes away.'

- 'I'm not trying to get out of meeting the goals on Leanna's individual plan. My concern is the way Leanna's special time is set up at the moment. It seems to be making her feel even less part of our playgroup.'

Some discussions get lively because practitioners express different views or incompatible opinions, or disagree over how to resolve a problem facing the team or service. Some of the problems that arise in equality practice are complex and there is no way through them that avoids every difficulty. This kind of problem is called a dilemma and can feel impossible because, whatever option you choose, there will be at least some negative consequences.

The problem-solving approach is to have a full discussion with involved colleagues. Individual childminders can draw on the support and listening ear of an adviser or network co-ordinator. You can even use the aid of a paper and pencil, and talk yourself through the options. Work through the following points.

1. What are my main options in dealing with this situation? Sometimes there will be two main routes.

2. Take each route in turn and explore the most likely consequences if you take this route. What is the upside of taking this route? Pull out the advantages, as well as what you anticipate could be the drawbacks.

3. Now follow the same process with the other option(s). Lay out all the details. It will not take ages, so long as you keep on task and do not get distracted into 'ah, buts' or how you may feel if . . .

4. Look carefully at the options, realising that dodging any choice is not an option. Which option most supports your key values for equality? If you are forced into a choice over what feel like competing equality values, then what are your priorities?

5. Now reflect on how you will put that option into practice. What will you, and colleagues if you have them, need to say and do? How will you deal with your feelings of unease or your desire to avoid unpleasantness?

SCENARIO

In a recent team meeting, Daniel and his team at Falcon Square after-school club have become more aware of the pressures on the children from their families. Two examples have arisen lately through children's conversations.

1. Lucy has developed a close friendship with Selena. They spend a great deal of time together at the club and during the school day.

Lucy has been invited to play at Selena's house and wants to go, but Lucy's parents find every excuse to refuse each invitation. There seems to be no reason except that Selena's family origins are Indian-Caribbean. Lucy's 'white' English parents have been heard making racist remarks when they think they are out of earshot of the staff.

2 Shamima is a popular girl at the club. She gets on well with many of the other children and is often asked to birthday parties or to come for tea. The staff recently overheard a conversation between parents about, 'There's no point asking Shamima to birthday parties. She never comes and her parents can't even be bothered to answer invitations.' Daniel has worked out that Shamima's parents respond only to invitations from other Muslim households.

Some of the club team feel Lucy's and Shamima's parents are equally rejecting and that Daniel should speak with both families. Other practitioners feel that the religious beliefs of Shamima's parents make their behaviour more acceptable. But what then of children who feel hurt because they regard themselves as Shamima's friend at school and club? The whole team struggles with the idea of whether rejection can ever be justified. They also face issues around how they should draw the boundary between what happens in the club and parents' personal decisions about family life.

Questions

1 **What are the main issues raised here? Practitioners in the Falcon Square team are taking different perspectives – what are these?**

2 **Is this a situation in which practitioners have a positive role to play and, if so, what might that be? What do you think Daniel should do?**

Boys and girls at play

Observation of children in early years settings or schools shows some differences between the preferred play of boys and girls. Boys, on average, engage in more rough and tumble than girls, and their games more often develop an element of play fighting. The concerned reaction of mainly female staff teams has led to attempts to redirect the boys' energy into other forms of play and sometimes to ban certain games. Other possibilities tend now to be discussed, as in the following examples.

- A proper consideration of whether the boys' games really are too 'noisy' or 'rough'. Can practitioners step aside from an outright ban and talk over with the boys where or when they play the games?

- Some ground rules may be appropriate, perhaps that there is no wrestling in the home corner or superhero pretend play happens out in the garden, rather than inside, and that sticks are not used as weapons.

- How far can you let play fighting go before you intervene? Practitioners are understandably concerned about children getting hurt. However, few play fights appear to turn into genuine aggressive attacks and children, girls as well as boys, seem well able to tell the difference. Boys seem to use physical rough and tumble as one way to form and sustain friendships.

TAKE ANOTHER PERSPECTIVE

There is now a more open professional debate about what can happen to children, boys in particular, when their pretend play is treated as a behaviour problem. How far have you considered these issues in your own practice (early years, the school playground or out-of-school care)?

- Do you operate a weapons ban? Do you extend it to any kind of superhero and goody/baddy play? Is the concern linked with what adults call 'rough play'?

- What are the genuine consequences of such a ban – especially if nobody is having a proper conversation with the children?

- What do you think so engages children about play around heroism or fighting the baddies?

- Practitioners are keen to use this engagement when sharing stories about legends and some moral tales behind celebrations. It is not surprising that children also direct this enthusiasm into their active play.

If you are thinking about making a change in your practice, then it would be useful to read further. Here are some suggestions.

- Paley, Vivian Gussin (1984) *Boys and Girls: Superheroes in the Doll Corner*. Chicago: University of Chicago Press.

- Holland, Penny (2003) *We Don't Play With Guns Here: War, Weapon and Superhero Play in the Early Years*. Maidenhead: Open University Press.

- You will find summaries in my books, *Understanding Children's Play* (2001) Cheltenham: Nelson Thornes, and *Understanding Child Development: Linking Theory and Practice* (2005) London: Hodder Arnold.

Teams develop resources offering involvement for all children

Use these ideas to pull out the main themes and, if possible, talk with a local team that has rethought its strategy. Bear in mind that practitioners do more than just lift the 'weapons play' ban:

- they observe the themes and actions in pretend play with an open mind
- they continue to deal constructively with genuine aggression.

DIVERSITY IN THE TEAM

The early years profession is far from being a mirror image of the population at large. Male early years practitioners are the most striking overall minority. Some settings in ethnically diverse neighbourhoods nevertheless have a mainly all-'white' team, although some teams are far more diverse. Steady emphasis on inclusion of children with disabilities has raised the possibility that the skills of disabled adults are probably under-used.

Recruiting and supporting practitioners

Equality issues can be addressed through reflection on how and where you place a job advertisement. You can word an advertisement to indicate an active welcome for applications from specified groups. It is a legitimate aim to create a more diverse pool from which to choose; however, applicants from particular groups must not then get favourable treatment within the shortlisting and interview processes. The only exception is on the basis of a genuine occupational qualification (see page 29). Think about your whole team when you consider under-representation. Consultations with children have shown that they think food is very important and they really value their outdoor space. From the children's perspective, the cook and the gardener are important people, as is the person who does important 'adult work' in the office.

Getting new team members is only part of the process; do you hold on to them?

- If you tend to lose your minority ethnic team members, what is going awry? Are there unchallenged assumptions or prejudiced attitudes within the team? Did a practitioner feel unsupported by colleagues when faced with parents who were racially abusive?

- Men in early years can share the experiences of females in predominantly male professions. Have two male practitioners left because they were fed up with being required to prove men could work safely in childcare, while tolerating sexist 'jokes' from female colleagues?

- Disabled colleagues might appreciate relevant support but will be irritated by assumptions that they need full-time special treatment. A colleague who is dyslexic should not be excused all report writing, but he or she needs to feel able to ask a colleague to look through a written draft. A colleague in a wheelchair will be able to undertake some physical games with the children, but perhaps not all.

It is important to tackle under-representation so that a team, or the local service as a whole, is a more accurate reflection of society. But then each member of staff or practitioner in a local service needs to feel properly included and not pushed into being a full-time representative of a grouping that is only part of their individuality. A disabled colleague will have opinions about many issues, not only disability. A male practitioner should not forever have to give the 'man's point of view'.

If you want to find out more:

- Lane, Jane (2006) *Action for Racial Equality in the Early Years*. London: National Children's Bureau.

- www.disability.gov.uk/dda/index.html.

- www.eoc.org.uk/EOCeng/EOCcs/Advice/guidelines.asp.

❖ www.legalservices.gov.uk. Download leaflets on equality and discrimination.

Using skills appropriately

There will always be some level of diversity within a team, even if personal identity by ethnic group membership appears to offer limited variety. One aspect to equality and diversity in the team arises from how you use individuals' knowledge and skills.

TAKE ANOTHER PERSPECTIVE

Practitioners with different professional and personal backgrounds can bring a fresh perspective, but this diversity needs to be coordinated effectively. It is not good practice if individuals are trapped inside a specialism or typecast because of particular skill or experience. Please consider the following examples.

▨ To what extent do you feel the way of organising is appropriate?

▨ If the use of the practitioner's skills is inappropriate, how would you explain your reservations to the team leader or other practitioners?

▨ What might be a more suitable use of this practitioner's talents?

1 Sarah's husband works for a Japanese firm and Sarah has joined him on two trips to Japan. Several Japanese families are living locally in company houses and have sent their children to the playgroup. The playgroup leader has asked Sarah to be key person for these children.

2 Alistair has a Scottish father and English mother. He has started to learn Gaelic and is keen on storytelling. Everybody else in the childminding network is monolingual. Alistair would like to offer some storytelling and songs in Gaelic for the crèche that supports network meetings.

3 Ayesha's family came from Trinidad. She is the only 'black' member of staff in the private nursery, which is in a relatively diverse neighbourhood. Ayesha has become aware that her room colleague seems to expect her to deal with the three 'black' parents, none of whom is of Caribbean origin.

4 Pete is the only practitioner in his community nursery with any experience of working with deaf children. The manager asks Pete if he will teach two colleagues basic signing and draw up a play programme for a profoundly deaf child who is about to join the nursery.

5 Nina spent several years in a city early years centre and has now moved to work in a nursery class serving a rural, mainly 'white'

locality. Two colleagues suggest in a team meeting that, 'Nina should lead us on the multicultural celebrations, because she's done all that stuff in her old job.'

6   Greg is a talented woodworker and coaches the local under-11s football team. The leader of his holiday play scheme asks Greg to take responsibility for both of these activities during the summer programme. The same request has been made for the past two years.

Equal status for team members

Diversity may arise within a team because of different professional backgrounds or job roles. Teamwork and equality practice can be undermined if a differential status has been allowed to develop between staff members. Specialist support workers, often employed for individual disabled children, need to feel and to be treated as full colleagues in a team. Practitioners in these vital roles are sometimes working with 'assistant' titles, such as Support Learning Assistant or Specialist Teaching Assistant. Titles matter less than equality of status and professional respect, but the word can be symbolic. SLAs or STAs will feel treated as lowly assistants if they are not invited to full team meetings. The wording and reality of their job descriptions should stress their work as crucial to ensure inclusion of a child within the nursery or school setting. The result can be non-inclusive if the emphasis is more on one-to-one support of a child, with the sense that child and assistant are a unit separate from everyone else.

In schools, it is very often a different group of people, not teachers, who take responsibility for break and lunchtimes in the playground, or inside on wet-weather days.

- The supervisors, or whatever their title may be, need to be fully involved in developing and reviewing a whole-school behaviour policy.
- Children whose disabilities affect their behaviour will be out in the playground, not necessarily accompanied by a support practitioner. Playground supervisors need to be fully informed about current strategies to support such children. They also need to know about practical issues of continence for some children, or emergency medication.

Men in childcare and early education

Women far outnumber men on the staff of early years settings, primary school teams, out-of-school services and in the childminding service. It is estimated that the early years childcare workforce is about 98 per cent female. When multidisciplinary centres draw their staff from a wide range of professions, they tend to have more male staff. Out-of-school settings

SCENARIO

The STAs at Clearwater Primary School have been very encouraged by the behaviour of Philip, the new head teacher. His first step was to welcome the STAs into the main staff room. The previous head had allocated them a small room that doubled as a place for wet coats and umbrellas. The group of practitioners had given themselves the ironic name of the Cloakroom Team.

Some of the STAs double as lunchtime supervisors, but this role is also covered by additional part-time staff. Philip begins to address what will be needed, in terms of pay or organisation of hours, to enable all practitioners to attend full staff meetings on a regular basis.

Under the previous head, non-teaching staff had tried and failed to get invited to staff meetings about the revised school behaviour policy. The head had brushed aside their concern that lunchtime supervisors were on the front line of dealing with challenging behaviour. There had also been a panic when nobody had informed the supervisory staff about a child with epilepsy. A dangerous situation had been avoided only because one lunchtime supervisor had a daughter prone to seizures and calmly took control. The final indignity had been when the previous head had refused to run off a copy of the school's inspection report for the Cloakroom Team. When challenged, she said, 'Official documents are for proper staff.'

Questions

1 **For what reasons was the previous head's approach unacceptable? What might have been her justification for the two-tier staff system?**

2 **Entrenched differences in status can be hard to challenge and shift. What else could the Cloakroom Team have done, if the problem had not been resolved by the change in head teacher?**

and playwork provision like adventure playgrounds tend to have relatively more men, because of their different professional tradition and links with youth work. Primary schools have more men, as teachers and classroom assistants, but the majority of staff teams are still female.

The predominance of women in work with young children is mainly explained by strong social attitudes that care and early education of young children is 'naturally' a female occupation. This bias over status is linked with a history of low pay and limited career prospects, although this situation has improved in recent decades. The pressure in the UK of the early twenty-first century to expand childcare provision has increased efforts to recruit and train more practitioners in total, including attracting more men into this career path.

Male and female team members

Children and adults come in two sexes and all children need to be able to relate positively to each sex. A mixed staff group, or a mainly female group supplemented by regular male volunteers, can be the most effective way of opening up possibilities for all the children and gently challenging the stereotypes. Any mixed team, or childminder couples, should be aware of how daily tasks are shared or delegated.

▩ Boys and girls need to observe female practitioners who make decisions within a mixed-sex team or childminder couples. Females need, *sometimes* (not non-stop!), to show physical confidence and willingness to take a risk or have an adventure.

▩ A balanced approach does not, of course, mean that Jof must always take the cooking activity and Sian leads lively ball games. Your aim, in using the opportunities of a mixed team, is to show children that men and women are well-rounded individuals.

▩ Sian can show enthusiasm about numbers or scientific investigation, and that she is willing to learn from all the children. Jof can be a great builder of dens with the children. But he also shows his caring side when a child is hurt or wants to confide how 'someone has been so horrid to me'.

▩ Practitioners of both sexes, in a centre team or within the family home as jointly registered childminders, can shown children how men and women can listen, learn from one another and defer to each other's opinion, without any implication that one sex is usually right and the other wrong.

Male colleagues should cover the same range of responsibilities as the female team members. Male practitioners should not be expected to take over the physically more active boys, nor to be the main one to set and hold to boundaries. Some individual boys may respond better to a male figure, so flexing to that observation could be an appropriate response in a team or for choices between two childminders. The male practitioner may be able to show this child that maleness can co-exist with respect for others and especially for females. A team will have to deal sensitively with any parent who homes in on one or two male practitioners, with the expectation that they will discipline less cooperative children.

Behaviour and conversation

Female practitioners must be ready to address their own assumptions and attitudes about males as colleagues and male carers in the home. Theory and practice still do not always match over gender equality. I have heard early years practitioners complain about the lack of men in the profession.

Then on another occasion the very same people make snide remarks about a male carer such as, 'He'll make someone a lovely wife one day.' Male childminders sometimes feel treated as an oddity, and not just by people outside the childcare profession. They recognise that male child carers of any kind are in the minority, but fairly resent having to deal with assumptions that they are marking time until they find a 'proper job'.

An existing team has to make male practitioners or volunteers welcome, recognising that some issues will need to be discussed. It is not only about 'Are we happy to share the same set of toilets?', although that can be a big issue for some practitioners. It is a considered balance between putting Steve at his ease as a new colleague and acknowledging honestly the experience of any person joining a profession filled mainly by the opposite sex.

Practitioners need to be aware of unspoken assumptions and expectations on the basis of gender. Team leaders and group facilitators will sometimes have to address situations like those outlined in the following examples.

- Colleagues should listen to male colleagues as much as to other team members. But do not ask or expect Steve to speak up on a regular basis, as a man, more than a female colleague. If Steve takes a while to warm up in a group discussion, he is not necessarily any more a 'shy person' than quietly-spoken Bella, who is sitting next to him.

- If a male colleague appears to dominate discussion, then the imbalance should be handled in the same way as with any more outspoken team member. A team leader or group facilitator needs to ensure female practitioners do not defer to a male, then complain later that he 'always takes over the discussion'.

- A male colleague may be able to give a fresh perspective, because he is a man, but he should not be expected to represent the whole male sex. A colleague of a different ethnic group from the rest of the team should not be pushed into this 'expert' role – by the same token, a male practitioner should not be required to explain the behaviour of other men.

- Be aware of staff-room or coffee-time conversation. A previously all-female group may have developed bad habits of complaining about men in general. It is not fair behaviour to make highly critical remarks about men and then say to a male colleague 'But you're different' or keep saying, 'Present company excluded'. It would be unacceptable if Steve were a 'black' colleague, so it is not acceptable because he is a man.

- If there is more than one male practitioner in a team or a network group, let them talk together without a fuss. Some female practitioners react with 'Now they're ganging up', when they would not say the same about two female colleagues.

TAKE ANOTHER PERSPECTIVE

Females in predominantly male occupations report the same kind of frustrating experiences as those highlighted in the examples in this section. They are also aware, like male practitioners in early years, that their standards of work and behaviour are judged not just on a personal level, but also as an interpretation of the impact of their sex. In male-dominated professions or organisations, it is far too easy that Josie's outburst is interpreted by a group stereotype: 'Typical woman, they get all emotional!' On the other hand, Joe's equally impassioned rant is seen as the behaviour of an individual: 'That's just Joe sounding off again.'

This dynamic around a minority is unjust, but fairness will never be improved until teams recognise what is happening. Females sometimes resist acknowledging the reality: that this pattern is also imposed by women on men in at least some early years, school and out-of-school services.

Support groups

Anyone in the minority in a profession can benefit from an appropriate professional network, and men in childcare have developed groups for mutual

SCENARIO

Liz and her deputy, Jonathon, have worked hard to build a supportive atmosphere within the team at Crest Road Early Years Centre. Recently they have introduced the technique of mirroring to team and room meetings, as a means of building direct understanding of 'what it feels like to me'.

Darren feels that Maddie, a relatively new team member, does not fully trust his skills with the babies. He has given her time to settle and used words to reassure her, saying, 'No, it's fine, thanks. I'll change Razia', when she presses help on him. In a room meeting supported by Liz, Darren first asks Maddie, 'Can I show you what I mean?' Then he stands very close, leans over and starts to offer advice, mirroring what Maddie does to him. The demonstration is brief and Darren moves back immediately to his seat. Liz helps the conversation that follows.

Finding out more
The idea of mirroring is described by Bill Rogers as part of guiding school-age children towards more positive patterns of behaviour. See, for example, Rogers, Bill (ed.) (2004) *How to Manage Challenging Behaviour.* London: Paul Chapman Publishing.

support. Local 'men in childcare' networks have developed, as well as some drop-in groups specifically for male childminders. There is a parallel with facilities to support fathers who are the primary family carer (see page 237).

Women in traditionally male-dominated professions have found value in similar formal or informal contacts. There have also been supportive networks for professionals whose family origins are from minority ethnic groups. Of course, sessions should not become whingeing shops, but individuals who are in a significant minority, for whatever reason, welcome the opportunity to air ideas and get some perspective. There is reassurance in hearing, 'It's not just you who gets . . .'. The aim is that there comes a time when such support is not needed because practitioners, whatever their group identity, feel fully included.

Genuine child protection

Increased awareness of child abuse has complicated the issues around male practitioners. Some teams and local authorities have developed rules limiting the care responsibilities of male practitioners. When challenged, some teams or advisers have resolved the issue by applying these inappropriate rules to all practitioners. Some decision-makers have been resistant, although not openly, to employing men in childcare at all. Such an approach is ineffective for child protection, discriminatory towards men and the no-touch policies are potentially damaging for young children (see also page 153).

A major misunderstanding arises from the inaccurate claim that 'most abusers are male'. Men predominate in sexual abuse but not in physical abuse, neglect or the emotional abuse of children. Some sexual abuse is also perpetrated by females. Women can be cruel to children and neglectful of their needs, so banning men is no way to deal with child protection in early years. All settings need clear procedures for taking on paid employees and volunteers, and a working atmosphere in which children, parents and practitioners feel able to raise any concerns.

If you want to find out more:

‡ Lindon, Jennie (2003) *Child Protection*. London: Hodder & Stoughton.

‡ Owen, Charlie (2003) *Men's work: Changing the Gender Mix of the Childcare and Early Years Workforce*. London: Policy Paper 6, Daycare Trust.

‡ Rolfe, Heather (2005) *Men in Childcare*. Occupational Segregation Working Paper, Series No 35, Equal Opportunities Commission www.eoc.org.uk.

SCENARIO

At Falcon Square after-school club, Daniel, the team leader, and five-year-old Lucy are sitting on a garden bench when she asks, 'What's a perv?' Daniel replies, 'I'll answer your question, Lucy. But first can you tell me what made you ask?' Lucy says willingly, 'My grandad says that blokes must be pervs if they want to work with little children.'

Daniel is faced with a tricky situation, but decides that Lucy's question deserves an answer. He replies, 'Well, that word is used for people who want to hurt children. I want to be here with you all because I really enjoy working in a club. Maybe I need to have a chat with your mum and dad. I'm sad to think that anyone in your family might be worried.'

Daniel decides that he needs to approach Lucy's parents about the conversation and will raise the issue with the rest of the team to let them all know how he handled the situation.

Questions

1 **Have you faced a similar situation?**

2 **Might there be any further concerns when Daniel explains the incident to his colleagues?**

PROFESSIONAL BEHAVIOUR AND SOCIAL LEARNING

Everyone brings to adulthood the results of learning within their own childhood. Professionalism is about addressing when you need to be flexible in your own habits of language and behaviour, and also in understanding those of your colleagues. You cannot know everything, nor can you manage daily professional life, frozen in anxiety about unintentionally giving offence. Your responsibility is to learn more, within the knowledge that many social and cultural traditions change over time. Similar issues are raised in the context of partnership on page 233.

Patterns of communication

Broad patterns of verbal and non-verbal communication are laid down in childhood, as children learn their family way. Individual families are affected by the ethnic group and cultural background of the adults, but there is usually a great deal of variation within any group. In open discussion, individuals may fairly counter with, 'We never did that in my family.' Any examples in this section, or other parts of the book, are possibilities and not firm predictions.

Same language – different use of words

You and your colleague can both be fluent in one language, yet use the same words to convey a different meaning. I was initially taken aback by a friend from Guyana (one of the mainland South American Caribbean countries). My friend would remark, 'You lie!' when I said something that surprised her. It took me more than one uneasy conversation to realise she was not suggesting what I said was untrue. Her words were the equivalent of 'You're kidding me!' or 'You don't say!' However, I had other friends whose country of origin was Guyana who did not use that phrase. There are many different ethnic and cultural traditions in Guyana and I never worked out whether my friend's phrase arose from her cultural group. It could have been exclusive to her own family, as indeed I use phrases that are particular to my own family upbringing.

LOOK, LISTEN, NOTE, LEARN

Collect examples of use of words that could cause misunderstanding if colleagues lack the confidence to check out meaning. Here are some ideas to start you off.

- English usage in much of the UK, especially by females, includes heavy use of 'sorry'. This word in context often means, 'Excuse me' or 'What a rotten thing to happen to you', rather than apologising for something that is your direct responsibility or fault.

- In the UK, the phrase, 'Would you like to lay the table for snack time?' is often a request, not an open question. I was unaware of this subtle usage until a practitioner, fluent in English and who came originally from Thailand, explained the situation in a group discussion. She had worked out, by her colleagues' reaction on several occasions that they were not expecting her to say, 'No, actually, I'm busy doing . . .'.

- Courtesy operates in different ways around the world and some cultural traditions avoid saying 'No' to a request, since this reaction is rude. The word, 'Yes' then means 'I've heard what you said' and not necessarily, 'I agree' or 'I'll do what you ask.'

Questions

1. What other examples have you encountered – in your work, personal life or on holiday in countries where you are less familiar with traditions?

2. What about in discussion with colleagues or fellow students? Bear in mind that no cultural pattern or habit is better or worse; you are exploring differences.

On the other hand, I have experienced many examples of the phrase used in Scotland, 'Where do you stay?', which means 'Where is your home?' English speakers based in England launch into a confused conversation about hotel bookings, because English-English tends to be, 'I'm staying in the Acacia B&B.' On reflection, I think the Scottish meaning for 'stay' is more logical.

Body language

Showing the soles of your feet, with or without shoes, is considered rude behaviour in several countries located, from the European perspective, in the Middle East and Far East. Beckoning gestures using fingers or whole hands are tricky, because around the world some gestures are definitely just for using with children or even pets, and are not at all polite if used between adults. Some colleagues, raised in these cultures, may be as prone to say 'But isn't it obvious?' as people raised in the UK, who take their own experience as the template for 'normal'. Colleagues should all be generous with each other, allowing that the other person did not intend to offend – unless there are clear indications that someone set out deliberately to be disrespectful or offensive.

There are broad cultural differences over volume, expressiveness in tone and supporting gestures. Some, not all, children and adults raised in parts of the African continent and the Caribbean have a more forthright style of delivery, with generous arm and hand gestures. Some colleagues will have been raised in a social or cultural group where children were taught to moderate their volume and keep gestures to a minimum. Neither is right or wrong; they are just different.

TAKE ANOTHER PERSPECTIVE

Good professional practice is even-handed on equality, and practitioners need to recognise how unfamiliar styles can provoke interpretations that are inaccurate.

I was part of a very productive discussion in which some practitioners expressed their reasonable frustration that it was not all right to be judged as 'loud' or even 'aggressive' for a more lively style. However, the part of the group (me included) who were taught to control their gestures started to share experiences from early school days. We recalled being told, 'Don't wave your hands around like that!' and even being made to sit on our hands to prevent fidgeting.

▪ In a colleague group, where everyone is now a fellow grown-up, it is fair to seek understanding and compromise that leaves each individual respected for their communication style and creates a comfort zone for everyone.

- A useful guideline is to be ready to check, using phrases such as 'I think I may be getting the wrong idea here. Are you telling me that . . .?' Be willing with a colleague, or in partnership with parents, to say, 'I'm afraid that I've offended you. But I really don't know what I've done.'

- You can encourage in an open way with, 'Please tell me what has happened between us.' Your words, backed up with body language, need to communicate courteously that you can see the result, but you do not understand the cause.

If you want to find out more:

You will bring up a lot of links by Googling 'cultural differences', although much is related to business and diplomacy. I found some useful material on www.cps.gov.uk/publications/docs/visitrep02.pdf.

10 Partnership with parents and families

Early years, school and out-of-school practitioners need to aim for a friendly relationship with parents, but it is still a professional relationship. The overall aim of a friendly, working partnership fits well with equality practice. You have a continuing obligation to deal with all the parents in an even-handed way. There will be differences between yourself and individual parents, and some sources of diversity may feel like a wide gap. Professional practice is to recognise and deal with feelings of unease or confusion that may block partnership. One way to dissolve the blocks will be to extend your own knowledge and be willing to discuss issues.

> **The main sections of this chapter cover:**
>
> ✴ **first impressions**
>
> ✴ **diversity within family life**
>
> ✴ **continuing partnership.**

FIRST IMPRESSIONS

All early years, school and playwork practitioners need to consider how they welcome prospective users of the service. The early contacts and first impressions are important and these are only partly created through communication between the adults. Good practice in creating an inclusive environment for children will show positive attitudes to parents through resources and events on the day they first visit.

Friendly communication supports partnership

Welcome and open communication

Good partnership is led through communication. From the beginning of your working relationship it is important to show that you would genuinely like to get to know families and their children. You develop familiarity with each other over time. Of course, you are not obligated to find out everything in the first meeting. Continued partnership is supported by opportunities for relaxed conversation, just chatting.

Families will realise that you are genuinely interested in them and their children without wishing to interfere in family life. Be prepared to share some personal information in return. If you are expressing an interest in a parent's country of origin, it is perfectly reasonable that they ask, and you answer, similar questions about where you spent your childhood. If any conversations raise issues of boundaries between professional and personal life, be prepared to reflect on how to draw limits, and discuss these with colleagues or an adviser.

There will always be some sources of diversity within practitioner and parent groups, and some of those sources of group identity may not be shared. For example, it is very often the case that an entire nursery team is female; yet some of the parents closely involved with their children's nursery life will be fathers. In neighbourhoods with significant language diversity, it is likely that some languages will be spoken by some parents but by none of the staff team. You do not have to share specific sources of personal identity in order to make friendly contact.

Considerate decisions may be made about personal ways to make a parent or family feel welcome and to ease communication.

- More group settings now are aware of being actively father-friendly, and that means more than sticking up one picture of a man holding a baby.

- Some parents will have children with disabilities; some parents will themselves have a disability. Good practice in partnership responds to the individuality of families and their needs. But parents of disabled children will not want a specialist version of partnership that treats them as different in every way.

- Perhaps no practitioner in a team has any personal experience of family life as Travellers or Gypsies, but lack of knowledge should not be a block; there are many resources on which you can draw (see page 67).

Temporary, closer partnerships within a group setting should not act in an exclusive way. Any specialist group sessions, or other form of contact, should work to help parents feel more included in the setting or service.

You do not want special initiatives to highlight a set of parents as permanently different, or appearing more favoured, in comparison with other parents. Adults can be as prone to object, 'It's not fair; they're getting more than us!' as their young children.

Of course, it would be unacceptable for practitioners to develop a closer, or warmer, partnership on the basis of any kind of group identity of practitioner, parent or other family carer (see the scenario on page 206). It is inevitable that you will feel more comfortable with some individual parents, and they with you. But you have a responsibility to judge priorities in your work in a professional way.

- Practitioners should not spend more time with individual parents, simply because they are 'people like me' – whatever the basis for this sense of fellow-feeling.
- If you work in a diverse neighbourhood, then there will be parents with whom you do not share the same ethnic identity, cultural background, language or faith. It would be poor practice for anyone to develop a different kind of relationship with parents who happen to share their own cultural background or faith.

Early visits and settling-in time

Many group settings have a pattern for contact between parents and practitioners before a child's first official day. Childminders often offer a family-home version of much of the following.

- An invitation for parents, probably with their children, to visit before taking up the offer of a place. Some nurseries offer open evenings or a tea party for 'new parents'. I would suggest rethinking this phrase, if you use it. Most parents are only 'new' to your service, they are almost certainly not new to parenting or family life.
- Materials that you show to explain about your service need to be accessible for anyone. Even if you and a parent share a fluent language, it is still more effective to have visual as well as written material to show 'what goes on here'.
- It is appropriate partnership practice with parents who already to use your service that you check whether they are happy for photos showing their children to be part of any brochure, album or illustrated ring-binder file that is available to legitimate visitors.

Early contact can be used appropriately to consider your resources. You might ask, 'I would really like to add to my book shelf. Could you tell me about your family language? I'd like to find suitable dual-language books.' This positive approach is different from implying to parents that their arrival will require immediate purchases with a reluctant comment like, 'Now I'll be Sadaf's childminder, I suppose I'd better get some special books.' In a similar way, you are not buying jigsaws featuring disabled children just because Tyrone has joined your setting, and he had one leg amputated as a result of damage in a car accident. In some cases, though, Tyrone's arrival may make a team aware of a significant gap in resources. However, the jigsaws are for everyone, as are any dual-language books.

Sharing the care of children

Friendly partnership with parents is crucial if you are to take good care of their children. Many of the practical points explored in Chapter 6 need to emerge through open communication with parents and other family carers from the very beginning. Babies and very young children will not be able to tell you about family diet or important issues over clothing or hygiene. Even slightly older children, with spoken language, may be uneasy about appearing to disagree with what a practitioner is about to do with or for them.

You need to create an atmosphere that leads parents to feel confident you really want to know and understand. Your first contacts with any individual parent should be a time when you are as concerned to hear about their child as you are to explain the way you work in your childminding practice, nursery or after-school club. Partnership needs to recognise situations that call for more specific questions. It is important to be honest if you do not know what a child is likely to need, or if you do not understand what a parent has just told you about care routines. Do not be uneasy about starting another conversation with, 'I'm really not sure what makes meat halal. And if we can't find the right kind of butcher, what would you rather we did?' It is far better that you struggle with mild awkwardness now than take an option that will create avoidable annoyance to this family – or significant embarrassment for you, or your colleagues, in the future.

Parents of children with a disability have many concerns and questions in common with all families: Will their child be safe and genuinely liked by staff? Will he make friends? What will happen if she wets herself? However, if children have a disability, then it is professional to have a proper discussion around some special issues.

- You need to know about this child's individual needs. It does not matter if you have previously worked with children with this disability or health condition. You still have to understand fully how Shireen's epilepsy affects her or the consequences of hemiplegia for Leroy.
- Approach the conversation with honesty, not pretending that the child is 'just like all the others' but avoiding a focus on 'difficulties'. It

is the difference between the courteous question, 'What should I know about Monica's diet?' and the blunt statement, 'I see Monica's diabetic; I suppose there'll be problems about food.' The second phrase is as unacceptable as saying to Omar's parents, 'This business about Ramadan; it's bound to be difficult with the fasting.'

- You need to understand fully about health issues: any regular medication; whether children are vulnerable to infection; how to recognise an emergency for this child and what to do.

- A child's key person in a nursery will lead the care, but all the information must be shared effectively with anyone else who could come into contact with the child. The same applies to schools and breaktime staff. What happens if Rashida has a serious asthma attack and the playground supervisors have no idea what to do?

Families with disabled children come from the full variety of ethnic groups and cultural backgrounds. Awareness of these issues needs to co-exist with equality focused on disability. Practitioners need to be aware of unchecked assumptions. For instance, Rashida's extended family lives a hundred miles away and her mother copes without family back-up. Leroy's mother is a lone parent yet she has an active support network of family and friends. Work with children with disabilities within autistic spectrum disorder often aims to help them manage more eye contact. However, within some cultures, children are not encouraged to engage in significant eye contact with adults because it is judged to be impolite staring.

You might be thinking over whether it will be sensible to prepare the children already in your home or group for the child's arrival. Perhaps a child's disability is likely to lead to comments and questions from other children. It is dishonest to pretend that there is nothing unusual about Leroy. He needs to use a wheelchair for anything more than short walks and may be the first child with a visible physical disability to join the nursery. You could discuss briefly with Leroy's mother what you plan to say.

It is possible that parents will not find out that their child has a specific disability until he or she has spent some time in nursery or with a childminder. Some parents may have been anxious for many months about their child's development or pattern of behaviour. But they have been told that their child will 'catch up', 'grow out of it' or that there is nothing wrong and they are worrying unnecessarily. Such parents may be relieved that their concerns have been supported and now perhaps someone will help. Other parents may have been unaware and are shocked to be told, however carefully, that all is not well with their child. A well-established partnership with the family will ease this sensitive situation.

Cultural diversity in names

For everyone, a name is part of your personal identity. It can feel anything from mildly discourteous to downright offensive if people make little effort to say your name properly, or persist in versions that you do not want to be called. Children deserve full attention and effort to say their name correctly. Partnership with parents is a vital route, especially with younger children who are less likely to say, 'Why do you keep calling me Steven?' and to stress, 'It's Se-jee-ven.'

Many of the practical issues that arise over names from a range of different cultural traditions are covered by general good practice. However, these issues may not be highlighted until you encounter names unfamiliar to you.

  * It is good practice to ensure that you spell and say correctly the names of all the children and their parents. The guideline of 'If in doubt, ask' sums up courteous behaviour applicable to partnership with every family.

  * If a personal or family name is unfamiliar to you, and initially you find it hard to say, then make yourself a reminder note on how to pronounce it correctly. Children themselves are often happy to drill you in practice.

  * In many cultures there are some names that can be given either to boys or girls. The sex of babies and toddlers is not always obvious. If you are in any doubt about names unfamiliar to you, then find out politely.

  * Ensure that you write down the names of both parents, if there are two in the family. UK families do not necessarily all share the same surname, even when parents are married to each other.

The European system of naming is far from universal. Most cultural traditions give names in addition to a single personal name. But many do not include the idea that all members of a family will share one common name – the European 'surname'. Not everyone, by any means, places the personal name first. So you need to check with parents the name by which you should address a child. Some families describe this as the 'calling name'. Here are some examples but, as you might guess, there is considerable diversity within as well as between cultural traditions.

  * Chinese naming systems have traditionally put the shared family name first, a generation name may follow and then a personal name. So, if Shek Gai Wai is about to join your home as a childminder, the most likely situation is that Shek is her family name, Gai indicates that she is a child in the family and Wai is her personal name. Vietnamese families follow a similar pattern.

- Hindu families place the personal name first, followed by another name such as bhai (brother) or devi (goddess). When children have a name that could be given to a boy or a girl, the second name will specify their sex. For instance Anu Kumar (prince) Sharma is a boy, whereas Anu Kumari (princess) Patel is a girl. The last name for Hindu families is a shared family name that indicates the family's traditional status and occupation. This system led to many people having the same last name and Hindu practice is to record the father's or husband's name for extra identification.

- Sikh tradition broke with Hinduism and with the system that last names reflect the caste system. Devout Sikh families will still not use a last name. Children have a personal name, usually followed by Kaur (princess) for a girl and Singh (lion) for a boy. Surinder Kaur may also have a last name, by which all the family is known. Otherwise, Surinder's father should be called Mr Singh and her mother Mrs Kaur.

- Muslim boys are often given a personal and a religious name (one of the names of Allah). The religious name often, but not always, comes first and adult men would usually be addressed by both names. Children are called by the personal name; it would be offensive to use only a boy's religious name as his calling name. So Muhammad Hamid Sheikh has a religious first name, a personal second and Sheikh is the family name. Girls are not given a religious name, so Hamid's sister is Razia Sheikh.

Families from a variety of backgrounds may choose to change the order of names, or agree on a shared family name, out of consideration for confused practitioners or to make daily life more straightforward in the UK. Families who follow Islam do not traditionally have a shared family name. But in the UK many Muslim families use hereditary names denoting social position or religious grouping, or use the father's personal name as a surname.

Names matter

Practitioners should follow the child's and parents' wishes over how a child is known, if this name is not his or her full first name. Some children prefer to be called by a shortened version of their name, or they have more than one personal name and choose to be known by the second one. Certainly, practitioners should never shorten or change a child's name (or a colleague's for that matter) to avoid the small amount of effort needed to learn the proper name.

Be sensitive in your first conversations with a family. If a family has previously experienced discourtesy about how to say or spell their name, they may tolerate simplification for an easy life. Sometimes parents want to avoid embarrassing a practitioner who has made the mistake more than once in this conversation. You can acknowledge that a name is unfamiliar to you with comments like, 'Can I make sure that I am saying your daughter's name correctly?' Avoid any suggestion that a name is 'odd'. Neither is a child's name 'difficult'; you are finding it hard to say because of unfamiliarity.

All languages do not include the same range of sounds and some blends can be hard to pronounce, although first-language speakers will not grasp the potential difficulty in what is 'normal' to them. If you genuinely cannot manage to say a child's name accurately, then explain the situation to parents and children. Young children sometimes struggle with patterns of sound. If your name is a challenge for any children to say, then it is your choice to simplify it.

TAKE ANOTHER PERSPECTIVE

In the UK the most familiar naming system has been that of one or more personal names followed by a family surname. The cultural tradition of calling the first names 'Christian names' arises because Christianity has been the world faith that has most shaped UK society.

A long-standing religious tradition, in some Protestant denominations, is to christen babies as a symbol of their entering the church community. This ceremony established the idea of a 'Christian name'. However, all world faiths do not 'christen' and nor does every Christian denomination – some prefer to baptise adults, because they are able to make the decision to commit.

In a diverse society, with many faiths and many families who do not follow a given religious faith at all, the phrase 'Christian name' is no longer appropriate. 'Personal name' is a more accurate description.

DIVERSITY IN FAMILY LIFE

Variety in family composition cuts across ethnic and social group diversity. Partnership with parents should be based on respect for different ways to run a family and without assumptions about who is likely to be counted within any given family group. Some children are raised by their two birth parents but some will be cared for by a lone mother or father. Some grandparents have stepped in to take parental responsibility. Some families will be formed by new relationships and step-parents and step-siblings will be part of the family. Some children may have been adopted or are in a long-term foster placement.

Male family carers

There are considerably more fathers in the nursery or school grounds than was the case with previous generations. But, with a workforce that is still predominantly female, fathers say that they can still feel like the exception. Female practitioners need to be aware of their own attitudes and offer respect for male carers such as fathers.

- Watch out that you do not assume that this is a temporary arrangement and ask when the child's mother will be coming.
- Male carers may be lone parents or may be the primary carer in a two-parent family. Some families organise their time so that both parents share in taking children to and from a childminder, nursery or school.
- Communicate directly with the parent in front of you and avoid the less respectful habit of using fathers simply as a channel for sending messages back to the child's mother.
- When both parents come, avoid addressing most remarks to the mother or always asking her questions about health or routine.

If you have a mixed male-female team, some fathers may be more comfortable talking with a male practitioner. It would be appropriate to respect this preference over a settling-in period, but a male practitioner should behave in ways that enable this parent to feel more at ease with other team members. Fathers should not be directed towards a male practitioner as a matter of course, no more than parents should automatically be guided towards conversation with a team member who shares their ethnic group identity or faith.

Of course, it is important not to assume that the shape of partnership changes radically for fathers. However, it is professional to reflect on how far daily exchanges or invitations for different types of involvement are underpinned by the unspoken assumption that 'parents' actually means mothers. A special event for fathers and other male carers can help to get the ball rolling. It may be a 'Dads' day', special 'Fathers' evening' or 'Bring a dad to nursery' event. Combined social and information events can be a relaxed way for practitioners in a team to hear from male family members what they would like to do or would be willing to do if asked.

It can help to have newsletters or family noticeboards that ask for a wide variety of help and cite some specific tasks rather than a general welcome to get involved. I saw a very effective noticeboard in one primary school. It had a general message about how much the school, including the nursery, welcomed parents' involvement. Then an array of about ten photographs showed named fathers, mothers and different family members busy with different recent projects and tasks.

Gay and lesbian families

Gay and lesbian parents are a group with a great deal of individual variation, just like any social group of people. They may feel understandably under pressure or scrutiny about their sexual orientation and the negative reaction of some people to their raising children. So you may not necessarily know that an individual parent is gay or lesbian. These mothers and fathers will want to talk to you about the wide range of issues that affect children and that they share with their fellow parents. They will want you to relate to them in their social role as 'parent' to their children. Their sexuality may not arise as an issue, any more than your own sexual orientation or whether you have a current partner.

Children do not seem to be confused about their own sex or in finding an appropriate gender identity; certainly there is no reason to assume that their emotional development is affected. Children's emotional stability and well-being depends on how they are treated by adults, not those adults' sexual orientation. Living in a gay or lesbian family does not appear to push children's later choices about sexual orientation one way or another. As many gay and lesbian parents point out, they were raised by a heterosexual couple.

If you are uncertain how to deal with children's comments or questions, then talk with the parent(s). They will have experience and preferences about how their family is described. Parents could be valuable in helping you decide how best to reply when one child says to another, 'You can't have two mummies' or asks, 'Is Mike your daddy's lodger?' Children can be made unhappy or feel isolated if their family situation is met with hostility or offensive amusement. In an unwelcoming local community, children may feel they have to be secretive about their family. Children are rarely comfortable keeping secrets that prevent their talking about what is important to them.

For all the changes in society, there is still a considerable amount of hostility towards people who are gay, lesbian or bisexual. Insults based on sexual orientation are part of the offensive vocabulary of many school-age children. Outright rejection is also strong in some social and cultural groups, and actively promoted by followers of some world faiths. This equality issue is another area in which you need to be clear about the prevailing values of your practice. You will not be able to please everyone and adult hostility will almost certainly be reflected in children's comments, especially by school age.

Partnership and disability

Bear in mind that some parents will themselves be disabled. In some cases they will be the disabled parent of a disabled child, but not necessarily.

Good practice in partnership does not become entirely different when parents are disabled. Many of the adjustments are more generally inclusive.

It is as important that you build an individual relationship with disabled parents as with individual children who are disabled. Practitioners are sometimes told that they should not treat the child of a disabled parent as a child in need. This advice is somewhat confusing, unless the meaning is unpacked. When there is disability in the family, the situation should not be treated as nothing but 'problems'. However, children whose parents are disabled have individual needs that deserve attention – just as with the siblings of disabled children. Family life for everyone is shaped by the presence of disability, as recognised by the Children (Scotland) Act 1995, which defines children as 'in need' when anyone within the immediate family is disabled.

SCENARIOS

1

In St Agnes Pre-school, Suzanne does not object to being known, at least sometimes, as 'Ricky's mum' – it is a normal part of life with young children. But Suzanne objected to how Sophie, a practitioner who has now left, had sometimes referred to her as 'the one in the wheelchair'. The parish council had already installed a ramp to ease access to the hall, but Suzanne's arrival with Ricky had shown that the narrow entrance lobby also posed problems.

In the early weeks, Suzanne expressed appreciation to Michelle for her approach along the lines of, 'How can we make pre-school life straightforward for you?' Suzanne simply wished to get on with the task of being a mother to Ricky. In the same conversation she raised her frustration with Sophie who tended either to ignore her or to insist on 'helping' without first asking whether Suzanne wanted any support.

2

Parents may have learning disabilities rather than physical disabilities. The kind and extent of learning disabilities vary considerably, so it is impossible to make broad generalisations. In Clearwater nursery class, Helena is ready to offer advice and support to Marie, whose learning disabilities mean that she is uncertain how best to care for Thomas or what kind of play resources are suitable for a nearly four-year-old. Young children can be very protective towards their parents, and Thomas already notices that his mother behaves differently from other parents. Helena is aware that Thomas could become a young carer for his mother. Helena wishes to help Marie to accept support from the local family support team.

> **Comments**
>
> ■ Appropriate support for disabled parents will never be a single template. You develop partnership with individual parents and families.
>
> ■ Are you aware of support teams or facilities in your area? Collect information on services that could be useful to parents like Suzanne or Marie.

CONTINUING PARTNERSHIP

Good practice in partnership allows for variety and offers an active respect to parents. The vast majority of parents are interested in their children, concerned about their wellbeing and closely involved in their lives. Parents will have a different perspective your professional outlook – they need to be focused on their own child – but otherwise you will have much in common.

Clear communication

Unless parents have specific early years professional experience, they will not necessarily grasp how 'learning through play' is an effective approach for young children. Bafflement about what you are doing and why can be shared between families of different ethnic groups and cultural background, as can pressure over literacy or numeracy. Some parents may expect the after-school club to operate as an extension of the school day. Even if you offer space and some resources for children to do their homework, club practitioners are not taking parental responsibility for the quality or accuracy of children's work.

TAKE ANOTHER PERSPECTIVE

Unspoken assumptions can also make communication more complicated. Liz Brookner observed the experiences of families over one reception year in an urban primary school. She described how well-intentioned practice, like the class teacher's open-door approach to communication, did not work to include the Bangladeshi families. The staff did not seem to have realised how much the children learned at home, nor that many parents had serious reservations about the effectiveness of school for their children.

Families from a range of cultural or national backgrounds may appreciate a more formal approach to first contacts with a setting, talking about their children or ways to raise confusions or concerns. The UK approach, especially in early years, tends to be informal, with the expectation that parents will simply approach practitioners or 'know' that they are welcome. Some parents prefer a more definite request for specific involvement, with the option, of course, of declining.

- Brookner, Liz (2002) *Starting School: Young Children Learning Cultures*. Buckingham: Open University Press.

Communication to show and tell can be less straightforward when you do not share a fluent language with parents. A lack of shared language complicates communication, and even good interpreters may not fully understand the ideas that you need to have explained and to understand in your turn. However, miscommunication is still very possible when you speak a shared language. The best way forward is to offer different channels of communication and to have an open and flexible working definition of partnership. Open days or evenings can work well for some parents as a way to experience the general approach of a group setting to children's learning. Parents often appreciate seeing the rooms set up and enjoy some of the experiences in a hands-on way. Such opportunities can be well supported by straightforward explanations from practitioners about 'what your child can learn from . . .'.

Adult literacy

Another approach to communication is through a family noticeboard, newsletter or other regular summary. Written material ideally needs to be in the main local languages. It will help everyone if you make generous use of visual materials to illustrate your messages. But practitioners need to recall that illiteracy, or a limited ability to read and write, is a hidden problem for many adults, across social and cultural groups. Traveller and Gypsy parents have often had disrupted schooling in their own childhood. However, a wide range of adults have developed strategies to cover their inability to read, such as 'I haven't got my glasses' or 'My wife deals with all that.' Sometimes, of course, these statements are true. A sensitive approach will benefit all parents, including those who cope with dyslexia: a disability that affects how children and adults are able to process written language.

All written material, and spoken exchanges too, need to be expressed in straightforward language.

- All professions have special words and phrases that are jargon to outsiders. Early years, school and playwork practitioners are no exception, and some degree courses have encouraged the use of academic terms.

- Considerate attention to use of words will benefit partnership as a whole. Parents who share a fluent language with you are unlikely to follow what you mean by 'gross motor development', let alone 'gender equity'. Fellow adults, working in their less fluent language, will be utterly perplexed.

- Newsletters or other written material will be done now on a word processor. It should be very easy to run off some copies in a large font size, if that will enable some parents to read the text. It would be wasteful of paper to run off every copy in that larger font, though.

- Can you offer simple audio-tape versions of newsletters or other written communication? You could involve children in setting up a comfortable corner where anyone can listen to the tape, at the same time as looking at written, and illustrated, material.

Partnership over disability

Any setting or service has to find a suitable middle course between treating the presence of disabled or sick children as a problem, about which other parents should be 'warned', and an equally inappropriate stance of 'it doesn't make any difference at all'. You may have judged it sensible to prepare the children to welcome a child. If so, then be ready for parents who ask questions because their children have said, 'Tyrone lost his leg, you know' or 'We've got to help Debbie, 'cos she's got "tism".'

Be ready to answer factual questions from family members about 'Is it catching?' or 'Are you sure you'll still have enough attention for all the other children?' Avoid assuming parents are making an unreasonable fuss, unless their persistence or language supports an interpretation that they are prejudiced about disability. The presence of a disabled or sick child should not trigger a stream of letters home to all parents. However, there may be occasions when a letter is appropriate.

For example, Tom's disability involves significant behavioural or emotional difficulties. He had a prolonged outburst today that distressed and frightened other children. You should think seriously about writing to parents under such circumstances, otherwise the local grapevine will buzz and some parents will fairly ask why they had to pick up details from their own children. It would be courteous to let Tom's parent know that the letter will be sent. If this incident is not the first, you might also need to reflect whether you can genuinely meet Tom's needs without further support for your setting.

TAKE ANOTHER PERSPECTIVE

Within the parent group, as with colleagues in a team, there will be a broad variation in emotions, as well as knowledge, about disability and serious health conditions. There are many appropriate options between the two extremes of a slick sentimentality about disabled children ('so brave') and a grim hopelessness ('so terrible'). The wide range of emotions experienced by parents of disabled or very sick children can better be understood by reading some of the books suggested on page 189, as well as, of course, by listening to parents who wish to talk.

The other source of mixed feelings, for which practitioners need to be prepared, is the concern felt by colleagues or parents who are themselves pregnant or whose partner is expecting a baby. Usual anxieties about the wellbeing of your baby are heightened by an awareness of what can happen, however unlikely that may be statistically. I became personally aware of this issue through working with the staff of a unit for profoundly disabled children over the months I was pregnant with my daughter. Practitioners and fellow parents can care very much about individual disabled children, yet not wish for their experiences to be repeated for the adult's unborn child.

Explanation of values in practice

You start the process of explaining equality within the early days of partnership. Some questions, or challenges, may arise from parents at that early point. Some comments may be voiced later. Taking the example of equality over gender, some parents will share your views and be pleased to give active support for what you do. Some parents may appreciate a chance to express their frustrations, because they have been trying to extend a son or daughter's interests, against opposition from a partner or relative. However, some parents or other family carers will disagree with gender equality in practice, for reasons related to cultural or faith traditions. Some of these parents will be 'white' UK families, certainly not all from groups classified as minority ethnic.

You share with parents what happens in your service; you are not telling them what they have to do in their own family. Perhaps in Annop's home (or Wai-yung's or Benjie's for that matter) it is usual that his mother and sisters do all the domestic tasks. The boys may find it odd in nursery or your home that you expect them to do up their own coat and help at tidy-up time. Friendly conversation with a child's parent can help practitioners to understand the gap between the family pattern and nursery, club or your home as a childminder. With your patience and encouraging invitation, it is very likely that children will choose to be like their peers and follow 'what we do here'. Their behaviour is unlikely to change at home while they have 'their people' serving them.

TAKE ANOTHER PERSPECTIVE

Read through the following examples and consider how you might reply if a parent said this to you. You could compare ideas with a colleague or fellow student.

1   'It says in your brochure something about equal opportunities and gender. What exactly does that mean?'

2   'I don't want you to let my son do this needlework stuff. He's a boy; he should be playing with cars and trains, not doing embroidery. Are you trying to turn them into wimps?'

3   'Tasha's gran has been going on about your clambering frame. She has a thing about girls falling on their privates; she stopped my wife climbing when she was young. Is it dangerous?'

4   'I know all this gender stuff is very politically correct – very feminist and all that. But I think you should keep politics out of the nursery. They're innocent little children and you're trying to brainwash them.'

5   'I don't really mind about Jon playing with the dolls, because he's very young still. But his dad's really uncomfortable about it. What happens when he's a bit older, will you do football and things with him?'

6   'I agree that children learn very young. But they should be learning what will help them when they are grown up. And that means learning how to behave like a proper young lady or young man.'

Partnership through involvement in activities

You will have experience and knowledge, as will your colleagues in a team, but one possible aspect of partnership is to welcome parents and other family members as a good source of knowledge, skills, personal interests and experience.

Some parents may be pleased to spend some time in a group setting, others may not wish to be directly involved in daily group life or cannot organise their time in that way. Parents should be able to choose the extent to which they are involved. Some mothers or fathers will have more time, interest or the confidence to become involved with a project. However, parents and other family members may be happy to contribute materials for dressing up, do some baking, entrust family items to the display or join in with the garden make-over.

Parents are interested to hear how children learn with you

It would be poor partnership practice to judge parents' interest by whether they join just one or two options that are defined as 'parent involvement'. It is also very likely that the pattern for partnership will be different between childminding, early years centres, schools, clubs and other playwork settings. The 'involvement' aspect of partnership can work well, so long as you are ready to reflect on invitations, assumptions and unspoken expectations. Here are some thoughts.

- Avoid a restricted view that practitioners ask only Liam's family about anything Irish and Ujala's family about Indian dancing. These parents may be pleased to share their experience, but they will also have a range of personal talents and skills.

- If you would welcome food, then make an open invitation. It should not be the case that, 'All the Indian mums have to make samosas.' Perhaps Ujala's mother likes making sponge cakes. Do 'English mums' ever have to contribute 'traditional English food' and what is that assumed to be?

- Note also that adults are not necessarily experts on all their own cultural traditions. Try asking a random group of 'white' English parents about the origins of May Day celebrations, how to do some country dancing or make a traditional Lancashire hot pot. Many people will have very little idea.

- Avoid assuming that Saira's father will not want to join a rota of parents who come in to support craft activities needing careful supervision. Perhaps you hesitate with, 'It'll be too difficult – what with his withered hand.' Suitable equality practice is to include Owen in the invitation and be ready if he wants to raise practical issues about his chosen involvement.

- Chris's parents may be knowledgeable about thalassaemia, because of their son's condition, but they are unlikely to want to be pigeon-holed as the people who always speak up about any disability or

SCENARIO

Liz and her team at Crest Road early years centre are keen to use food and cooking as one way to establish shared ground between children and families who attend the centre. A series of successful events with families has made them aware of the more subtle issues around this aspect of partnership.

They now look back, wondering at their own naivety in assuming that every parent – actually mother – in families from a minority ethnic group would somehow be an excellent cook. The team do not change an open invitation for families to contribute food for special occasions. However, experience has shown that the vegetable spring rolls made by Yan-Ling's mother are just as soggy and tasteless as the mini quiches that Stephen's mother wants to send. On the other hand, practitioners have to be very strong to let children have first tasting of the fudge brownies that are a speciality of Nathan's father.

Jonathon brought a high awareness of children's feelings from previous experience in primary school. He recounted to the team how a seven-year-old had become very distressed in his class. None of the other children wanted to try the sweets that the boy's mother had made and sent in for the group. As soon as he saw the tears, Jonathon ensured that he ate some of the sweets. But, as he explained to his colleagues at Crest Road, the other children had not been rude or unkind. Jonathon recalled, 'In fact, one girl was patting Harjeet's hand. She was concerned that he was crying, but she still didn't want to eat his mum's sweets, and that was what upset Harjeet. It seemed to be that the sweets looked very different from what was familiar to the other children. I learned a lot that day about not just putting out food from home.'

Comment

- Consider what you might take from this scenario for your own practice – to confirm what you have already realised, but also to reflect on assumptions that perhaps you have not checked.

health issue. Perhaps Chris's father is itching to mend and extend your inadequate book shelves, but he does not wish to seem 'pushy'.

Personal histories

Any family that has moved country or continent within recent generations could be described as having a country of origin as well as their current roots. Some families classified as 'black minority ethnic' are of recent arrival in the UK, but some have lived here for many years, in some cases for generations. There will always be variety in how families view themselves, and practitioners need to be aware of their own unchecked assumptions (see also page 112). It is important, and courteous, that you do not make assumptions about children's allegiances. For instance, you should ask a general question of a mixed group such as, 'Has anyone any connections with India?' rather than homing in on one child with, 'India's your country, isn't it, Rajiv?'

LOOK, LISTEN, NOTE, LEARN

Part of all children's personal identity is their family history. You could develop a project on family timelines. Whatever the extent of ethnic group diversity in your local community, you will be able to explore whether local families have moved around the country, or between countries. Several considerations will help you to make this project a positive experience.

■ Talk with parents about the plans for the project and reassure them, if necessary, that you are not delving into their family history out of nosiness.

■ Make sure that each family's timeline is treated with equal interest and respect. Families who have lived in the area for generations are as interesting as those who have family origins in other countries.

■ The families with strong local roots may take you towards an exploration of history for children. For instance, 'What was happening at the same time that Sara's great-grandparents were running the farm?' or 'Hamish's family lived here when the shipbuilding yards were still open.'

■ Families who have moved country recently, or in past generations, may be a direct way to make sense of geography for children, as may the experience of Traveller and Gypsy families.

■ Be aware and sensitive about refugee families whose moves will not have been a matter of choice, but forced by war and other political disruptions.

Dealing with misunderstanding or disagreement

There will always be some potential imbalance between practitioners and parents, or other family carers. Childminders and practitioners in group settings are responsible for following the policies that underpin good professional practice. No practitioner can flex on key values, however strongly a parent might feel to the contrary. Part of good practice, as a sole practitioner like a childminder, as well as a team member, is to know what is negotiable with parents and what is not. You will have a clear policy over discipline. Good practice in partnership does not mean you ever agree to handle a child's behaviour in a way that is emotionally or physically harsh. It does not matter how clearly parents give you permission to hit their children, nor whether they support this tactic by faith or cultural tradition.

SCENARIO

Over the last year Clearwater nursery class have been looking closely at their approach to girls and boys through the daily play activities. The rethink has been part of reflection for the whole school team led by Philip, the new head teacher. Within the nursery, the team decided to take a more active line in encouraging play to blur some children's firm ideas about what was girls' and boys' play, as well as what mummies and daddies usually did.

Philip has looked at the possibilities within the whole school staff team (mainly female) to promote diversity through adult role models. There have been active efforts to show that male practitioners can get involved in nursery opportunities like cooking and dressing up. They also worked to show the less enthusiastic boys that men enjoy reading and writing. The team has also looked at female practitioners, physically active play and how playground supervisors deal with games that have often been labelled as 'rough' and stopped. The team rewrote the school equality policy with more emphasis on gender, and have displayed the main ideas, with photographs of recent projects with the children in the nursery and main section of the school.

Over the next fortnight several parents asked to speak with Susan or Helena in the nursery. Two fathers do not think their sons should put on the wraps or the favourite feather boa from the extended dressing-up materials. A couple of parents are concerned that children are 'being made' to do activities more suitable for the opposite sex. One mother refers to the Clearwater policy on partnership and the commitment to respect families' religious and cultural traditions. Similar concerns are being raised by some parents whose children are in the primary school, although other families are very positive.

Questions

1 What are the main issues that Philip and his team face with this dilemma? With hindsight, could they have approached their new policy and practice in a different or better way?

2 Encouraging children to step across firm sex-role boundaries can worry families from a range of cultural or religious backgrounds. Have you faced a similar dilemma in your own centre?

A vital element in partnership will always be to explain to parents at the first meeting – through conversation and written material about your service – how some aspects of practice are non-negotiable. Further conversation will be necessary if events lead to potential disagreement. When parents and practitioners hold incompatible views with equal conviction, a discussion will not be easy but can be possible. Honesty, tact and respect for views that you do not share may help to bring about a working acceptance or compromise in most circumstances. If parents continue to ask that you meet requirements that are contrary to key values of your service, then regrettably there may have to be a parting of the ways. (See the example on page 119.)

It is crucial that you do not immediately assume that a parent is about to argue or be awkward. When parents voice concerns or questions, they are certainly not always cross. But a dismissive response to their first comment can tip even a courteous parent towards a sharp reply. You will experience individual differences in style from parents. Some differences may be shaped by that person's cultural background; some may be more about temperament.

- Some parents may find it hard to express a concern without cranking up the volume or using gestures that you feel to be excessive. Some cultural traditions are more forthright than others. It would be unprofessional to label a more lively style than your own as 'aggressive' or 'threatening'.

- Some parents will have trouble coming to the point. For personal or cultural reasons, they may be very concerned that they do not appear rude or unappreciative. They still have concerns that should be heard. You may need to look and listen beyond comments like, 'I don't want you to feel I'm making a fuss . . .'. You need to hear the unspoken 'but . . .' and invite the mother, father or grandparent to say more.

- The best approach will always be to listen to what a parent wishes to say to you. Ask open-ended questions so you can understand the key issues for this parent. Useful questions are often started with 'What . . .?' or 'How . . .?' or the request, 'Can you tell me more, please. I'm not quite clear what you don't like about . . .'.

- Once you have listened and understood, you can make a more appropriate response and that may include saying, 'Thank you for telling me about this. I need to think over what you've said [or talk with my colleagues]. I'll get back to you tomorrow [or another time in the near future].'

A professional approach to partnership means that you reflect on how far it is appropriate to adjust your behaviour in order to acknowledge the family cultural tradition. Sometimes you will appreciate opportunities to discuss choices in a situation with colleagues, a local adviser or network supporter.

It is professional to modify your preferred approach to using physical contact, how close you stand to another person or your comfortable level of eye contact, if your habits are making someone else feel less at ease.

SCENARIO

At Falcon Square after-school club, a mother whose son has just started takes Daniel to one side and says, 'I would have thought twice if I'd known you had a Muslim fundamentalist working here.' Daniel is genuinely perplexed and asks, 'Who is it you're talking about?' The mother gestures towards Josie, who was raised as Muslim but has only recently started to wear a close-fitting headscarf. She has married Quasim, who is happier if she covers her hair outside the home. Daniel replies, 'That's Josie. I think she was on holiday when you visited with Sean. Josie wears her headscarf as part of her faith but that doesn't make her extremist. Is that what you mean by "fundamentalist"?'

Daniel will need to judge whether Sean's mother wants, or needs, further conversation and whether Josie could usefully be part of that discussion. However, it would not be at all appropriate to agree to any request that Sean should have little to do with Josie. Nor would it be right to agree that Shamima or Gayatri, both from Muslim families, are only in contact with Josie. The same principle would hold in an early years setting where choices would be made about a key person for children.

Questions

1 Recent events globally and in the UK have increased the ease with which some people link Islam with extremism. How have you dealt, or would you deal, with similar comments in your own practice?

2 Effective partnership with parents may first need reflection in the team. Perhaps some practitioners are themselves swift to believe that some signs of religious faith, like a headscarf, are evidence of hardline views, whereas the crucifix worn by a Christian colleague is 'just a cross on a chain'.

It is also appropriate to use less informal modes of address, if parents or family carers do not wish to be called by their personal name. (Schools are usually more formal than early years or out-of-school provision.) However, be aware that in any kind of communication, it can indicate differential status if one person is always known as Mr or Mrs Johnson and someone else is always addressed as Jane.

When females are judged inferior

Discussion in this chapter and elsewhere in the book has recognised that gender equality applies to men as well as women. A man can feel very isolated as a father in an otherwise all-mothers drop-in or the 'token male' in an all-female team. Some communities have developed in ways that are hostile to men as fathers or any other role. This section now addresses the situation that can arise because some ethnic group and cultural traditions place considerably less value on females – girls and women – than on males.

Sometimes such a tradition is supported by interpretations from a world faith. In case any readers are leaping to conclusions, the faith in question is not inevitably Islam and all Muslims do not interpret the Qur'an in ways that severely limit female daily life. Some sects within Christianity and Judaism require women to remain in a subservient role. But there is not always a religious connection. Some Gypsy and Traveller communities encourage behaviour towards females that is hard for outsiders to interpret other than as discourtesy. In some groups, not all, it is usual for males to refuse to answer a woman until more than one time of asking. Practitioners need to understand patterns of behaviour from young boys but, of course, they may also experience communication that feels discourteous from fathers.

Female professionals within equality practice have struggled with the dilemma of showing respect to traditions whose followers decline to show active respect in return. To date, the most usual way of resolving the dilemma has been to weigh respect for ethnic group, cultural tradition or faith as more important than gender issues. People have also been the most anxious about accusations of being 'racist', and the easiest way out has been to skate over these issues. This situation is sensitive and littered with interpersonal potholes. But circumstances are not resolved by ignoring them, so I offer my views in the following section. Please read it more than once and use the ideas to support personal reflection and discussion in a team.

A respectful way of dealing with disrespect

There are limits to how far women should be expected to travel along the road of allegedly 'different yet equal'. Nor are such situations exclusively about gender; they are about right of respect for the cultural traditions of women who have learned they are of equal significance with men.

251

- It is appropriate professional effort that you seek to identify the underpinning reason for what feels like discourtesy to you. Your responsibility is to understand the sources of behaviour, to realise that at one level the words and actions are not directed at you personally.

- This realisation may help you stop searching for what you have done or said that appears to have annoyed this father or other male family member – or whatever other emotion you are using in a struggle for interpretation.

- At another level, this male reaction is disrespectful because it is utterly impersonal. Female practitioners can receive a standard pattern of response, regardless of their own behaviour and professional skills.

- Equality practice would direct you to challenge such a pattern if it were on the basis of skin colour or another ethnic group marker. The behaviour is no more acceptable on the basis of gender.

Suppose you face a continuing situation where a male family member of a child in your care seems to feel he is justified in telling you, as a female, what is to be done with his child (or grandchild). The communication is not a conversation; it is a list of orders. Perhaps you are interrupted on a regular basis by a father who is not prepared to wait if you are talking with another woman. Perhaps a child's male family carer ignores you (and you are sure he is not deaf), or pointedly waits to reply until you have asked courteously several times to speak with him.

You allow generous time to establish partnership with families, as well as showing a consistent model of what is regarded as courtesy in your service or setting. Then it is appropriate to address what you observe to be happening on a regular basis. You might say with a level, yet firm, tone of voice:

- 'I appreciate that you prefer talking with Harry. However, I am the team leader of this nursery and on issues such as . . . it is appropriate that you talk with me. If you prefer, Harry can be part of that discussion, but I will lead the meeting and I will make the final decision.'

- 'Thank you for letting me know you want to have a word. I will be with you as soon as I have finished talking with Donna's mother.' . . . 'Mr Johnson, I will be able to listen to you when I have finished with Mrs Kelly.' . . . 'Mr Johnson, please do not interrupt us again.'

- 'Thank you for letting me know these important details about your son's care. I need to talk with his key person and then I'd like to get back to you.' . . . 'I have heard what you would prefer and we discuss such issues in the team. I am not able simply to say "yes" to what you want.'

If the working relationship becomes tense and very awkward, you may ask for a meeting to discuss the situation. You need to approach the situation as a problem to be resolved and not as a matter of fault-finding. It may help to have a colleague also present, although you need to weigh up whether that will seem too formal or an attempt to 'outnumber'. Hold to an assertive approach with statements like:

- 'I understand that you feel it is acceptable to tell me that I "must do" something – like yesterday when . . . However, I experience your words and gestures as discourteous to me.'
- 'I realise that you feel it is quite all right to ignore me until I have spoken at least three times to you. I wish to show respect for your cultural tradition, but I feel placed in an impossible position. In my cultural tradition, your behaviour would give a clear message of discourtesy. I want to try to find some way out of this that leaves us both reasonably comfortable.'
- 'I wish to show respect for your cultural tradition [faith], but not to the point where I feel disrespected just because I am a woman and you are a man. This situation is giving me problems around . . . and I would like to find a way through.'

Bear in mind that many adults, from a wide range of social and cultural backgrounds, have not had much experience in taking an assertive, rather than aggressive, approach nor of constructive approaches to conflict resolution. This kind of approach is characterised by statements that are honest about your own feelings, show respect for the other person's perspective and yet make it clear that you are not content for matters to carry on in the same way (see the examples on page 209). The aim of this kind of discussion is to reach an easier pattern of interaction. You are very unlikely to change deep-rooted habits. Just be pleased if family members will adjust their behaviour enough to make daily conversation more constructive.

TAKE ANOTHER PERSPECTIVE

It is important to bear in mind that some people, from any social or cultural background, are just plain rude. There may be personal reasons, insecurities or previous experiences underlying their behaviour, but it is not related to their group identity.

Allow for this possibility and avoid assuming there must always be an explanation arising from cultural tradition just because this person belongs to a different ethnic group, nationality or faith from you.

Some parents appreciate informal drop-in sessions

Supporting parents

When families experience a supportive partnership, they may well ask you for advice or guidance for further information. Part of continued professional development is for you to extend your knowledge but just as much your skills of how to find more information. Nevertheless it is important to be aware of boundaries to partnership.

■ Confident and experienced practitioners may need to be careful not to take over from families. You offer support; you do not step into the parent's role.

■ You can share your knowledge of local support organisations or sources that are more national, but it is the family's choice what they follow up and what decisions they make.

■ It can be valuable for you to keep a folder of local information, especially in a group setting. But ensure that you update it regularly. The message to families also needs to be clear between information you provide about support agencies or organisations and active recommendation.

■ Some families – for example, refugee and asylum-seeker families – may need accurate legal advice. You may be able to suggest reliable sources of information, but be clear about the limits to your expertise.

A valuable role in partnership can be to put families in contact with other professionals who could offer expertise – for instance, to disabled children and their families. Some agencies will already be involved with a family and you will be informed through communicative partnership with parents. Be ready to learn from physiotherapists or speech therapists, so that you understand the work being done with children and can help where appropriate. However, a child's special needs may become clear during the time of your involvement, or it may be you who first raises concerns. Whatever the pattern of your involvement, it is important that talking with other professionals is never seen as more valuable than talking with children and their parents.

Of necessity, many parents become relative experts in their child's disability or health condition. If you make time to talk with and listen to them, you will extend your knowledge in general and, very important, you will understand far more about what this disability or health condition means for this individual child and family. However, not all parents of disabled children are experts, or feel as if they are.

- Good practice will be to have conversations with parents in which you give time and attention to learn from them, but also share what you know.
- Show your willingness to support parents in finding out more, either about their own child's individual needs or about the condition in general.
- Do not assume that parents will have heard about a relevant support organisation. Some parents manage with very little support or information, until they make contact with an early years setting.

You may also be a much-appreciated support for parents who are trying to weigh up advice from different sources, some of which may not be compatible. The professionals involved with a family are supposed to work cooperatively, but some parents find themselves dealing with different sources of information and firm views about how best to help their child. Some professionals are empathetic and supportive, others have a limited idea of ordinary life with a disabled child (or more than one disabled child) and the practicalities of juggling different priorities, including the needs of siblings.

If you want to find out more:

- *Contact a Family*, 209–211 City Road, London EC1V 1JN. Tel: 020 7608 8700; www.cafamily.org.uk. Offers useful guides under the title *Making a Difference* and is often able to link up families for support even when children have rare syndromes; there is also material available for download from its website.

- Dickins, Mary with Denziloe, Judy (2003) *All Together: How to Create Inclusive Services for Disabled Children and their Families*. London: National Children's Bureau.

- *Disabled Parents Network*, Unit F9, 89–93 Fonthill Road, London N4 3JH. Tel: 08702 410 450; www.disabledparentsnetwork.org.uk.

- *Early Support*, a joint initiative by the DfES, DoH and Sure Start, offers a wide range of materials. *The Family Pack* (free for practitioners in England) has parent-friendly layouts for gathering information during early meetings. There is also material to download at www.espp.org.uk.

- *Family Rights Group*, The Print House, 18 Ashwin Street, London E8 3EL. Tel: 0800 731 1696; www.frg.org.uk. Advice for families involved with social services.

- *Fathers Direct*, Herald House, Lamb's Passage, Bunhill Row, London EC1Y 8TQ. Tel: 0845 634 1328; www.fathersdirect.com. A national information centre about fatherhood.

- Kahn, Tim (2005) *Fathers' Involvement in Early Years Settings: Findings From Research* www.pre-school.org.uk.

- Lindon, Jennie and Lindon, Lance (2000) *Mastering Counselling Skills: Information, Help and Advice in the Caring Services*. Basingstoke: Macmillan.

- *Parentline Plus*: Tel: 0808 800 2222. Offers advice and information to anyone supporting a child; check for your local office by telephone or on the website www.parentlineplus.org.uk.

- *Pink Parents*, The D'Arcy Lainey Foundation, PO Box 417, Oldham OL2 7WT. Tel: 0161 633 2037; www.pinkparents.org.uk. Particular focus on gay and lesbian parents.

- *National Family and Parenting Institute*, a short guide on the Joseph Rowntree Foundation report (see below): *Think Parent: Supporting Disabled Adults as Parents*; www.nfpi.org/disabledparents.

- Olsen, Richard and Tyers, Helen (2004) *Supporting Disabled Adults as Parents*, a Joseph Rowntree Foundation report; www.jrf.org.uk/knowledge/findings/socialcare/n34.asp.

INDEX